SCIENCE IN VIEW

JACK FIELDHOUSE

STUART ROBERTSON

OXFORD UNIVERSITY PRESS

Oxford University Press, Walton Street, Oxford OX2 6DP

Oxford New York Toronto
Delhi Bombay Calcutta Madras Karachi
Petaling Jaya Singapore Hong Kong Tokyo
Nairobi Dar es Salaam Cape Town
Melbourne Auckland

and associated companies in
Berlin Ibadan

Oxford is a trade mark of Oxford University Press

Reprinted with corrections, 1987, 1988, 1989, 1990

ISBN 0 19 914237 8

To our families for support and encouragement, without which this book would not have progressed beyond the first few pages.

Jack Fieldhouse and Stuart Robertson
Firrhill High School, Edinburgh

Printed in Hong Kong

Introduction

To the Teacher

The majority of school science courses recognise the importance of students' own experiences and interests. Four main fields of science are covered in **Science in View**: Healthy Bodies, Energy, The Environment, and Materials. These fields have been written to support the Scottish Standard Grade Science Course. However, such is the importance of these four fields, the book is a valuable asset for any pupil-centred science course.

Each topic is organised in double-page spreads which can be used as the basis for a lesson. Experimental details and results are used extensively for the development of information-handling and problem-solving skills. The experiments described could form the starting point for student practical investigations. However, class practical work has deliberately not been given. This will allow the teacher the freedom to select the practical back-up most appropriate to the interests of the students and the resources available.

The book is illustrated throughout and in many cases the student is required to consider the illustrations in order either to develop knowledge and understanding of the topic or to develop skills. It is also comprehensively indexed and the students are encouraged by the text to use it.

Each double-page spread contains a variety of questions which allow the student to develop skills in obtaining and presenting information, carrying out calculations, suggesting and describing experimental procedures, drawing conclusions and making predictions. These questions are also valuable for assessment of these skills and could be used to build up a profile of a student's progress.

With particular reference to the Scottish Standard Grade Course it should be noted that the book contains a thorough coverage of the specific objectives in knowledge and understanding relating to the compulsory topics. Equally important, the text has been designed to develop the skills of information handling and problem solving. The questions cover the Extended Grade Related Criteria for these skill areas and have been colour coded to correspond to the three main levels of performance (Foundation, General and enhanced General or Credit). Success with questions coded ■ suggests a performance at Grade 6, ■ at Grades 5, 4 or 3 and ■ at Grade 2. However, this coding is provided merely as a guide and it is expected that teachers will wish to bring their own expertise to bear on this.

To the Student

Science is an important part of your life. This book is intended to help you realise why.

Most people are interested in staying healthy and living in pleasant surroundings. Having a good time whilst you are alive also depends on the sensible use of energy and available materials. Making the right choices is important and **Science in View** will help you to do that. We hope you enjoy using it.

Contents

Healthy bodies

The environment

Energy

Materials

HEALTHY BODIES

This section is about your body and the sort of decisions you might make which will affect its health. In it you will learn about human variation, dental health, the link between food and health, smoking and solvent abuse, your heart and circulation and the factors which influence fitness.

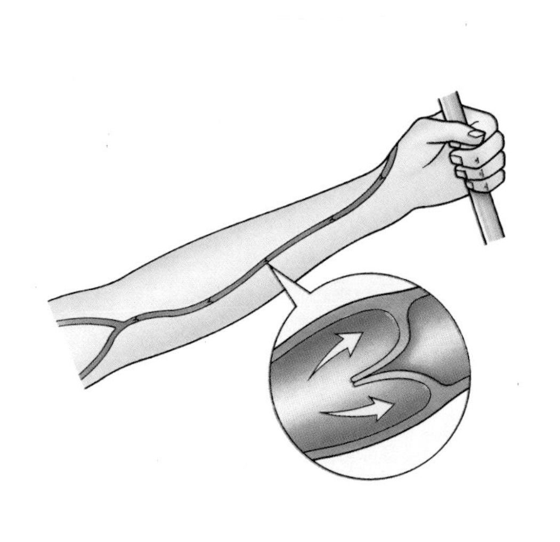

We're only human

Human variety

The photograph shows four of the many kinds of **human beings** in our world. The women look different in several ways. However, no matter where they come from, all human beings are alike in many ways.

1 Which two words above mean 'men and women'?

2 List 4 ways in which human faces are alike.

3 List 4 ways in which human faces may be different.

Human faces — alike, yet different

Every human being is special

British people sometimes say that all the Chinese look alike. The Chinese probably say the same about the British! However, people *do* differ from each other in many ways. The differences include sex (male or female), eye colour, age and weight. There are even differences between 'identical' twins.

One interesting difference between people is the pattern of ridges in the skin on their finger tips. These ridges help you to grip firmly on small objects. Whenever you touch anything the ridges leave a **fingerprint**. This is a pattern of greasy sweat. The police have records of the fingerprints of about three million people in Britain. Any fingerprints detected at the scene of a crime are compared with those on police records. In this way it may be possible to identify a criminal even if there was no witness to the crime. The photographs show three main sorts of fingerprint pattern.

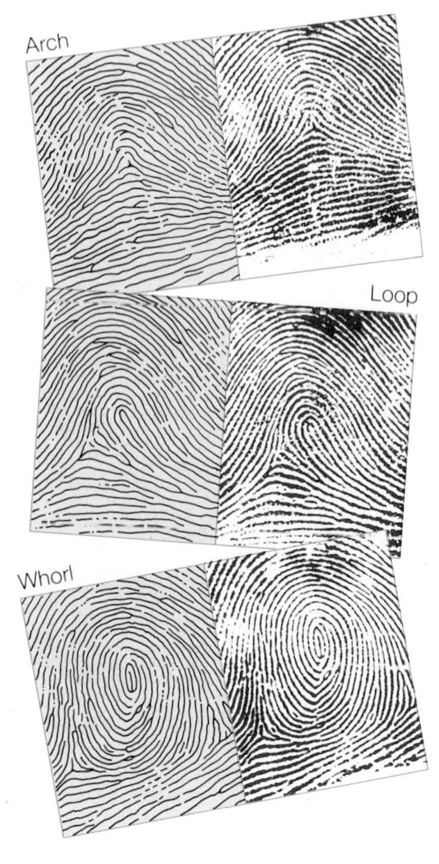

4 Name the three main sorts of fingerprint pattern.

5 Use the photographs to help you describe the sorts of patterns that you can see on your own finger tips.

6 Explain why the police fingerprint *every* finger of a suspect and not just one.

Describing differences

DUNNBURGH DRAGGERS PULL IT OFF

Pulling some facts together

DUNNBURGH DRAGGERS tug-o'war team heaved its way to an easy victory in the county championships yesterday by beating their old rivals, Munntown Manglers, in straight pulls.

Winning skipper, Eddie Evans, weighing in at 90 kilograms (kg), was full of praise for his lads. The team, according to mighty Colin Clarke (100 kg), is 'over the moon'. Three good reasons for Dunnburgh's run-away win are cousins Dave Dawson, Alf Adams and Frank Ford, each of whom tips the scales at 80 kg. New-boy Bob Binns (90 kg) nearly missed the match due to a strained thigh: isn't he glad he didn't! Henry Hall, also 90 kg, the 'grand-dad' of the team at 55 reckons he can still show a thing or two to the team's 17 year-old 'baby', Gerry Gibbs (70 kg) – even if it's only drinking champagne out of that well-deserved cup!

Name	Weight (kg)
Alf Adams	80
Bob Binns	90
Colin Clark	100
Dave Dunn	
Eddie Ev	

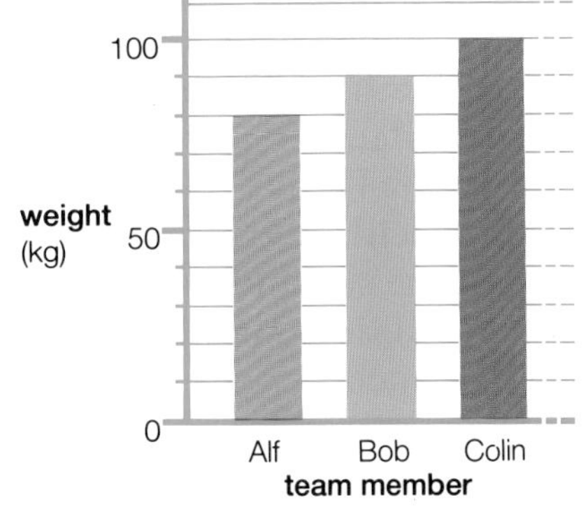

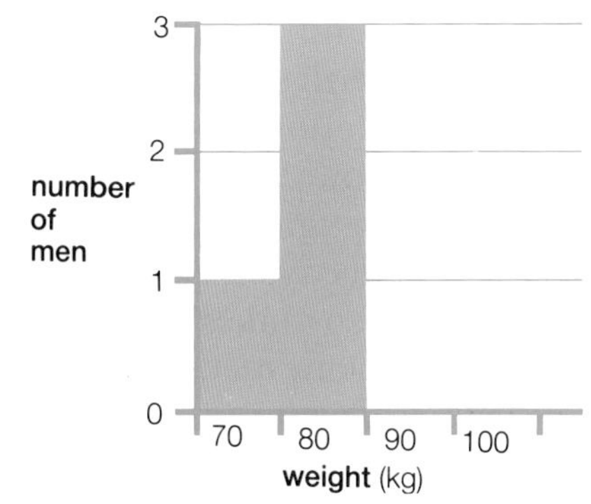

Tables

The trainer of Dunnburgh Draggers could record the weight of each team member in a **table**, part of which is shown above.

1 Copy and complete the table to show the weights of all eight men.

2 Which man is lightest and what does he weigh?

3 What is the average weight of the eight men?

Bar charts

Part of a **bar chart** is drawn above. The weight of each man is shown by the height of the column drawn above his name.

4 Copy and complete the bar chart to show the weights of all eight men.

5 Which two weights are most common?

6 How many men weigh more than 70 kg?

Bar graphs

Part of a **bar graph** is drawn above. It shows the number of men having each weight. For example, 3 of the men weighed 80 kg.

7 Copy and complete the bar graph to show the team's weights.

8 Which two weights are least common?

9 How many men weigh less than 90 kg?

Healthy teeth and gums

A healthy mouth

Smile please!

A healthy mouth feels good and what's more it looks good. Teeth are obviously important for eating, but they help you in other ways too. They play a part in speaking. Another way of saying 'hello' is with a nice smile!

Tooth decay

Tooth decay is the most common disease affecting British school-children: an average 14-year old will have seven teeth affected by decay. About 40 per cent (%) of British adults have lost all of their teeth and have false ones. Tooth decay spoils your looks and causes you pain; but it *can* be stopped.

1 In a class of 20 British 14 year-olds, how many teeth are likely to be affected by decay?

2 In a group of 20 British adults, how many are likely to have lost all of their teeth?

The causes of tooth loss

It is warm and moist inside your mouth and there may be bits of food around. **Bacteria** (germs) find it a good place to live. They mix with saliva and stick to your teeth and gums forming a yellow-white material called **plaque**. The remains of food in your mouth often contain sugar. The bacteria in plaque use sugar as a food and produce **acid**. Acid attacks teeth and decays them. Tooth decay is one cause of tooth loss. The acid also makes the gums red and swollen. They shrink back from your teeth and the bone that anchors your teeth in the jaw is destroyed. Gum disease is one reason for bad breath but it also causes tooth loss.

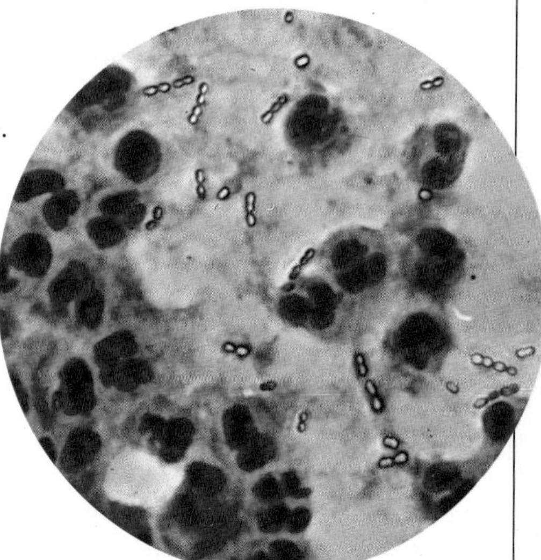

Bacteria in plaque

How to keep your teeth

First you can choose foods and drinks which contain less sugar. Most of the sugar that you eat is 'hidden' in sweet foods, as the table shows. Secondly you can choose to brush your teeth and gums thoroughly and regularly to remove plaque and the remains of food. Brushing helps to stop gum disease but it also helps to stop tooth decay and so does the sort of toothpaste you use. This is explained on page **7**.

3 Give three reasons why germs find the inside of your mouth a good place to live.

4 Which two diseases cause the loss of teeth?

5 Draw a bar chart to show the 'hidden' sugar in the foods listed in the table.

Food	Sugar content
tube of mints	5 teaspoons
jam tart	4 teaspoons
can of cola	7 teaspoons
bag of nuts	0 teaspoons

'Hidden' sugar

Teeth types

The structure of a tooth

The photograph shows the kind of tooth you have at the back of your mouth. The **root** is anchored in your jawbone. The **crown** sticks up above your gum.

The drawing shows the inside of the same tooth. The **enamel** covers the biting surface: it is the hardest material in the human body. Most of the tooth is made of **dentine**: this is hard, but not as hard as enamel. The **pulp** is the soft centre of the tooth. It contains the nerve and blood supply of the tooth.

1 When a dentist pulls someone's tooth out: the person is given a pain-killing injection and there is a lot of bleeding.
Use the information above to explain this.

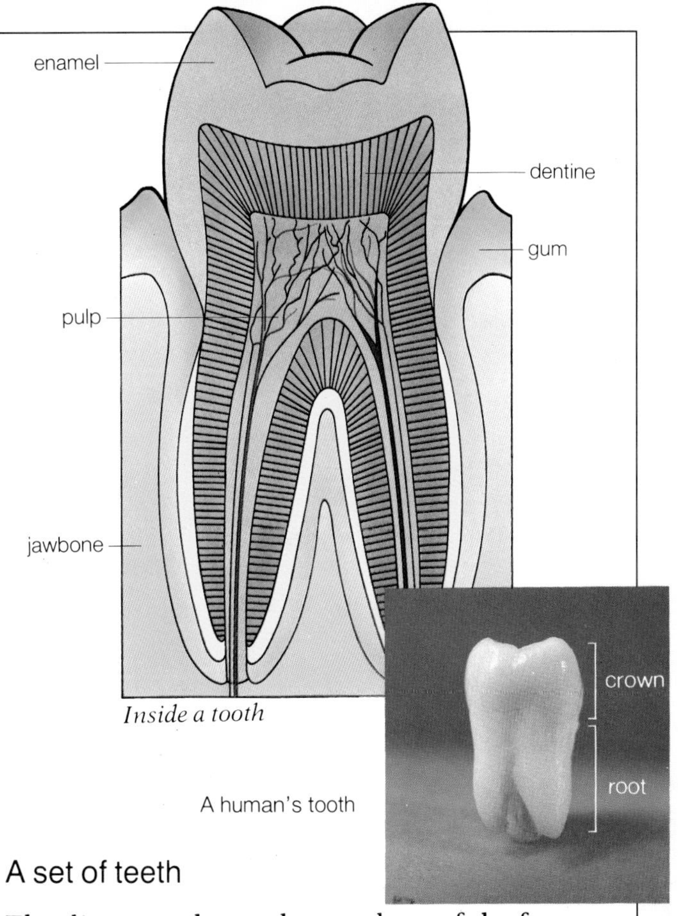

Inside a tooth

A human's tooth

Your four types of teeth

The diagram below shows a human skull with the teeth in place. **Incisors** are chisel-shaped teeth: they bite and cut off food. **Canines** are pointed teeth: they tear off food. **Premolars** and **molars** have flattened, bumpy crowns: they chew and grind food.

2 Which teeth do you use to:
a bite a piece off a biscuit
b chew a piece of meat?

3 Imagine eating a crusty bread roll. Describe how your four types of teeth would help you do this.

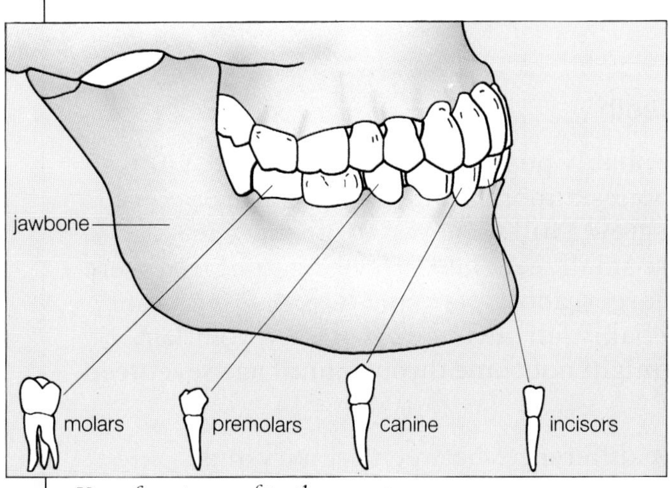

Your four types of teeth

A set of teeth

The diagram shows the numbers of the four types of teeth in a full adult's set.

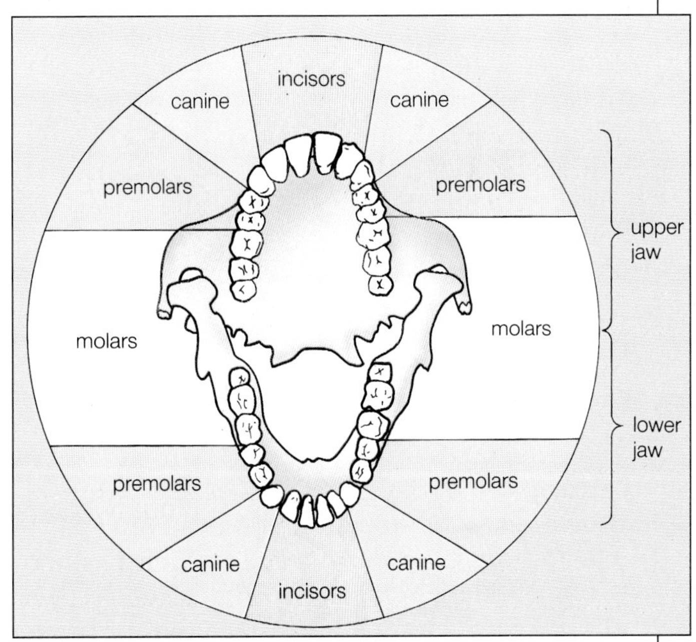

A full adult set of teeth

4 How many teeth are there in
a the upper jaw
b the lower jaw
c the full set?

5 How many of each of the four types of teeth are there?

Open wide

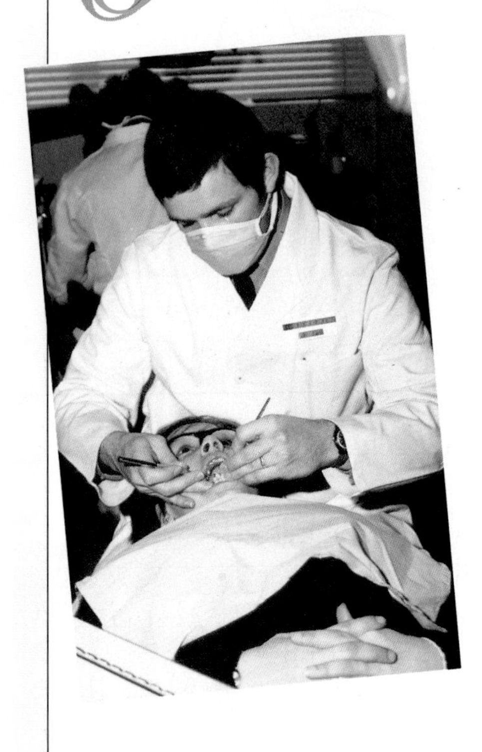

Dentists and decay

Until the middle of the 19th century the only way of dealing with a painful tooth was to have it pulled out. If you lived in a town then a barber might do this for you. If you lived in the country then you might have to wait for a visit from a travelling tooth-puller.

There are now about 20 000 **dentists** in Britain. You can get free check-ups under the National Health Service (NHS). Adults pay for treatment but children don't. Your dentist will advise you on how to care for your teeth. He, or she, will look out for decay and give **fillings** to stop the loss of teeth. It is a good idea to visit your dentist for a check-up about every six months.

1 Why should you visit a dentist for regular check-ups?

2 About 50 million (50 000 000) people live in Britain. Calculate the number of people per dentist.

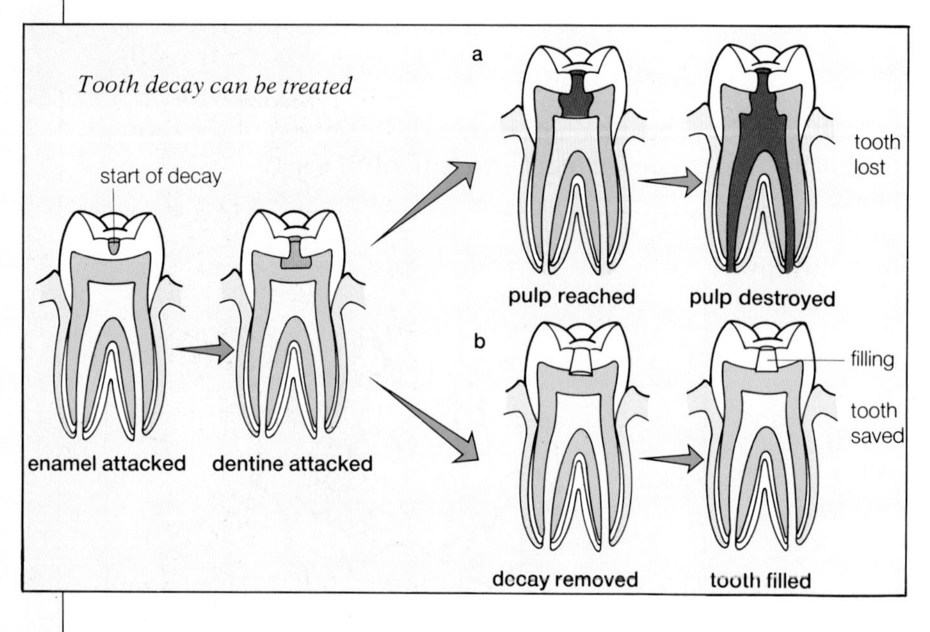

Tooth decay can be treated

Fillings help save teeth

The diagrams show what happens to a decaying tooth: (a) if it is left untreated, and (b) if it is treated by a dentist.

3 Which part of a tooth usually decays first?

4 Write a few sentences to describe the decay and loss of a tooth.

5 Write a few sentences to describe how a decayed tooth can be saved by a filling.

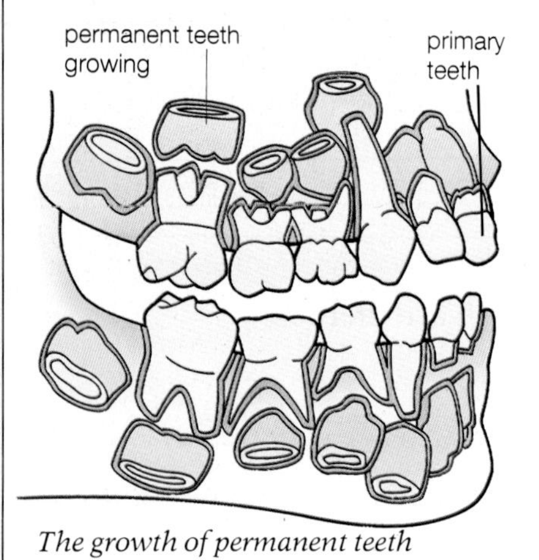

The growth of permanent teeth

Your two sets of teeth

Your first tooth probably pushed its way through the gum when you were about six-months old. By the time you were two, or three, you grew a full set of twenty **primary teeth** (baby teeth). These small teeth had to last you until they were replaced by your larger, adult, **permanent teeth**. Your first primary tooth probably fell out at about age six; your last permanent tooth might not come through until age seventeen, or later.

6 Write down two differences between primary and permanent teeth.

Defeating decay

Fluoride and tooth decay

Tap water contains many dissolved chemicals, including **fluoride**. The line graph shows the results of an investigation. It compares the number of decayed teeth in 12–14 year-old children with the concentration (strength) of fluoride in their drinking water. For example, children who drank water containing 1.0 grams (g) of fluoride for every 1000 litres (l) of water (a concentration of one unit) had, on average, about 3 decayed teeth.

1 About how many decayed teeth did children have if they drank water with a fluoride concentration of:
a 0.5 units, and **b** 1.5 units?

2 What happens to the amount of tooth decay when the fluoride concentration is increased from 0 to 2.0 units?

Should fluoride be added to your water supply?

Some authorities now add small amounts of fluoride to their water supplies. Tooth decay has become less common where the water is **fluoridated** in this way. Most people agree that fluoride strengthens tooth enamel and helps stop tooth decay, especially in children. Many toothpastes contain fluoride. But not everyone agrees that water should be fluoridated!

4 Say whether Alice and Betty agree with adding fluoride to water.

5 Talk to your friends about what Alice and Betty say and then write down **your** opinions about adding fluoride to water supplies.

6 Look back over pages **4** to **7** and then list what you should do to keep healthy teeth and gums.

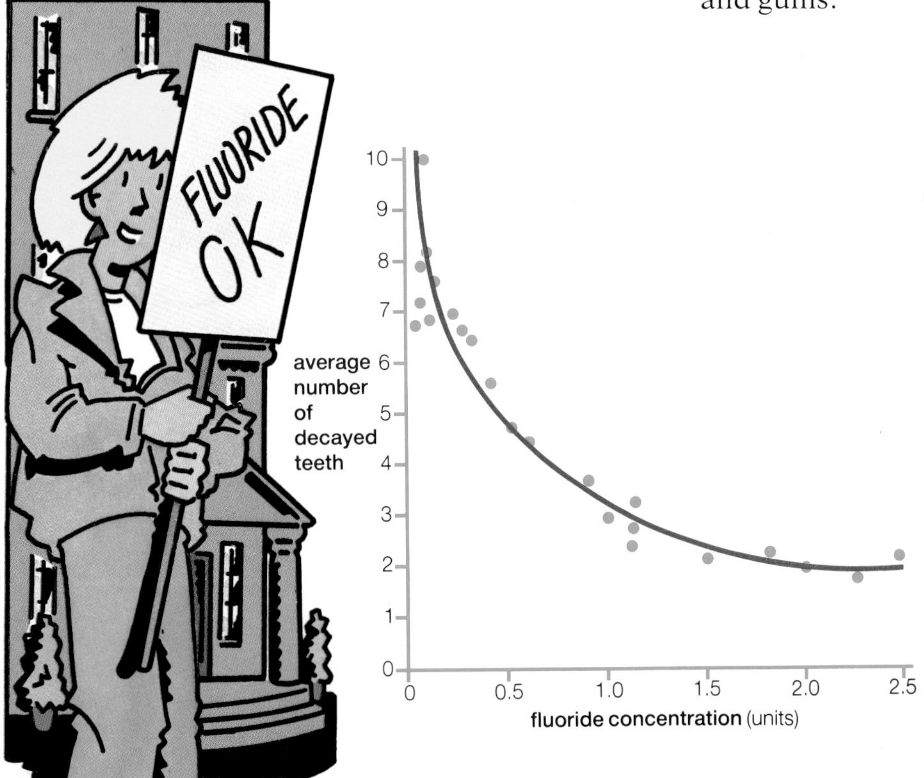

Alice Addit says "How can anyone be so daft as Betty? It has been proved that fluoridation stops tooth decay. Less tooth decay means less toothache, and you look a lot better with healthy teeth. Think of the cost in taxes to pay for dental treatment. I want my kids to keep their teeth: false teeth are no substitute for the real thing."

Betty Banit says "People like Alice really annoy me! Why should everyone be forced to drink fluoride? It is well known that a high concentration of fluoride is poisonous and even low concentrations might cause health problems. The cost of fluoridation would be enormous — why should the water I use for washing have expensive fluoride in it? I say watch what you eat, and your teeth will be all right."

Food . . .

Why you need food

Most people in Britain have enough to eat. No one is likely to starve to death. An average person eats half a ton of solid food each year, and drinks 110 gallons of liquid.

Your body needs food to:

- **grow**
- **repair**
- **get energy**
- **keep healthy**

You're all on a diet!

The word **diet** simply means 'the things you eat and drink'. The diagram shows the food that a **varied diet** normally contains.

1 Using the diagram explain what is meant by a varied diet.

2 **a** List the foods you ate yesterday.
b Do you think you had a varied diet? Explain your answer.

Measuring how much energy there is in food

One way of measuring how much energy there is in food is shown opposite. As the food burns, heat energy is released. This warms the water. The more energy there is in the food the more heat energy is released, and the hotter the water gets.

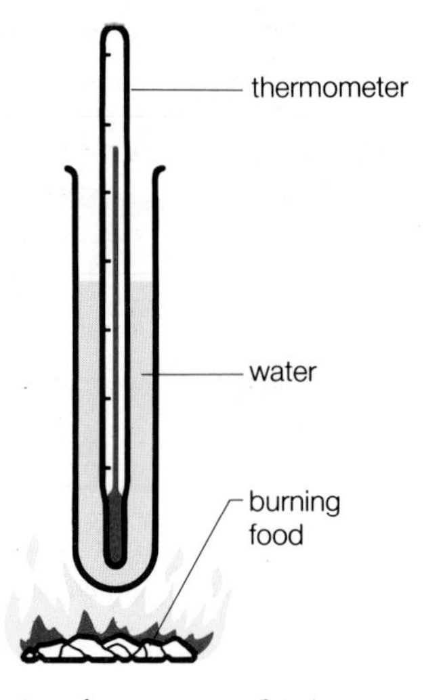

Measuring the energy in food

3 Why is a thermometer used in this experiment?

4 What two measurements would you make to find the increase in temperature of the water?

5 A lot of heat would escape and not help to warm the water.
a In what way would this affect the results?
b What could you do to reduce the loss of heat?

6 How would you find out which of two different foods contained the most energy?

. . . Glorious food

milk 770 kJ

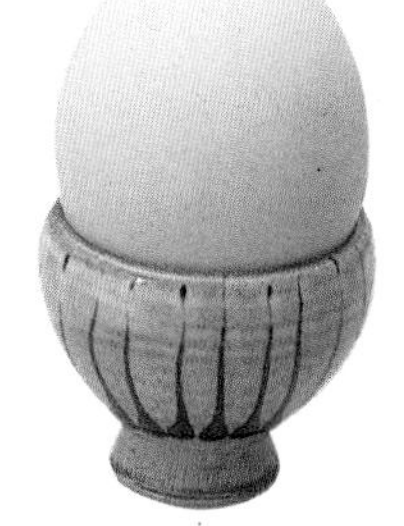

egg 157 kJ

butter 252 kJ

yoghurt 315 kJ

roll 756 kJ

apple 188 kJ

The energy contained in some familiar foods

The energy in familiar food

The energy in food can be measured in units called **kilojoules (kJ)**. (One kilojoule is quite a small amount of energy. The energy released when a match burns is about 4 kJ.) The photograph shows you how much energy there is in some familiar foods.

1 How much energy is there in a snack of ½ pint of milk and an apple?

2 How much energy is there in a breakfast of two boiled eggs, a buttered roll and a yoghurt?

The energy needs of four different people

The energy you need

How much energy you need depends on:

- **how big you are**
- **how active you are**
- **how fast you are growing**

The diagram to the left shows you how much energy is needed each day by four very different people.

3 Why is more energy needed each day by:
  a the boy than the girl?
  b the boy than the male office worker?
  c the male labourer than the male office worker?

4 Which of the four people will need to eat the most food each day? Explain your answer.

Fighting the flab

One out of three

If you regularly eat food containing more energy than you need, the extra food is stored in your body as fat and you become **overweight**. One out of three adults in Britain is overweight. Fatty foods contain a lot of energy compared with other foods. So, staying slim means taking care not to eat too much fat and also foods containing a lot of sugar! Meat, butter, and cheese have a high fat content — even lean meat is 10 % fat. Cakes, biscuits, and sweets have a high sugar content.

Being overweight is a problem

Joan always said that being fat kept her jolly — until she started getting pains in her chest. Her doctor explained that being overweight *could* help cause high blood pressure and heart disease, but said that Joan's heart was quite healthy. He advised her to lose some weight though, and Joan decided to take his advice.

1 Why was Joan worried about her chest pains?

2 Which foods should Joan cut down on, and why?

Careful slimming is a good idea for overweight people. Most people only need to stick to a varied diet and simply not eat too much. Trying to lose too much weight, too quickly, can be dangerous.

I was 19 stones . . . .

. . . . but now at 10 stones I feel much better

Some normal-weight people become so worried about their weight that they starve themselves. They have an illness called **anorexia**.

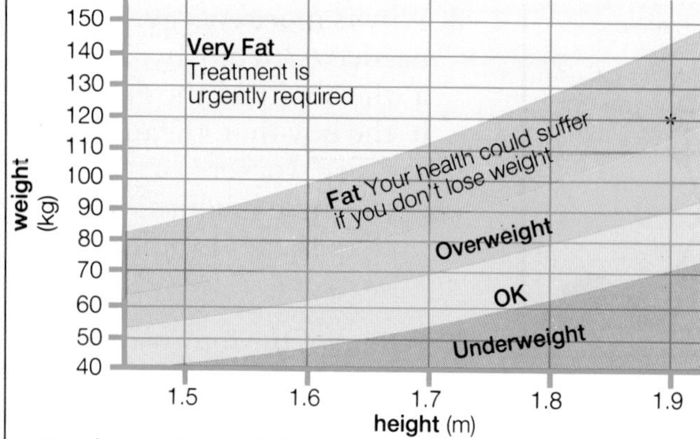

Height/weight graph for adults

Figuring it out

Stephen is 1.9 metres (m) tall and weighs 120 kilograms (kg). His position on the diagram is shown by *. So, Stephen is fat and his health could suffer if he doesn't lose weight.

3 Explain why being heavy doesn't have to mean that you are overweight.

4 Use the diagram to comment on:
Alice, 1.5 m and 100 kg.
Brian, 1.8 m and 60 kg.
Colin, 1.6 m and 55 kg.
Daisy, 1.7 m and 80 kg.

Food for thought

Plants are an important source of food

In the richer countries of the world, including Britain, animals are a major source of food. Most people enjoy eating meat, cheese, eggs, etc. In poorer countries a much bigger part of the people's diet comes from plants and meat is a luxury. A diet which is mainly from plants can be just as good as our diet. The bar chart compares the **protein** content of some foods from animals and some foods from plants. Protein is needed by your body for growth and repair.

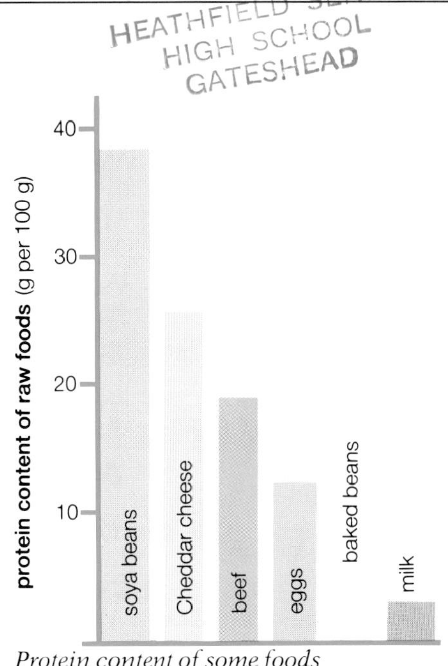

Protein content of some foods

People who *choose* not to eat meat are called **vegetarians**. Their religion may forbid eating meat, or they may not want to eat animals. Vegetarians who eat cereals, eggs, cheese and milk as well as vegetables and fruit will have a good, varied diet. But vegetarians who *only* eat fruit and vegetables have to take care that their diet contains everything needed for good health.

Fibre in your food

The important thing most likely to be lacking from a British person's diet is **fibre**. This is the part of bread, cereals, vegetables, and fruit which is not digested. Bread, cereals, fruit, and vegetables usually contain quite a lot of fibre. These foods are useful as part of a slimming diet as they fill you up without providing lots of energy. Scientists believe that the fibre in your diet helps prevent diseases of the gut, and may even help prevent heart disease.

Fibre foods

Food additives

Manufacturers are allowed to add certain substances to food for colouring, flavouring, or preserving. Such substances are called **food additives**. The labels on most pre-packed foods must list all ingredients, including additives (look at the example opposite). The higher up the list something appears, the more of it there is in the food. Food additives are usually listed in a way which explains their use and gives their chemical name or reference number.

Use the information to the right to give:

1 The purpose of additive E102.

2 The chemical name of an additive which enhances, that is 'brings out', flavour.

3 The additive present in the highest concentration.

then they melt in your mouth'

INGREDIENTS

Potato starch, vegetable oil and hydrogenated vegetable oil, potato flour, salt, autolysed yeast, flavouring, hydrolysed vegetable protein, cheese, onion, flavour enhancer (monosodium glutamate), pepper, colour (E102, E127), antioxidant (E320).

TP24/O

Food additives

Using alcohol

Dear Susan,
Thankyou very much for the lovely flowers on my birthday. We had a family get-together, a nice meal, and a couple of bottles of wine. I got a bit tipsy - but it was a great day!
Love,
Isobel

Percentage alcohol in some alcoholic drinks

Sensible drinking

Most people drink with their friends sometimes. Used in this way, **alcohol** does no harm. It relaxes people and helps them get on with each other.

% alcohol in a drink

1 UNIT OF ALCOHOL =

A measure of alcohol

How much alcohol?

The photograph above shows the percentage (%) alcohol in four kinds of drink. Another way to show this is by a **pie-chart** like the one above. The size of the 'piece of pie' compared with the whole circle shows the percentage of alcohol in the drink.

1 Which of the four kinds of drink contains the:
  a biggest % alcohol
  b smallest % alcohol?

2 Which of the four kinds of drink does the pie-chart show?

3 Draw a pie-chart for a drink with 25% alcohol.

Keeping count

The photographs opposite shows the amount of alcohol in some common drinks. This amount is called **one unit**. Doctors recommend that you should not drink more than 20 units of alcohol in a week, with no more than 5 units on any one day.

4 Isobel had a sherry before her meal and two glasses of wine with it. David had a pint of beer before his meal and two single whiskies afterwards. How many units of alcohol did each drink?

Mis-using alcohol

Dear Sandra,
I just had to write to you. Being all alone I found that a couple of drinks each day made life seem better – but now it's a couple of bottles! I feel so awful. Please help me.
Alison

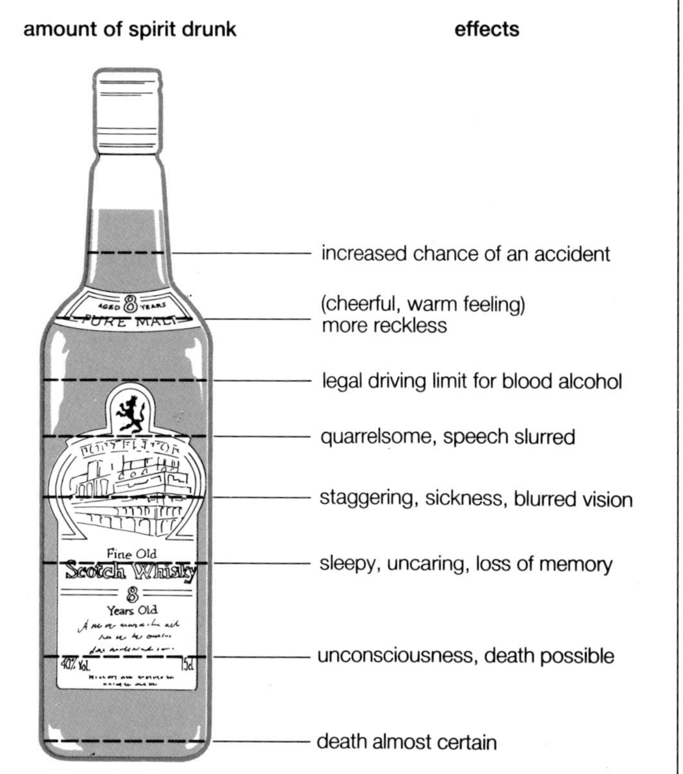

More drink means more drunk

Dangerous drinking

Drinking doesn't solve your problems — it just makes more problems. Alcohol is a **drug** and too much drinking can cause **addiction**. **Alcoholics** depend on alcohol, but they can be helped.

Blood alcohol level

When someone drinks alcohol it gets into their blood. **Blood alcohol level** is measured in milligrams (mg) of alcohol per 100 millilitres (ml) of blood. Each unit of alcohol drunk raises the blood alcohol level of an average person by about 15 mg/100 ml. The **liver** removes alcohol from the blood, but takes about an hour to deal with one unit of alcohol.

Using a breathalyser to check blood alcohol level

1 What blood alcohol level would be caused by drinking four units of alcohol?

2 What blood alcohol level would be caused by quickly drinking two and a half pints of beer, and how long would it take for the liver to remove this?

Only an accident?

The misuse of alcohol can cause violence, crime, family problems and health problems such as stomach ulcers, liver damage, and heart disease. Alcohol dulls the brain and makes accidents more likely. The line graph to the right shows how the chance of a driver having a road accident depends on his blood alcohol level. The **legal driving limit** for blood alcohol is 80 mg/ml, but the only really *safe* level is *no* alcohol.

3 What is the increased chance of an accident for a driver with a blood alcohol level of 130 mg/100 ml?

4 What is the increased chance of an accident for a driver with the legal alcohol limit in his blood?

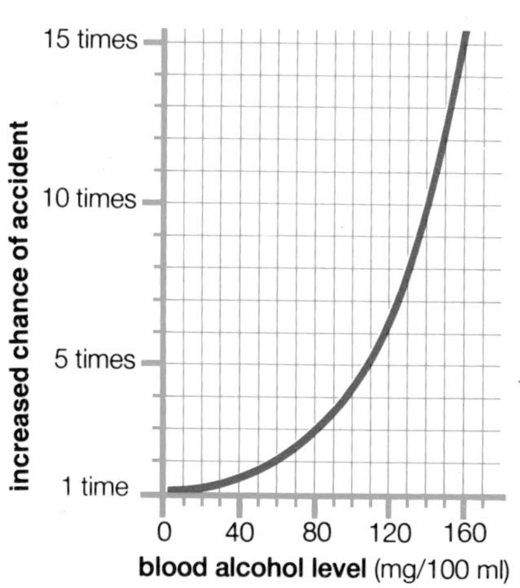

Blood alcohol and accident risk

Take a deep breath

Why bother breathing?

The air around you is a mixture of gases, one of which is **oxygen**. Your body needs oxygen to release energy from the food you eat. You can stay alive for several weeks without food, a few days without water, but only about five minutes without oxygen.

During **breathing** you take in air, from which your body gets the oxygen it needs.

A day's breathing would blow up an enormous balloon

Where the air goes

As you breathe in, air goes down your **windpipe** to your **lungs**. The diagram shows where these parts are in your body. The photograph is an X-ray of someone's chest. You can see their ribs as well as their lungs and heart.

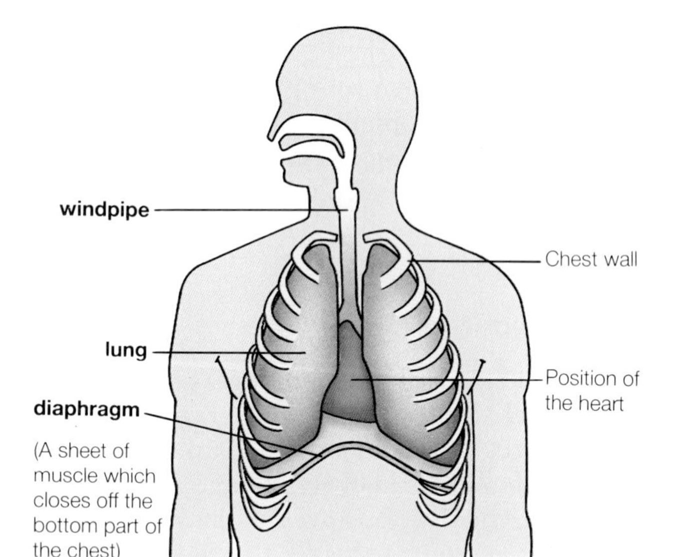

The human breathing system

A change of air

You breathe in and out about 15 times per minute when at rest. Each breath contains about 0.5 litres of air. In your lungs some **oxygen** passes from this air into your blood At the same time the gas **carbon dioxide** passes from your blood into the air, and is breathed out. Carbon dioxide is one of the wastes which your body produces.

Inhaled (breathed in) air contains about 20% oxygen, 80% **nitrogen**, and a tiny amount of carbon dioxide. **Exhaled** (breathed out) air contains about 15% oxygen, 80% nitrogen, and 5% carbon dioxide.

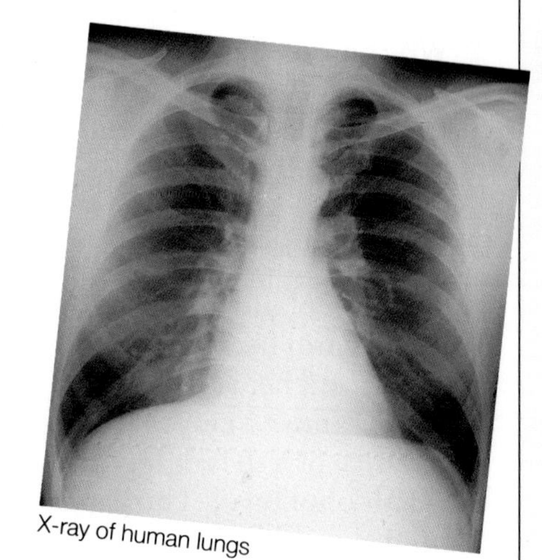

X-ray of human lungs

1 What volume of air do you breathe in and out in 1 minute at rest?

2 About what volume of air do you breathe in and out in a day, when at rest?

3 The pie-chart shows the gases in inhaled air. Draw a similar pie-chart for exhaled air.

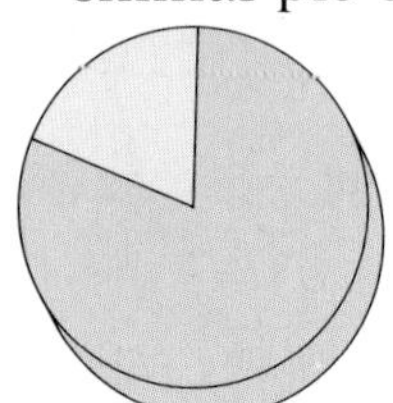

Gases in inhaled air

4 Explain why you breathe faster when you are running than when you are resting.

Breathing deeper

How you breathe

The changes which cause you to breathe in and breathe out are shown in the diagram.

- **Breathing in.** When the muscles between your ribs **contract** (tighten), your **ribs** are raised and your chest expands. At the same time, your **diaphragm** muscle contracts and flattens. The space inside your chest gets bigger and the air pressure inside your lungs gets less. Air comes into your lungs from outside.
- **Breathing out.** When the muscles between your ribs **relax**, your ribs are lowered. At the same time, your diaphragm muscle relaxes and pushes upwards. The space inside your chest gets smaller and the air pressure inside your lungs gets higher. Air is pushed out of your lungs to the outside.

Luckily, you don't have to think about all this! It happens automatically.

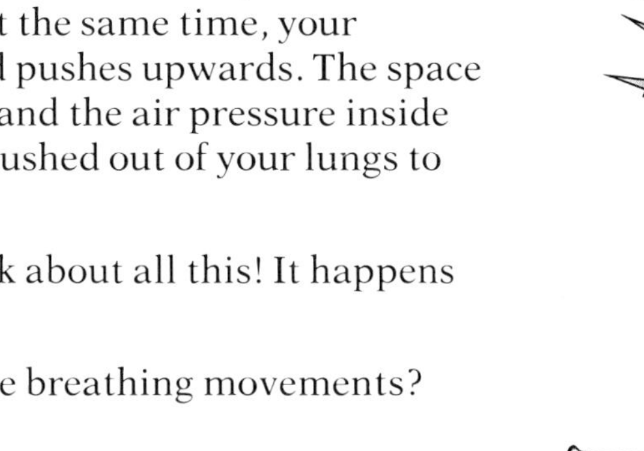

Breathing in

Breathing out

1 Which muscles bring about the breathing movements?

More about breathing

The diagrams show your breathing system in greater detail. Your windpipe and other **air passages** are lined with sticky **mucus**. This traps dirt, and germs which may be in the breathed-in air. The tiny '**hairs**' beat to and fro' and sweep the dirty mucus up to your throat where it is swallowed. The air passages end in little bags called **air sacs**. These have very thin walls and are close to tiny blood vessels. Oxygen passes from the breathed-in air into your blood at the air sacs.

2 Name one sort of air passage.

3 The diagram shows a magnified view of an air sac and some blood vessels. How will the blood at B differ from the blood at A?

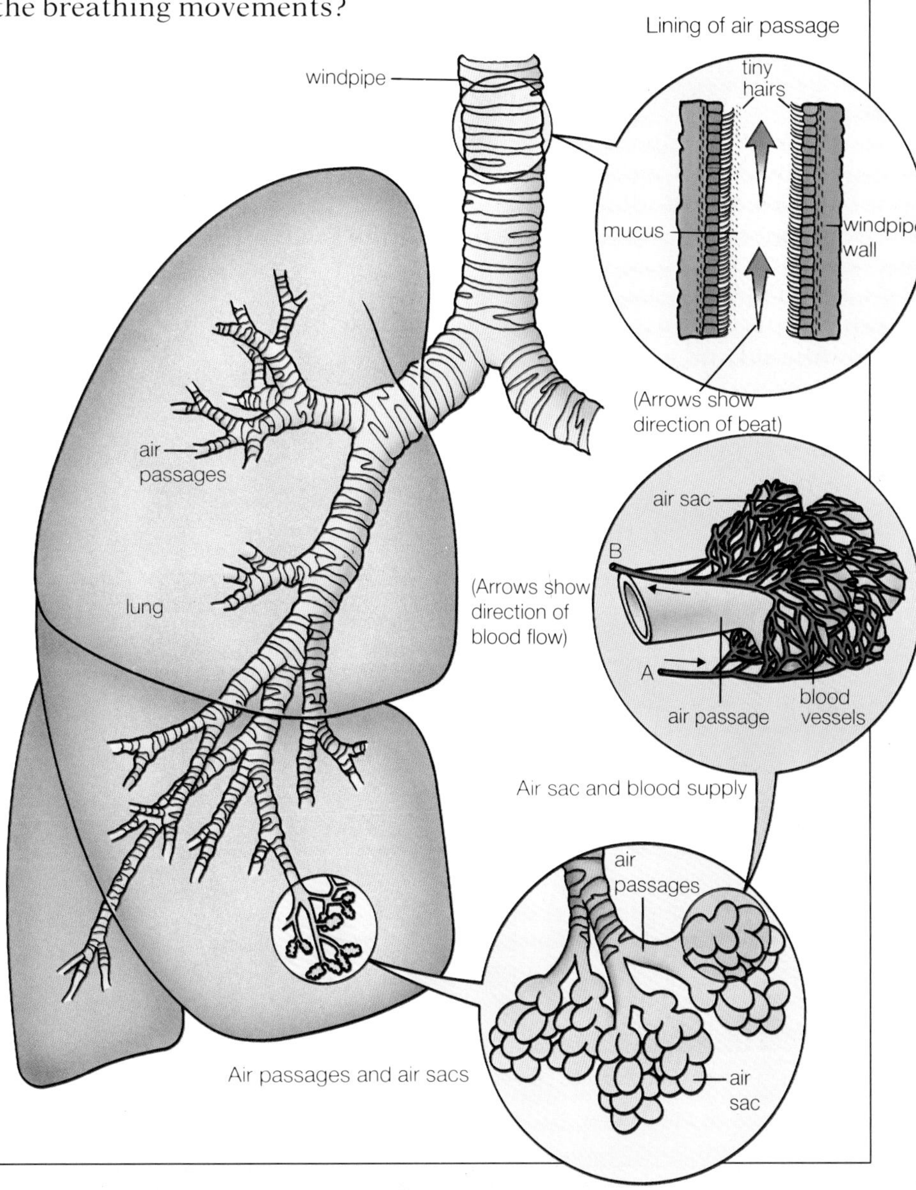

Investigating breathing

Checking on carbon dioxide

The experiments summarise two ways in which you can test for the presence of carbon dioxide.

1 Which chemical goes cloudy when carbon dioxide is bubbled through it?

2 What colour change would you expect to see if you bubbled carbon dioxide through some bicarbonate indicator solution?

3 If the bicarbonate indicator changes colour *quickly* from orange-red to yellow what can you tell about the amount of carbon dioxide in a sample of air?

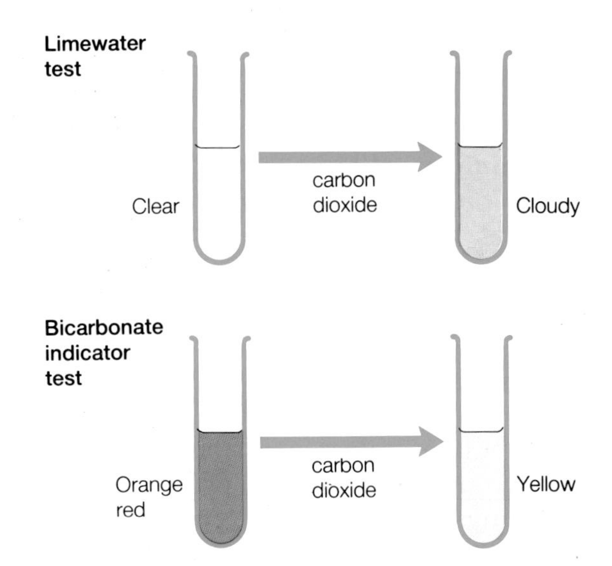

Tests for carbon dioxide

An experiment on breathing

The diagram shows apparatus which you could use to compare the amount of carbon dioxide in inhaled and exhaled air. When you breathe in through tube 1, air is pulled in through tube 2 and bubbles through the liquid X in **A**. When you breathe out through tube 1, air bubbles through the liquid X in **B** before being pushed out through tube 3.

Suppose that you did use this apparatus to compare the amount of carbon dioxide in inhaled and exhaled air.

4 What would you use as liquid X?

5 As the apparatus is drawn, the experiment would not be a fair one. Explain why not, and say what change you would make.

6 Suppose that you carried out a fair experiment and breathed in and out several times through tube 1. What results would you expect? Explain why.

7 In what way might running before the experiment affect your results? Explain why.

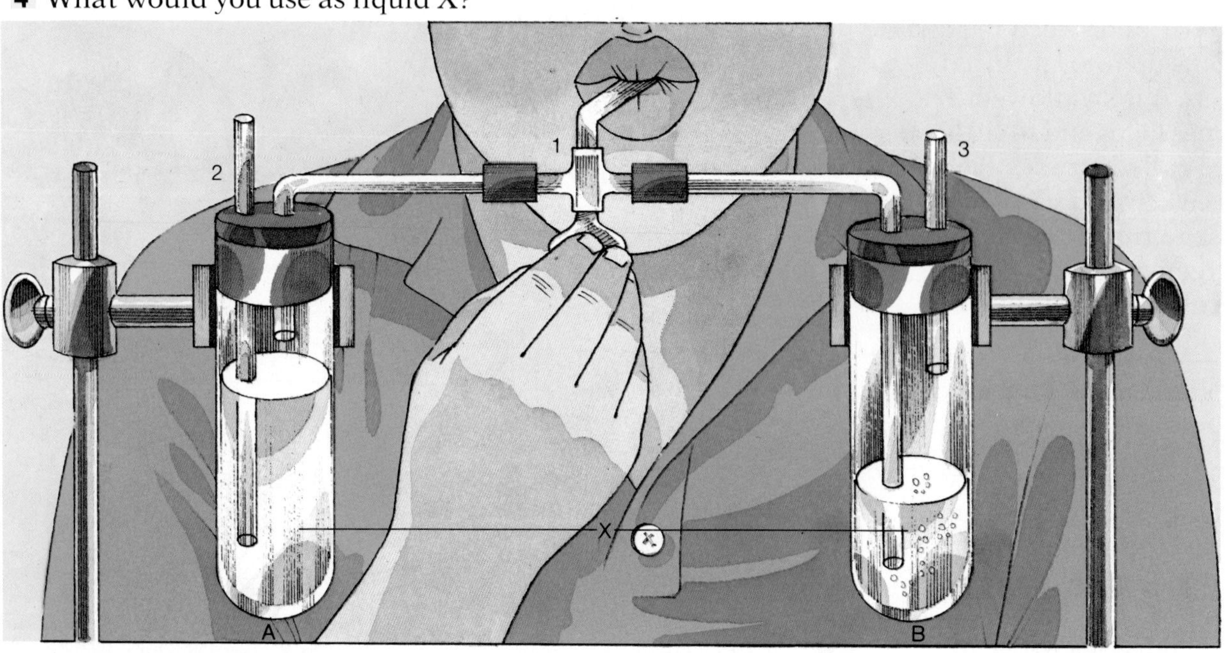

Comparing the carbon dioxide content of inhaled and exhaled air

Breath of life

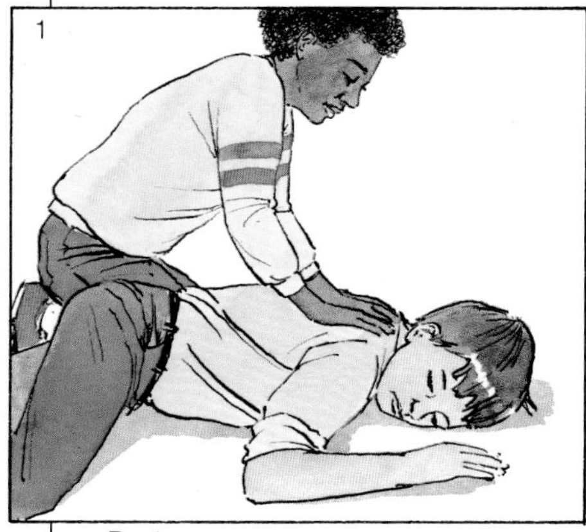
Back pressure

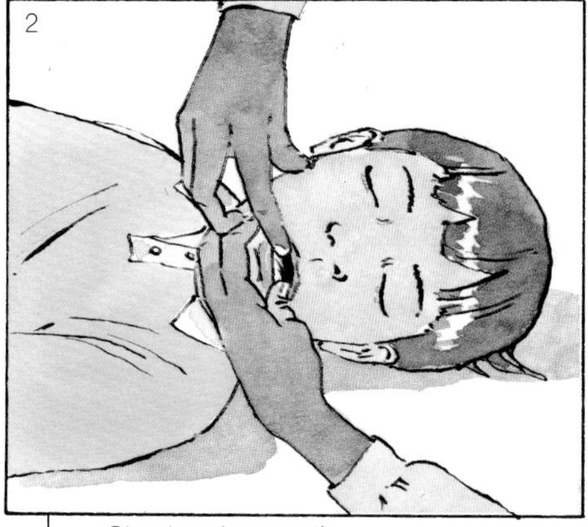
Clearing the mouth

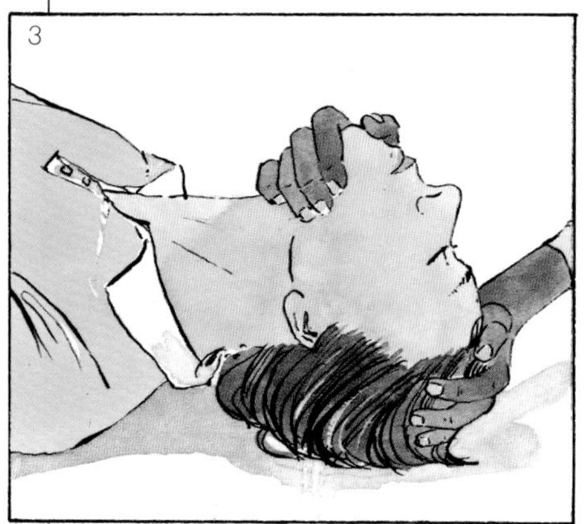
Positioning the head

Artificial respiration

When Charlie felt like a bit of peace and quiet he would set off for a day's fishing. One day he made a very important catch!

Charlie had been fishing for about an hour when he heard splashing. 'Just kids again', he thought: 'chucking in rubbish. That will really scare the fish away.' But next he heard screaming. Someone was in trouble. He sprinted to where the noise had come from. Now all was quiet, and a boy's body was floating face-down in the water. Charlie felt scared but he knew that he must act quickly. He dragged the boy out and checked for a heart-beat. So far, so good! He pressed down hard on the boy's back a few times and then turned him face up. He watched for some movement of the boy's chest and listened at his mouth. No luck! Charlie tilted the boy's head back until his chin was in the air, and made sure that his mouth was clear. He crouched down and held the boy's chin with one hand and pinched his nose closed with the other. Charlie sealed his mouth over the boy's and blew gently, removed his mouth and watched the boy's chest fall before blowing again. The next ten minutes seemed like hours. Slowly though the boy began to breathe for himself again. Charlie's efforts had been rewarded.

Drowning, gas poisoning, and electric shocks can all kill by stopping your heart beating or your breathing. Giving **artificial respiration** to someone means helping them to start breathing again. The **kiss of life** is one way of doing this: it is quite simple to learn at a first-aid class, and could help you to save a life.

1 How did Charlie try to get water out of the boy's lungs?

2 Why did Charlie pinch the boy's nose?

3 How was Charlie sure that the air he blew out had gone into the boy's lungs?

4 Describe how the kiss of life is given.

5 The kiss of life works because exhaled air has quite a lot of oxygen in it. Use the index to write down the percentage of gases in inhaled and in exhaled air.

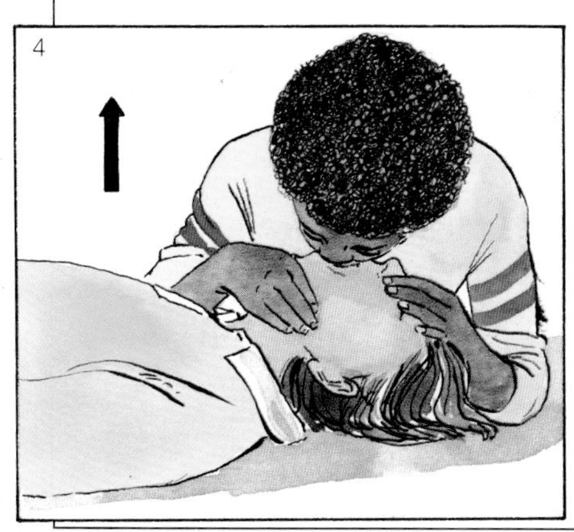
Kiss of life

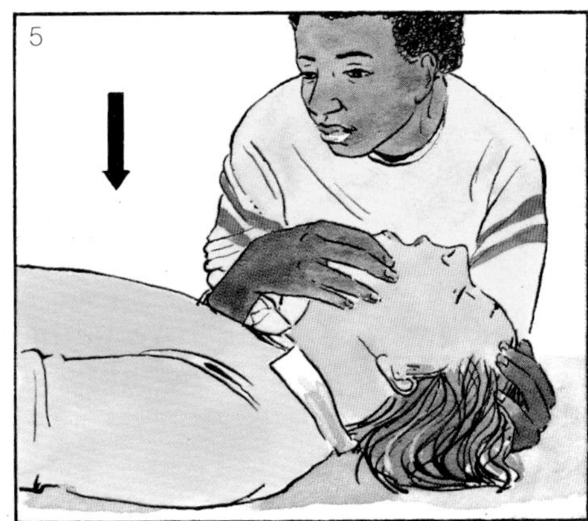
Breath check

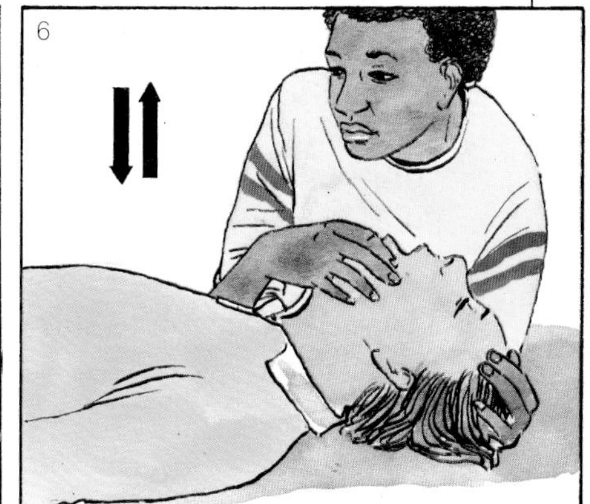
Breathing restored

Gone in a puff of smoke

Breathing can be dangerous

Sometimes you can't avoid breathing in harmful substances. Dangerous chemicals can get into your lungs. From there they may enter your blood and pass round your body.

But some people breath in harmful substances on purpose. They may take up **glue-sniffing**, for example. This can make them do things which are dangerous to themselves or to others. The chemicals they breathe in are poisonous — glue-sniffing can kill! A lot more people risk their health by **smoking**. Tobacco smoke contains **tar**, **nicotine**, and **carbon monoxide**, all of which are harmful. Non-smokers can't avoid these harmful substances altogether; breathing in other people's smoke can be dangerous.

Second-hand smokers

Smoky city

1 Use the photographs to name two ways that harmful chemicals get into the air.

2 Where in your lungs do chemicals enter your blood?

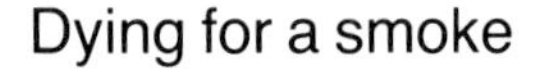

Dying for a smoke

It has been estimated that of 1000 young men who smoke:

1 will be murdered,
6 will die in road accidents, and
250 will die early as a result of smoking.

This table shows the death rate from **lung cancer** among men smoking different numbers of cigarettes per day.

Number of cigarettes smoked per day	10	20	30	40
Deaths per 10 000 men	6	16	21	30

Cigarette smoking and lung cancer

3 What is the death rate from lung cancer among men smoking 30 cigarettes per day?

4 How does the number of cigarettes smoked per day seem to affect the death rate from lung cancer?

5 Draw a line graph to show the results in the table.

This table shows the death rate from lung cancer among men who gave up smoking cigarettes.

Years stopped smoking	2	6	10	15	20
Deaths per 10 000 men	10	5	3	2	2

Stopping smoking and lung cancer

6 What is the death rate from lung cancer among men who have stopped smoking for 6 years?

7 Describe how giving up smoking cigarettes seems to affect the death rate from lung cancer.

8 Draw a line graph to show the results in the table.

Tar-get

Everybody isn't doing it!

Most people in Britain *don't* smoke: over 60% of men and women are non-smokers. There are about 10 million ex-smokers.

The **nicotine** in tobacco smoke is a drug which some people get addicted to. It paralyses the tiny 'hairs' in the lining of the breathing passages: this can give you a **smoker's cough**, or cause **bronchitis**.

The **carbon monoxide** in tobacco smoke gets into your blood and makes it harder for the red blood cells to pick up oxygen.

The **tar** in tobacco smoke sticks in your air sacs, irritates these and can eventually cause **lung cancer**. Smoking also seems to cause heart disease.

No smoking

1 Name 3 harmful things in tobacco smoke.

2 Find out the price of 20 cigarettes and then work out how much would it cost you to smoke 20 cigarettes each day for the next 10 years at this price.

Testing for tar

The apparatus shown in the diagram can be used to find out how much tar is formed when a cigarette is smoked. The suction pump draws air through the cigarette, and the tar gets trapped in the cotton wool. If you weigh the cotton wool on a sensitive balance before and after the experiment then you can work out its increase in weight: this is the weight of tar.

burning cigarette

To suction pump

cotton wool

Measuring the tar content of a cigarette

The Government publishes figures comparing the amounts of tar produced by different brands of cigarette. Some of these figures are shown in the table. The amount of tar reaching the smoker is given as milligrams per cigarette (mg/cig).

brand	**tar** (mg/cig)
Players No. 6 Extra Mild	9
Embassy No. 5 Extra Mild	10
Peter Stuyvesant King Size	13
Embassy Regal	16
Woodbine Virginia	18
Capstan Full Strength	25

Tar content of cigarettes

3 How much more tar (in mg) is there in a Capstan Full Strength cigarette than in a Players No. 6 Extra Mild?

4 Why should the cigarette be 'smoked' slowly in the experiment described above?

5 Describe how you would use the apparatus shown to find out how good the filter on a filter-tip cigarette is at trapping tar.

6 How much tar would you inhale if you smoked 20 Embassy Regal cigarettes each day for 10 years?

7 Draw a bar chart to compare the tar produced by four brands of cigarette from the table.

The living liquid

5 litres is a lot of blood

Blood is your body's transport system

Your body contains about five litres of blood. It is inside tubes called **blood vessels** which channel blood from one part of your body to another. Blood delivers food and oxygen to where they are needed. It picks up waste products and takes them to where they are got rid of. It also carries heat around your body.

Not just a red liquid

The photograph shows blood through a microscope. **Red blood cells** pick up oxygen from your lungs and carry it to the rest of your body. **White blood cells** fight any germs which might get into your body. **Platelets** help stop you losing blood from damaged blood vessels. They form **clots** which plug the damaged parts. The liquid **plasma** forms about 55% of blood. It is mostly water, with chemicals dissolved in it. Plasma carries dissolved food around your body, and blood cells.

Microscopic structure of blood

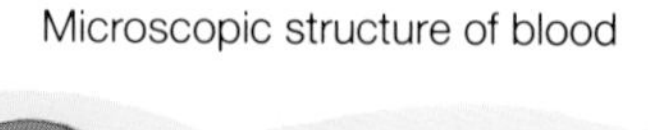

The diagram shows the main parts of blood.

1 Identify the parts labelled W, X, Y, and Z, and write a sentence about each saying what it does.

2 Draw a table to summarize the information you obtained in question 1.

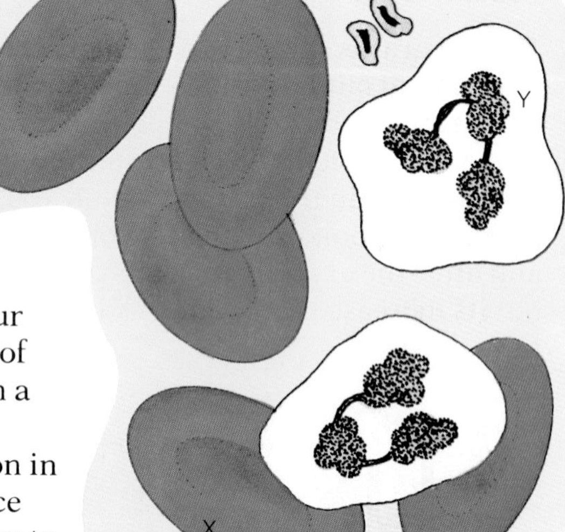

The main parts of blood

More about your blood

Most of the blood cells are made in the **marrow** inside your bones. There are about a million blood cells in each drop of blood: they are all very, very tiny. Red blood cells contain a chemical called **haemoglobin** which joins with oxygen. Haemoglobin contains **iron**, so if you don't get enough iron in your diet then fewer red blood cells can be made to replace those that wear out. A lack of red blood cells will cause you to feel tired and to look pale: you will be suffering from **anaemia**.

If some blood is spun round and round very fast in a tube, the red blood cells sink to the bottom of the tube. The diagram shows two lots of blood (1 and 2) which were treated in this way. One lot of blood was normal, the other was from an anaemic person.

3 Which of the two lots of blood had more red cells?

4 Which of the two lots of blood came from an anaemic person? Explain your answer.

5 Explain *why* an anaemic person often looks pale and feels tired.

Spun blood

The same, but different

Giving blood

Losing a lot of blood, because of injury or illness, can be fatal. The photograph shows a **blood donor** giving blood. The blood drains from a blood vessel in his arm into a collecting bag. In an emergency, blood may be given directly from one person to another. But usually, donated blood is kept in cold storage until needed. The second photograph shows a patient being given blood by means of a **blood transfusion**.

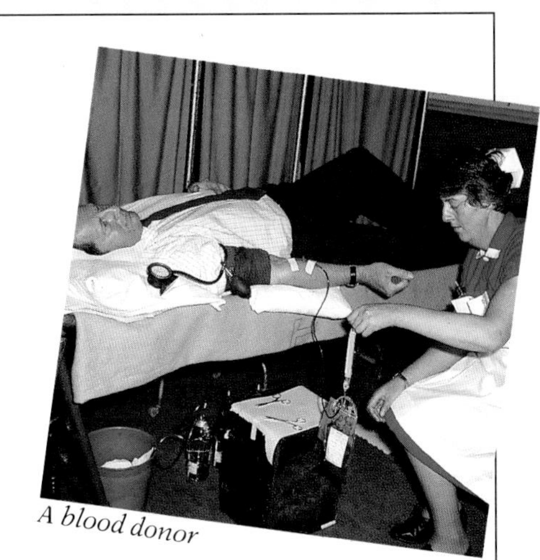

A blood donor

BLOOD GROUPS

WHEN Bjorn Svennson's tyre burst, he was doing 120 mph. His car went out of control and hit a crash barrier. It landed on its side a long way down the track.

The ambulance team knew the blood groups of all the drivers in the race, including Bjorn's. The desperate fight for his life would have been lost within minutes if blood of the right group had not been available.

Bjorn has one thing to say to blood donors. 'Thanks.'

About 1890 it was discovered that there are different **blood groups**. If someone is given blood of the wrong group it may make his red blood cells stick together: small blood vessels may get blocked, and this can kill.

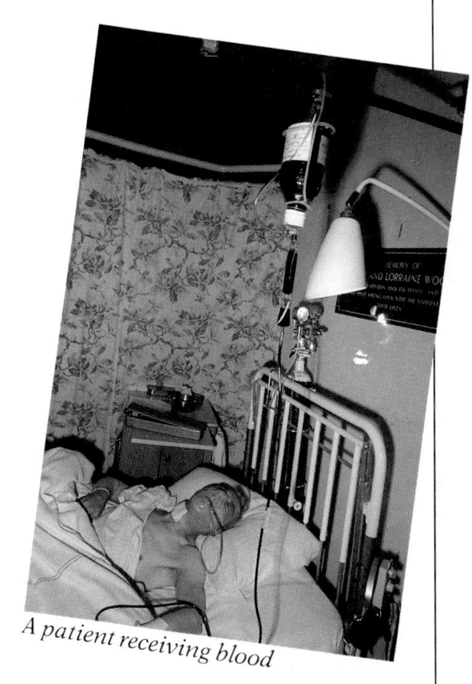

A patient receiving blood

Blood groups throughout the world

The four most important blood groups are called **A**, **B**, **AB**, and **0**. Everybody in the world belongs to one of these. The table shows how the percentage (%) of people belonging to these groups differs from country to country.

1 What % of Scots belong to blood group 0?

2 Which country has the lowest % of blood group B?

3 Many people think that the Chinese and the Japanese are very closely related. Does the information in the table agree with this? Explain your answer.

4 The Welsh are closely related to the Scots and the Irish. What do you expect the % of blood group AB in Wales to be?

5 Draw a bar chart to compare the % of blood group AB in England, China, and Russia.

	% blood group			
Country	A	B	AB	O
Scotland	35	11	3	51
Ireland	32	11	3	54
England	42	8	3	47
China	23	26	6	45
Japan	36	22	9	32
Russia	36	23	8	33

World-wide blood groups

Germ warfare

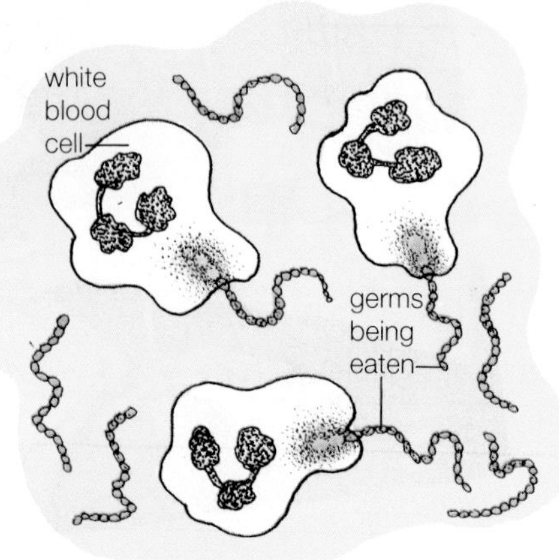

Germ-'eater'

Germs and disease

The tiniest living things are called **germs**. Most germs are harmless but some can cause **disease**. Different diseases, like flu and measles, are caused by different sorts of germ.

Your skin is a barrier, but if it is broken by a cut, for example, then germs can enter. Germs may also enter your body in the air you breathe and the food you eat. Once inside, the germs can breed and spread through your body. They make poisons which can cause damage or even kill.

1 Name 2 ways in which germs can get inside your body.

2 'Coughs and sneezes spread diseases!' Explain why this well-known rhyme is true.

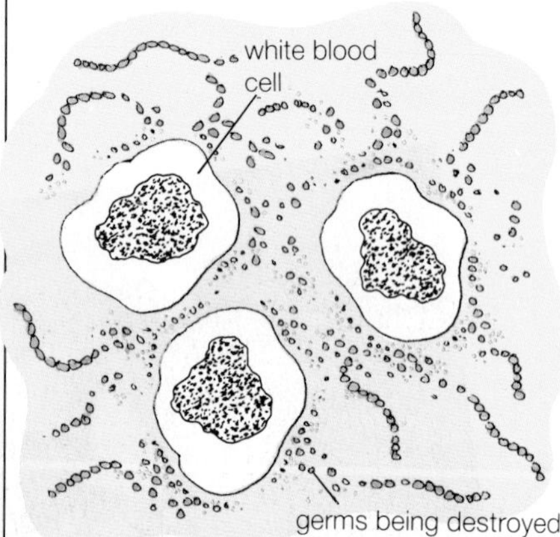

Chemical warfare

More about white blood cells

You read about white blood cells on page **20**. These cells defend your body against germs which have managed to enter. One sort of white blood cell 'eats' any germs it meets. Another sort carries out a kind of 'chemical warfare' against germs. It produces chemicals called **antibodies** which cause germs to break down and die. It also produces chemicals called **antitoxins** which cancel out the poisons made by germs. White blood cells are able to make different antibodies and antitoxins to deal with different sorts of germs.

3 What is main job done by white blood cells?

4 What is the difference between an antibody and an antitoxin?

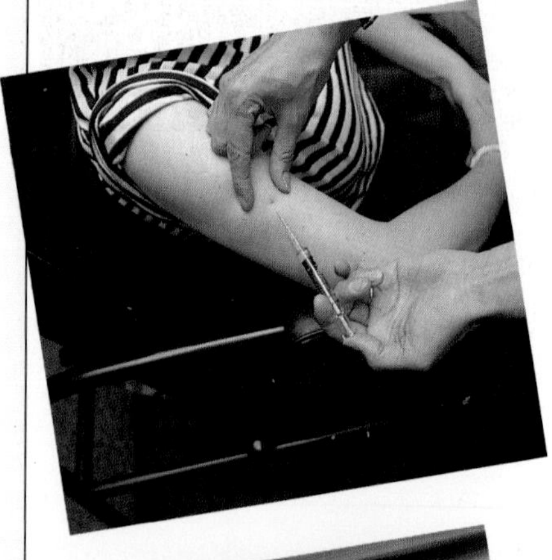

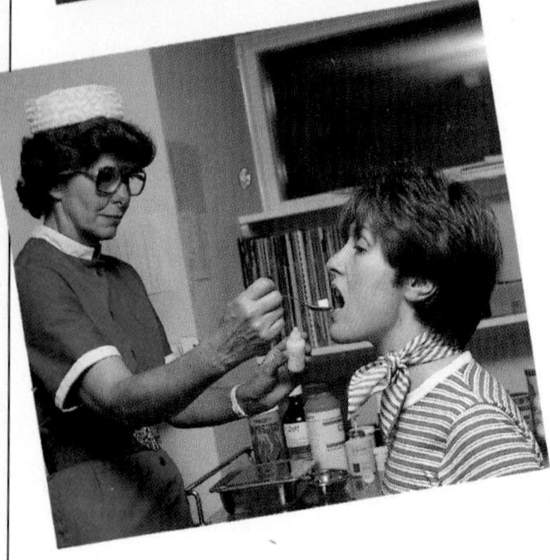

Immunity and immunisation

After any disease, the antibodies you made stay in your blood for a while. This gives you **immunity** (resistance) to the disease. You may be immune for a few weeks (as after 'flu) or for a lifetime (as after measles).
Doctors can give you immunity to some diseases by:

- Putting dead or weakened germs into you. These cause antibodies to be formed but can't give you the disease.
- Putting actual antibodies or antitoxins into you. This gives you quick protection in an emergency.

Giving immunity in these ways is called **immunisation**. Immunisation may be given by an injection, for example against measles, or by mouth, for example against polio.

5 What is meant by being immune to a disease?

6 Suppose you had to go abroad tomorrow to a country where a deadly disease was common. How might a doctor help you?

Prevention is better than cure

My name is James Phipps; I'm twelve years old and lucky to be alive. Four years ago, in 1796, people were dying like flies of a disease called smallpox. A doctor called Edward Jenner lived near our house in Gloucestershire. He had noticed that milkmaids never seemed to catch smallpox, although they did catch cowpox from the cows they milked. Jenner decided to find out if someone could be protected against smallpox by giving them cowpox – that someone was me! My mum agreed to let him try, so I suppose it was all right. He scratched some liquid from a cowpox blister into my arm: I got cowpox and felt a bit ill but I soon got over it. Cowpox isn't too bad a disease really. When I was healthy again, Dr Jenner scratched some liquid from a smallpox blister into my arm. I didn't catch smallpox – thank goodness! A few months later he tried again but I still didn't catch smallpox.

A risky experiment

1 Which two diseases are mentioned above?

2 What is the above writing mainly about?
- **a** The life of James Phipps.
- **b** How experiments are carried out.
- **c** An early attempt at immunisation.
- **d** Why smallpox is dangerous.

3 Explain why James Phipps didn't catch smallpox, using information from page **22**.

age	immunisation
from 3 months	dipheria, whooping cough, tetanus, polio } 'triple' vaccine
5–6 months	diphtheria, whooping cough, tetanus, polio (booster) } (booster)
9–11 months	diphtheria, whooping cough, tetanus, polio (booster) } (booster)
12–24 months	measles
about 5 years	diphtheria (booster), tetanus (booster), polio (booster)
girls of ages 10 to 14	rubella (German measles)
girls and boys at about 13 years	tuberculosis (BCG vaccination)
15–19 years (leaving school)	tetanus (booster), polio (booster)

The usual timetable for immunisations

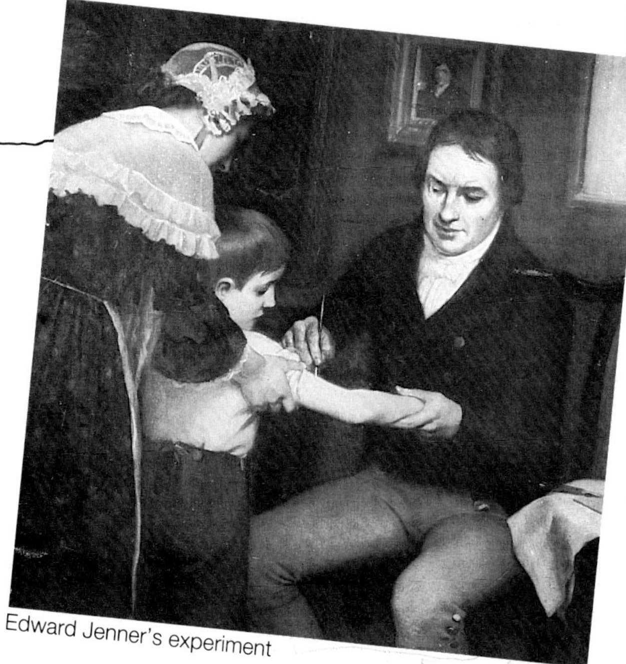
Edward Jenner's experiment

Timetabled immunisation

The timetable shows when British boys and girls are normally immunised. A **booster** immunisation 'tops-up' the level of an antibody which is already present.

4 Against which disease are girls, but not boys, immunised?

5 Write short notes about two of the diseases named, using books supplied by your teacher.

Have a heart

A job for life

The diagram shows the position of the **heart** in the body. It is slightly to the left of centre. Your heart is about the size of your fist. It is a blood-filled bag of muscle which acts as a **pump**. When the heart muscle contracts, your heart squeezes out blood; when the heart muscle relaxes, the heart fills up again with blood. This non-stop action **circulates** blood around your body. Your heart works all your life without rest.

There are miles of **blood vessels** in your body, through which your blood circulates. The diagram only shows some of the main blood vessels.

1 Explain why a chest injury can be very dangerous.

2 Look back at page **14**, and then explain how your heart is well protected inside your chest.

The position of the heart

Heart massage

If someone's heart stops beating they will quickly die unless it starts up again. This is because their blood circulation stops.

It is sometimes possible to restart a heart. The diagrams show the two stages of **heart massage**. You could learn these at a first-aid class. (*Warning*: *You should never try this on someone whose heart has not stopped — it could kill.*) A couple of blows to the middle of the chest are given first. These are followed by rhythmically pressing down on the chest and then relaxing. If the person has stopped breathing it will be also necessary to give the kiss of life.

3 What are the two stages of heart massage?

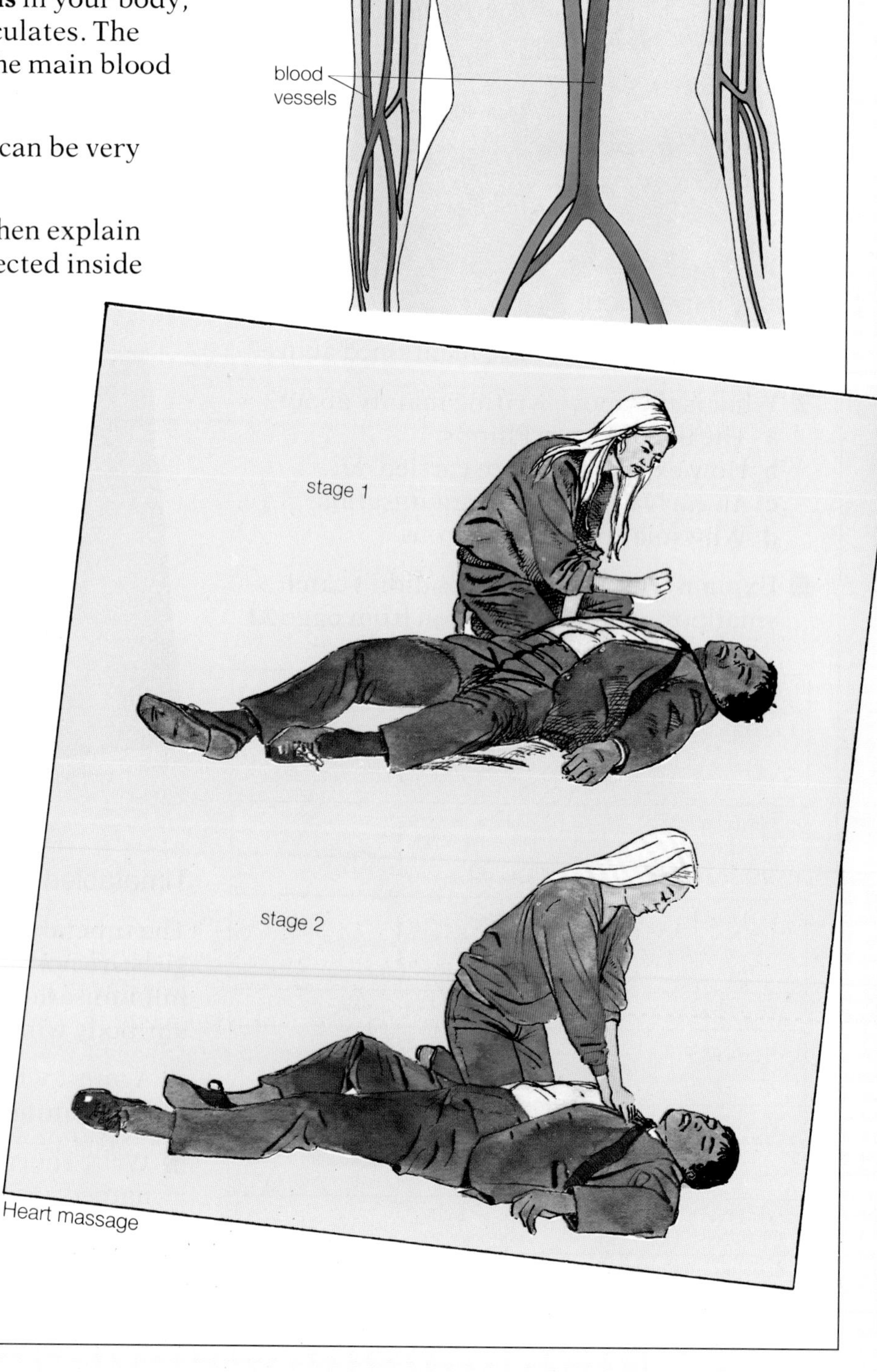

Heart massage

The blood stream

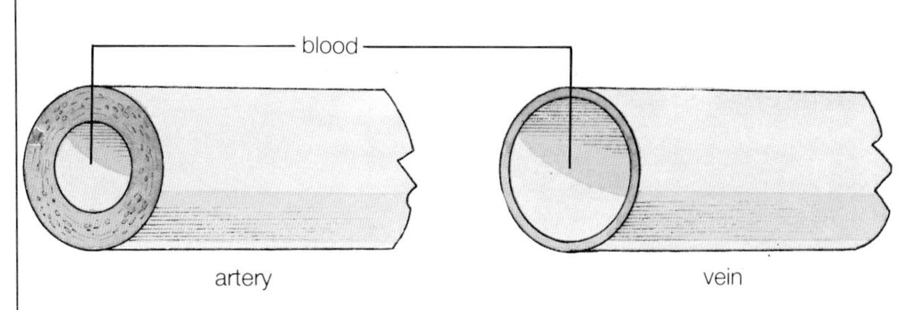

William Harvey investigates the circulation of blood

A one-way system

William Harvey was an English doctor who lived in the early 17th century. He was interested in the way that the heart moved blood around the body. At that time, scientists knew of two sorts of blood vessels; thick-walled **arteries** and thin-walled **veins**. They believed that the heart pushed out blood into both arteries and veins, and that when the heart relaxed blood returned to it by the same route. But Harvey was not sure. Harvey examined blood vessels in animals and humans. He showed that veins had structures in them called **valves**, which only let blood move in one direction — back to the heart. Harvey realised that the blood must be pumped out from the heart into the arteries and return to the heart in the veins.

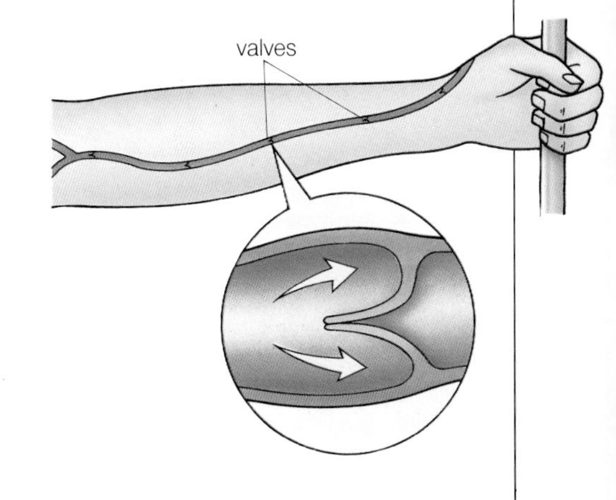

But Harvey was not able to show how blood passed from the arteries to the veins. It was not until after his death that a third sort of blood vessel was shown to make this connection. These blood vessels, called **capillaries**, are so narrow that they can only be seen by using a microscope.

1 What three sorts of blood vessel are named in the above writing?

2 What type of blood vessel has thick walls?

3 What is the above writing mainly about?
  a 17th century history.
  b The structure of arteries and veins.
  c Experiments on living animals.
  d The discovery that blood circulates.

Blood flow around the body

The diagram shows how the heart and blood vessels work together to **circulate** the blood. The arrows show the direction of circulation. Although the capillaries are microscopic, every part of the body has lots of them. Food and oxygen pass from the blood to the body-parts through these thin-walled capillaries.

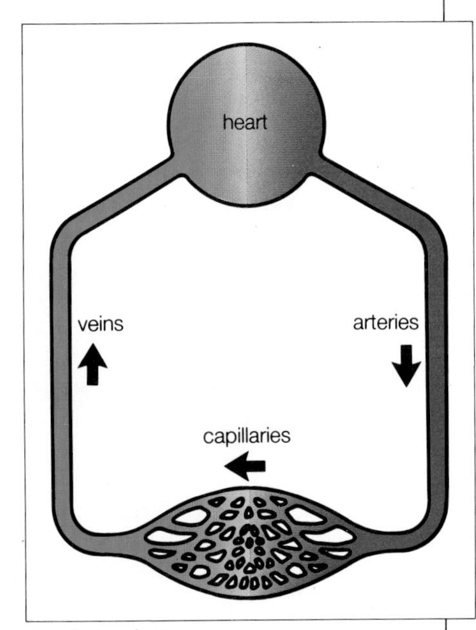

Blood circulation

4 What stops the blood circulating in the opposite direction to the arrows?

5 Write down the path taken by blood as it passes from the heart and back to the heart again.

More about circulation

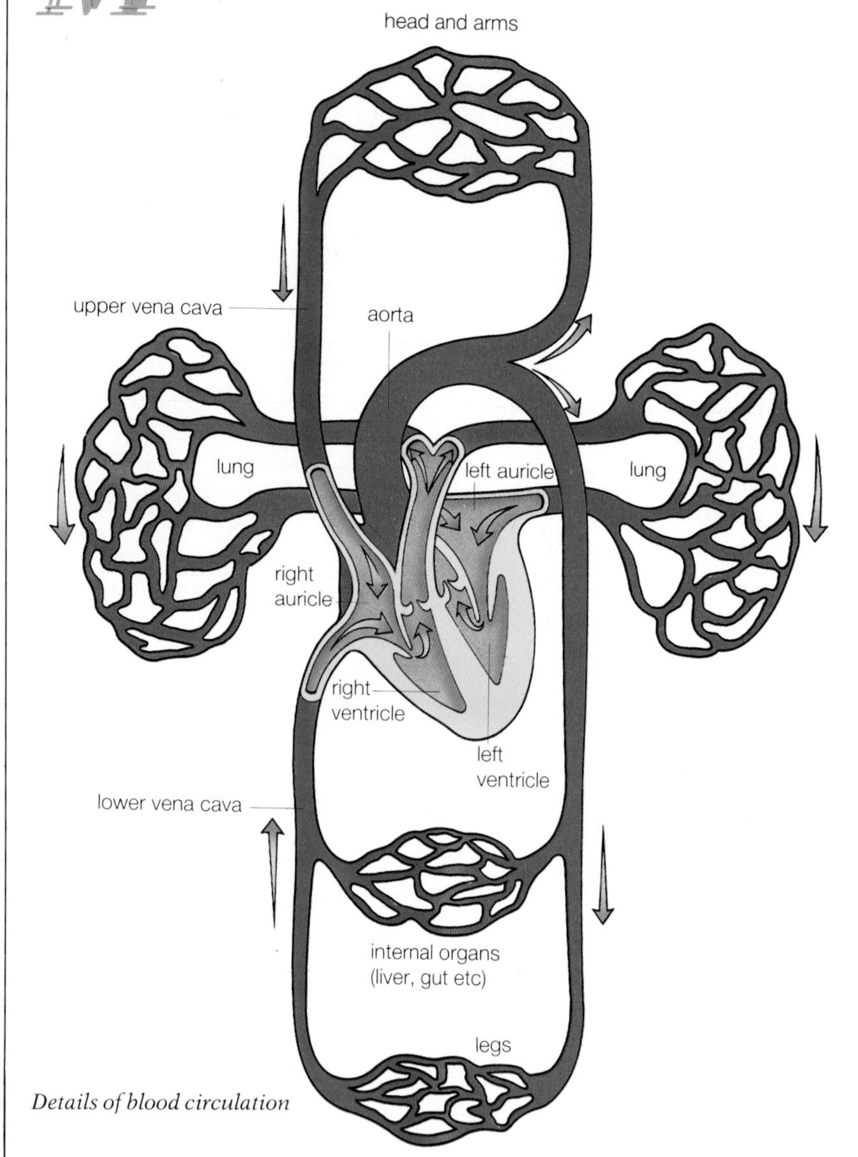

Details of blood circulation

Return trip

The diagram shows more detail of the structure of the heart, and of the way that blood circulates around the body. The arrows show the direction of circulation.

You can see that the inside of the heart is divided into compartments called **auricles** and **ventricles**. The diagram is drawn as if you were looking at someone face to face. This is why the left auricle, for example, is shown on the right.

1 Into how many compartments is your heart divided, and what are they called?

2 Imagine you are a red cell. Write down the path you would take as you circulated in the blood from the left ventricle and back again via the legs.

3 Which compartments of your heart will contain blood in which there is a lot of oxygen?

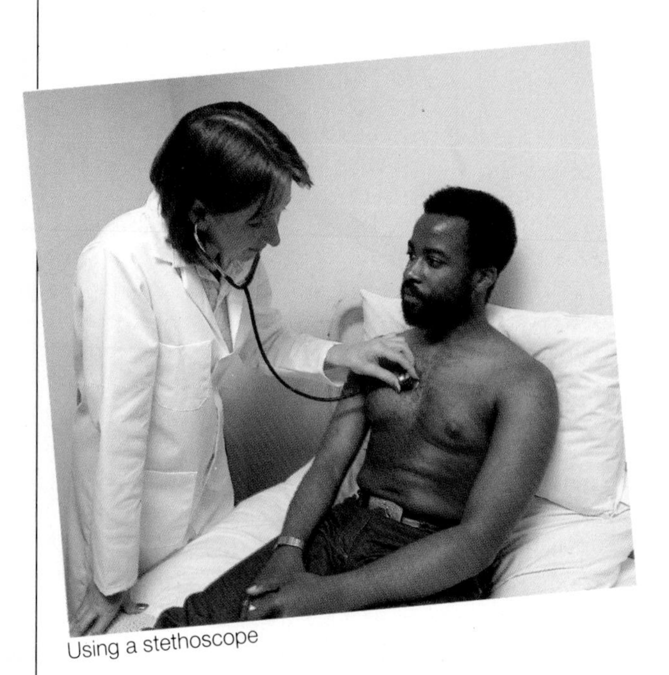
Using a stethoscope

Your noisy heart

If you put your ear to someone's chest you can listen to their heart beating. The sound is clearer when heard through a **stethoscope**. The noise is made by the valves in the heart opening and closing to control the flow of blood through the heart. Doctors can tell if your heart valves are working properly by listening to your heart beat.

4 What is a stethoscope used for?

5 Use the diagram to say where there are valves in your heart.

6 What else could doctors tell about your heart by listening to its beat other than if the valves are working properly?

Heart-throb

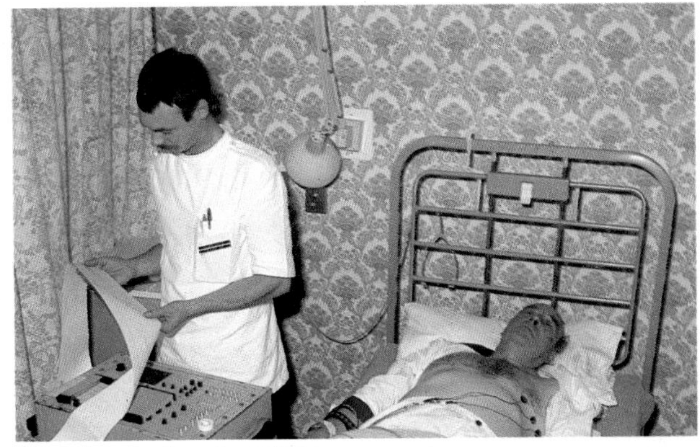
Recording the heart's activity

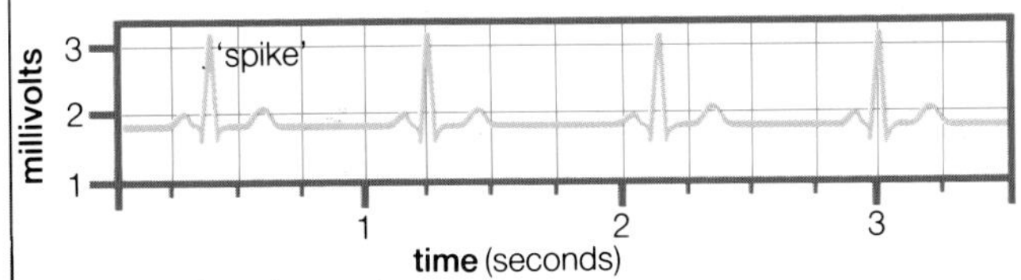

A normal cardiograph

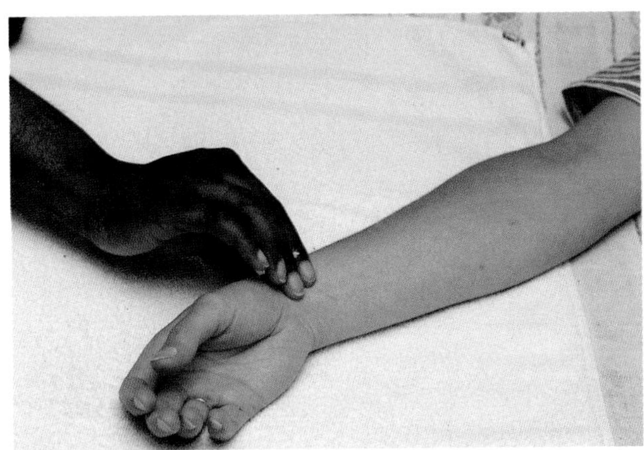
Finger on the pulse

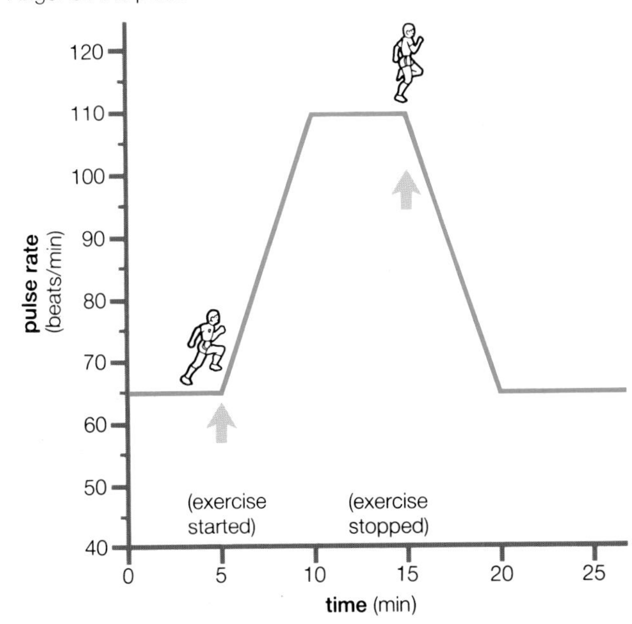

The effect of exercise on pulse rate

Checking the heart's condition

When your heart beats, small electrical changes take place. The photograph shows a patient having these changes measured. A recording of the changes on a chart is called a **cardiograph**, part of which is shown in the diagram below. Each 'spike' happens as the heart pushes blood out into the arteries. An unusual-looking cardiograph may be caused by an unhealthy heart.

1 How many heart beats are show on this cardiograph?

2 How would a weak heart be recognised from a cardiograph?

3 Use the cardiograph to work out the rate of heart beat in beats per minute.

Finger on the pulse

Each time your heart beats it pushes blood into your arteries and makes them swell-out a bit. If you put your fingers on someone's wrist as shown in the photograph, you will feel a sort of bumping. This is because you are squashing a small artery and can feel it swelling each time their heart beats. The regular swelling is called their **pulse**.

Your **pulse rate** is the same as the rate at which your heart beats. An average person's pulse rate is about 72 beats per minute, when at rest.

4 Robert's pulse rate is 68 beats per minute at rest. What will his rate of heart beat be?

5 Mary's pulse rate was 65 beats per minute, Joan's 67, Noreen's 88, Ethel's 75 and Anne's 55 beats per minute.
a Draw a bar chart to show these results.
b What was their average pulse rate?

6 The line graph shows how Mary's pulse rate changed over a period of time during which she took some exercise.
a What was her highest pulse rate?
b For how long did Mary exercise?
c What seems to be the effect of exercise on rate of heart beat? Explain why the body needs to respond in this way.

CHD

Coronary heart disease

The photograph shows the **coronary arteries** which supply blood to the heart muscle. As you get older, these arteries can gradually get blocked by a fatty deposit from your blood. This means that part of your heart gets less blood than it needs, causing **coronary heart disease (CHD)**.

One sign of CHD is a cramp-like pain across your chest. The pain may spread to your neck, shoulder, arm, or jaw, but usually fades if you rest for a few minutes. The pain is called **angina**. It can be eased by drugs, but it is a warning that you are more likely to have a **heart attack** than the average person. A heart attack is caused by the complete blockage of a coronary artery. Part of the heart is damaged by the lack of oxygen. The pain does not fade away with rest. In a severe heart attack the heart may stop beating and cause death if it can't be started again quickly.

The pie chart shows the causes of death in Britain:

1 What is CHD?

2 About what percentage of deaths is caused by CHD?

3 Give one example of an 'other cause' of death.

Heart attack — here I come!

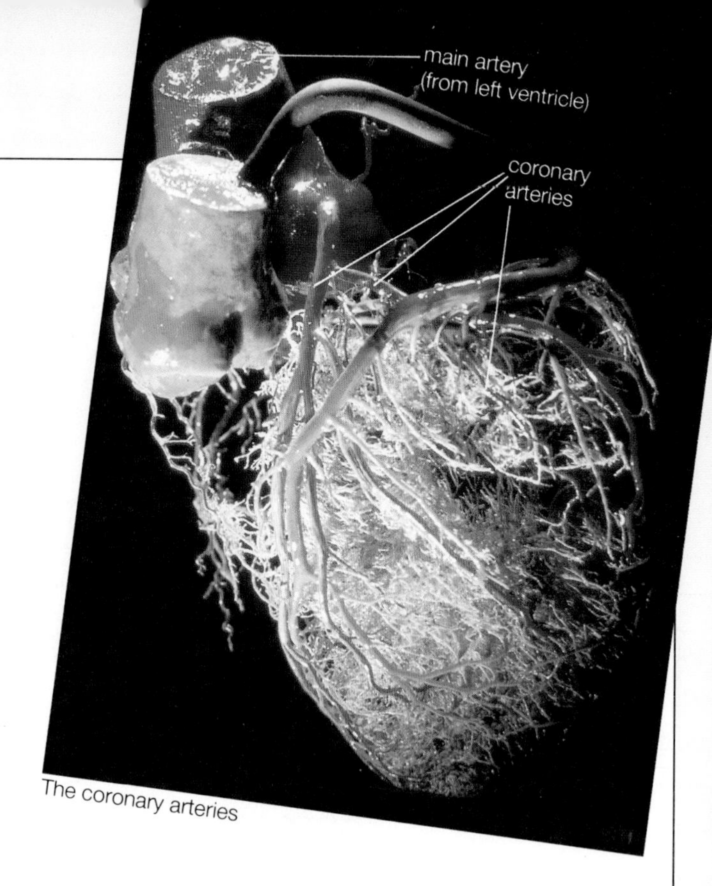

The coronary arteries

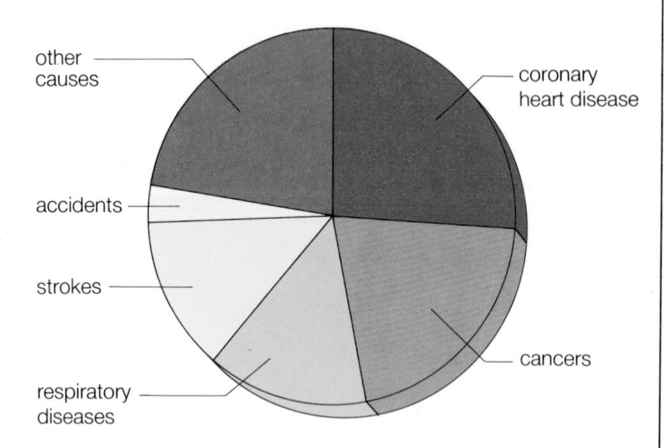

Causes of death in Britain

How to avoid coronary heart disease

- CHD seems to be more common in some families than in others.
- You are more likely to get CHD as you get older.
- Men are more likely to get CHD than are women.

You can't choose your parents, and there is not much that you can do about your age and sex! However, you can make choices about the way you live.

4 What sort of person is most likely to suffer from CHD?

5 Use the index to find out ways in which *you* can choose to avoid CHD. List what you find and where.

Problems, problems

Wrong place, clot!

The diagrams to the right show how a blood vessel can 'fur-up' inside. Furred-up arteries cannot expand so easily when blood is forced into them by the heart beat. **Hardening of the arteries**, as it is called, is one cause of **high blood pressure**. Sometimes blood-clots form inside furred-up arteries, and the blood supply to a vital part of the body may be blocked. A blockage like this is called a **thrombosis**. A thrombosis in a coronary artery could cause a heart attack: in an artery which supplies the brain it could cause a **stroke**, resulting in paralysis or even death.

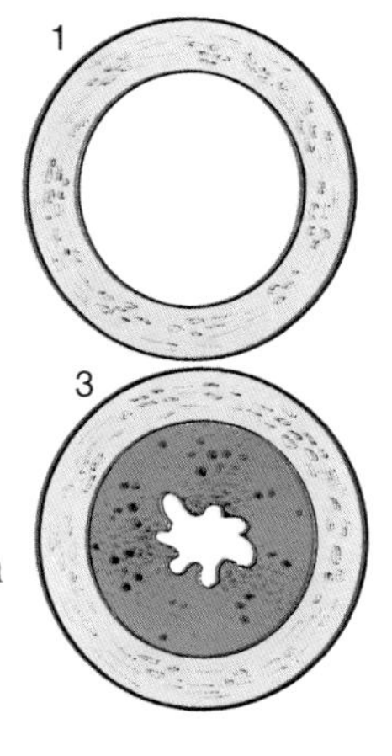

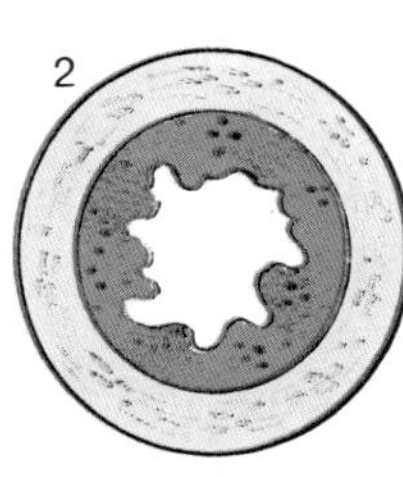

An originally healthy artery (1) becomes 'furred-up', (2), narrowing until it is easily blocked by a blood clot (3)

How arteries harden

Leaky valves

If the valves in your heart do not shut properly, your heart will not work as well as it should. A surgeon might be able to carry out a repair. Sometimes a faulty valve can be replaced with an artificial one, by an operation. An artificial valve is shown in the photograph. This kind of operation can't be done while the heart is beating, so the heart is by-passed and a **heart-lung machine** is used to do the work of the patient's heart and lungs during the operation.

Keeping pace

A healthy heart keeps a steady pace under normal conditions — it doesn't suddenly speed up or slow down. If someone's heart cannot keep a steady pace then sometimes they can be helped by having an operation to fit an artificial **pacemaker**. This involves fitting a small battery inside their chest. The battery produces a controlled supply of electricity to make their heart beat at a steady pace. The X-ray photograph to the right shows a pacemaker in position inside a patient's chest.

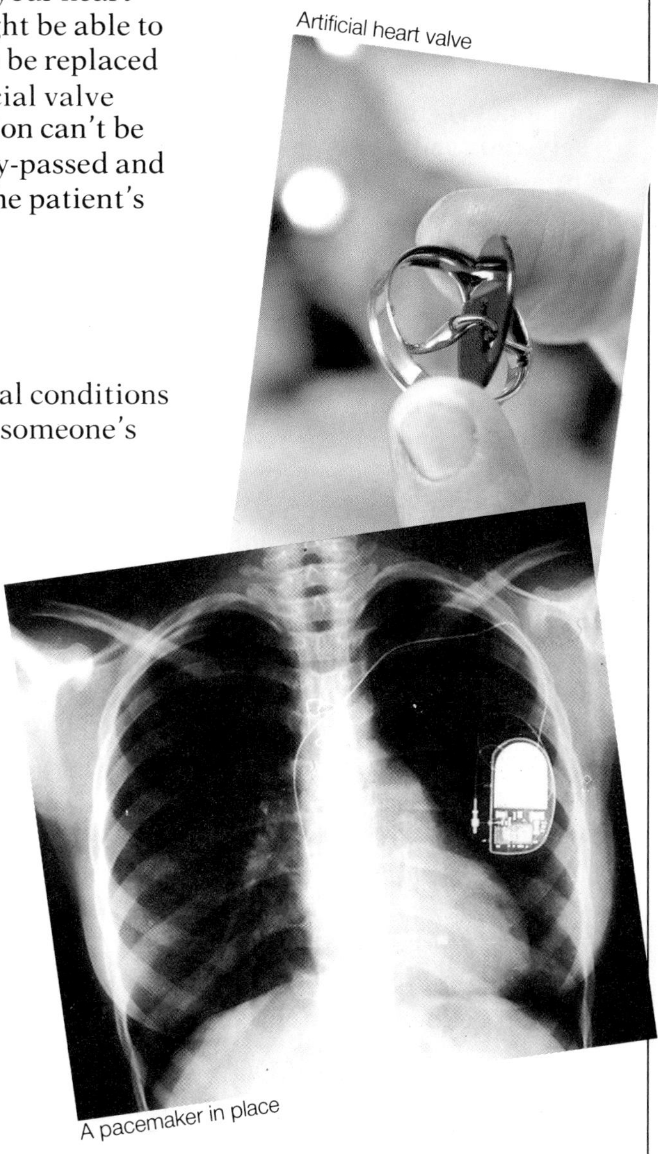

Artificial heart valve

A pacemaker in place

1 Why might a doctor check your blood pressure?

2 What is a coronary thrombosis and what could it cause?

3 What particular jobs does a heart-lung machine do for a patient?

4 Give an example of a situation where having a steady, unchanging rate of heart beat would be a disadvantage. Explain your answer.

Fit for life

Jogging

Physical fitness

There are three things which make up physical fitness. The photographs show people concentrating on developing each of these.

Stamina

Jogging is one way in which you can increase your **stamina**. Stamina is the part of fitness which **keeps you going** when you exercise hard. Exercises which develop stamina strengthen your heart. A stronger heart can beat more powerfully to supply your muscles with the food and oxygen they need. Also stamina exercises help you breathe deeper and easier.

Yoga

Weight training

Suppleness

Yoga is one way in which you can increase your **suppleness**. Suppleness is the part of fitness which allows you to **move freely and easily**. Exercises which develop suppleness involve gentle stretching. They help you to avoid sprains and pulled muscles. The more supple you are, the less likely it is that you will suffer aches and pains caused by stiffness.

Strength

Weight lifting is one way in which you can increase your **strength**. Strength is the part of fitness which gives you a reserve of **muscle power** for unexpected heavier jobs such as lifting and shifting. Exercises which develop strength build up the size and power of your muscles. Strong muscles also help you to keep a trim shape.

All-round physical fitness is more important than concentrating on just one part.

1 What are the three things which make up physical fitness?

2 Jack starts each working day in the same way. Before breakfast, a few stretching exercises lead on to some press-ups and sit-ups. After breakfast comes his brisk walk to work.

Explain how Jack's start to the day helps his all-round physical fitness.

3 Describe the things which *you* do to help you keep physically fit. For each one, explain how it helps your fitness.

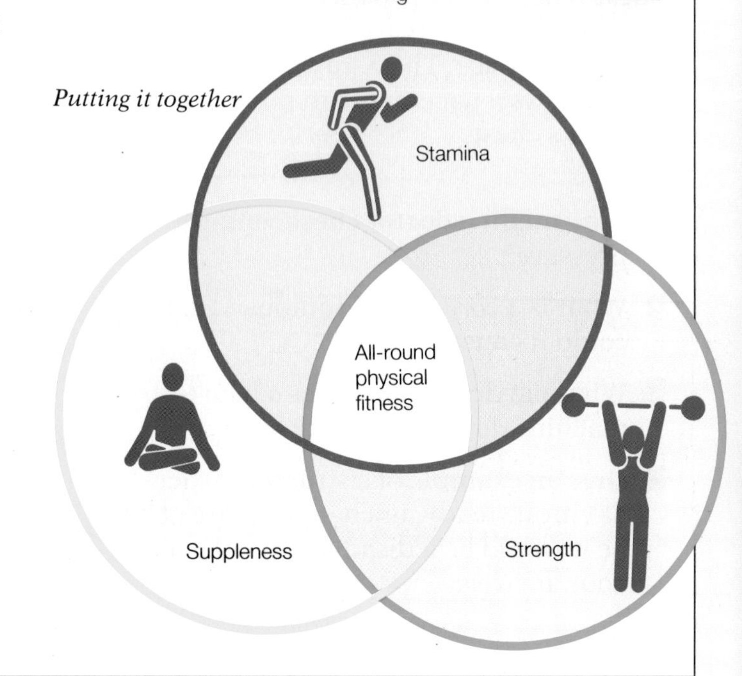

Putting it together

Making your mind up

Exercise is fun!

Exercising your choice

Exercise doesn't have to be hard work. As the picture shows, it can be fun! You don't have to stick to just one sort of exercise either. Variety is the spice of life. What *is* important is that you exercise:

- **long enough**
- **hard enough**
- **often enough**

A twenty-minute run which makes you breathe heavily, done three times each week is enough to improve your fitness. Taking exercise is easy when it becomes a part of life.

exercise	amount of benefit		
	Stamina	**Suppleness**	**Strength**
badminton	**	***	**
canoeing	***	**	***
climbing stairs	***	*	**
cricket	*	**	*
cycling (hard)	****	**	***
dancing (ballroom)	*	***	*
dancing (disco)	***	****	*
digging (garden)	***	**	****
football	***	***	***
golf	*	**	*
gymnastics	**	****	***
hill walking	***	*	**
housework (moderate)	*	**	*
jogging	****	**	**
judo	**	****	**
mowing lawn by hand	**	*	***
rowing	****	**	****
sailing	*	**	**
squash	***	***	**
swimming (hard)	****	****	****
tennis	**	***	**
walking (briskly)	**	*	*
weightlifting	*	*	****
yoga	*	****	*

* *no real effect*
** *beneficial effect*
*** *very good effect*
**** *excellent effect*

S-score

S-score

The table compares the benefits of different exercises.

1 Describe the way in which disco-dancing helps you keep fit.

2 Which sorts of exercise most help:
a stamina?
b suppleness?
c strength?

3 Which exercise most helps all-round physical fitness?

Summing up

You will have to make many **decisions throughout your life** which **will affect your health and fitness**.

4 Look back over pages **4** to **31** and list the main choices which you can make which will help you to lead a healthy, fit life.

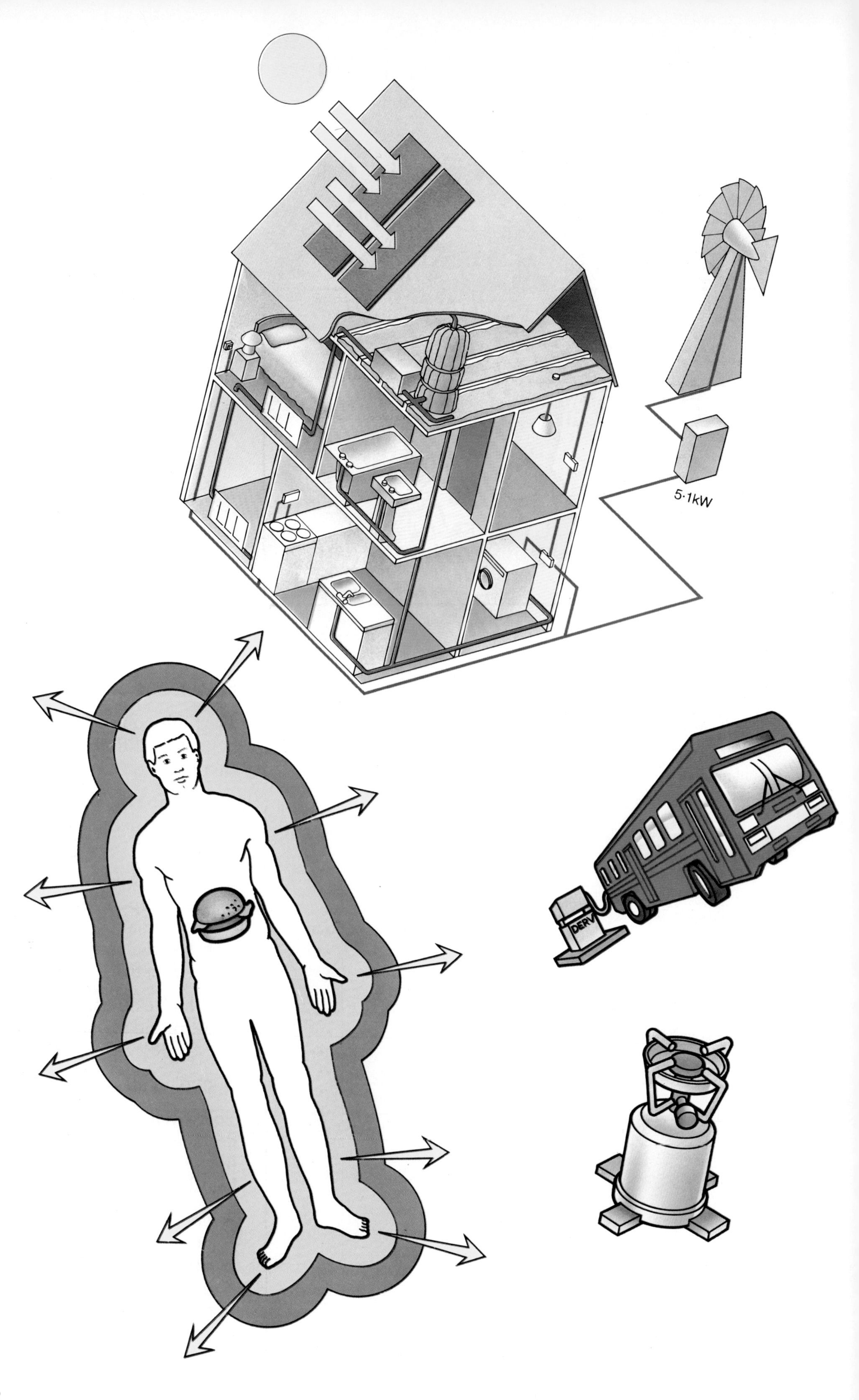
5·1kW
DERV

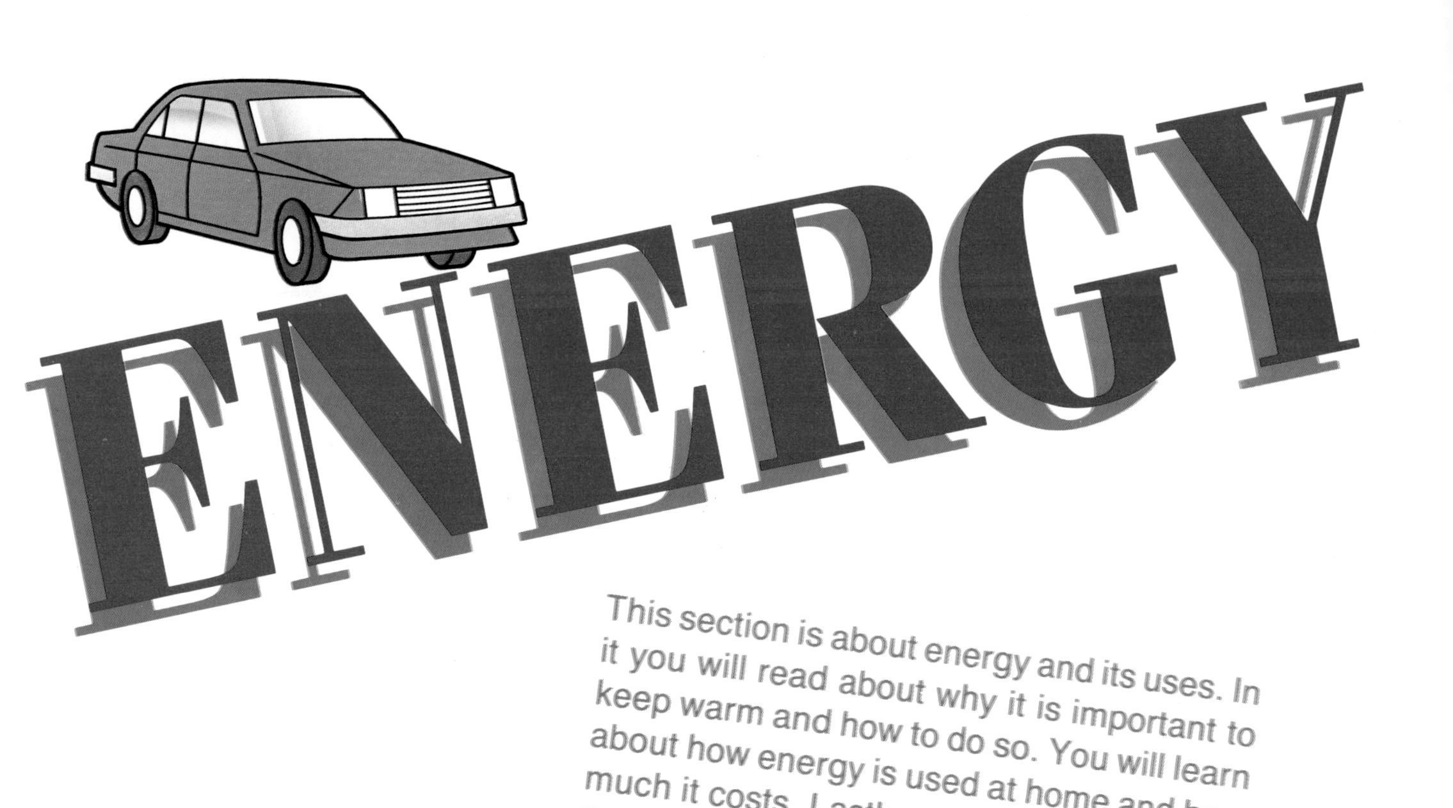

This section is about energy and its uses. In it you will read about why it is important to keep warm and how to do so. You will learn about how energy is used at home and how much it costs. Lastly you will find out about the fuels our energy comes from and why we must find new sources of energy.

Hot and cold

The temperature of the body stays at a steady 37 °C

Feeling the heat

How often have you heard someone say on a hot day 'I'm roasting' or on a cold day 'I'm freezing'?

Have you ever wondered what would happen if you rushed up with a thermometer and took their temperature?

Unless they were ill you would find that their temperature on the hot day was exactly the same as their temperature on the cold day. On both days you would measure about 37 degrees Celsius (written 37 °C). This is because the human body is able to keep its temperature steady.

Some animals such as fish and frogs are called **cold-blooded** animals. This does not mean that they are cruel. It means that their temperature stays the same as their surroundings. So on a hot day they are hot and on a cold day they are cold.

Humans, and other animals such as birds, are **warm-blooded**. The body temperature of a healthy person stays at about 37 °C no matter what the temperature of the surroundings. Being a warm-blooded animal means that your temperature is steady.

Keeping your cool

A Summer day in Britain can be as hot as 35 °C while a Winter day might be 0 °C or less. Our body temperature (37 °C) is *higher* than both of these. Heat flows from hot things to cool things so heat will flow out of our bodies to the surroundings. However, in hot surroundings, such as in strong sunshine, the body has to help heat escape by producing sweat. As the sweat dries it takes heat away with it.

1 Estimate the temperature of the surroundings in the photographs. Choose your answers from 0, 20, 35 and 80 °C.

2 What is the temperature of the people shown in each of the photographs?

3 Fred and his pet frog go everywhere together. The graph shows their body temperatures in a variety of different surroundings.

a Which line on the graph (A or B) shows Fred's temperature and which shows his frog's temperature? Explain.

b One day they go swimming together. The temperature of the water is 30 °C. What will be Fred's body temperature and what will be the frog's body temperature?

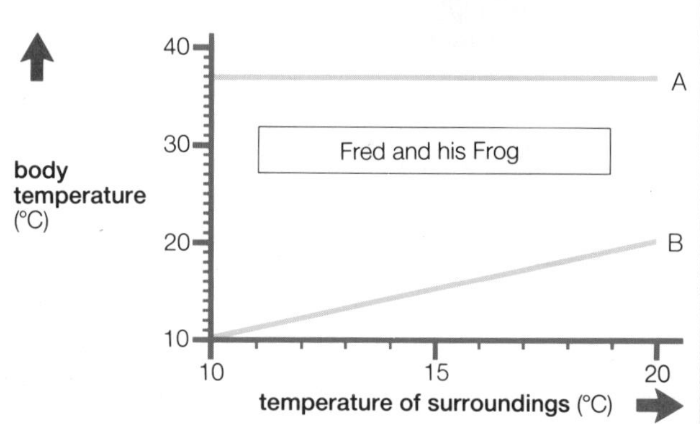

When things go wrong

Not quite right

Although your body normally can keep a steady temperature things can go wrong! For example, if you lose a lot of heat, by being lost in a snowstorm, your body temperature could become as low as 32 °C. When your body temperature drops like this you are said to be suffering from **hypothermia**. Hypothermia is very dangerous and can lead to death. However, people suffering from hypothermia can be saved by helping them to get warm again. Usually they are wrapped in blankets to stop further heat loss. Once in hospital they are carefully placed in a bath of warm water.

If you are unlucky enough to have a **fever** your body temperature could be 40 °C or even 42 °C. This high temperature speeds up the body's fight against infection.

Hypothermia and fever are two examples of your body temperature going very low or very high. But even small changes in temperature can have a big effect on your body. If your body temperature falls by as little as one degree you begin to shiver. This helps to heat you up again. People sometimes talk about feeling 'one degree under'.

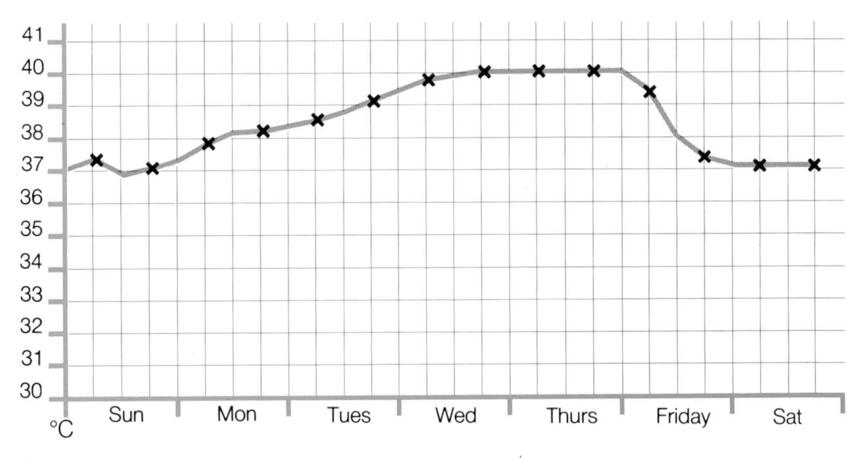

Use the temperature chart and the letter from John Smith to answer these questions.

1 How often was John's temperature taken?

2 What was the highest temperature reached?

3 When was John's temperature highest?

4 What was wrong with John when his temperature was high?

5 How long did John's high temperature last?

Dear Mum,
Thanks for the grapes. I was feeling much better after your last visit but things have not gone so well this week.
On Monday I started to feel a bit funny and my temperature went up. By Wednesday I had a bad fever although I do not remember much. Apart from the fact that I sweated a lot which soaked the new pyjamas you gave me. However, towards the end of the week my fever got better and by Friday evening I was almost myself again. I look forward to seeing you next week.
Love,
John.

Keeping warm

Fuel for the body

The temperature of your body is normally higher than the temperature of your surroundings. As heat always flows from a hot place to a cold place, this means that you are always losing heat. To make up for this loss of heat, energy must be put back into the body. This new energy comes from the food we eat.

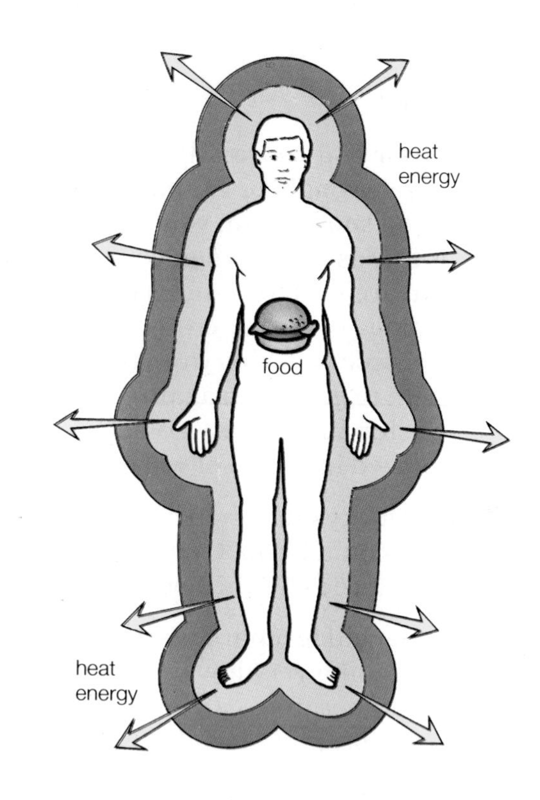

Energy supplied by food replaces energy lost to the surroundings

Energy in food

When something burns, it releases heat energy. You can use this simple idea to compare the energy stored in different foods. The apparatus shown can be used to do this.

A sample of food is burned in a special spoon held close to a test-tube. The heat makes the air in the test-tube expand.

The expanding air pushes out the plunger of the syringe. By comparing how far the plunger moves for different foods you can compare the energy stored in the foods.

In an experiment to compare the energy stored in 3 different foods, 3 samples of each food were burned. The numbers shown in the table are the distances moved by the plunger.

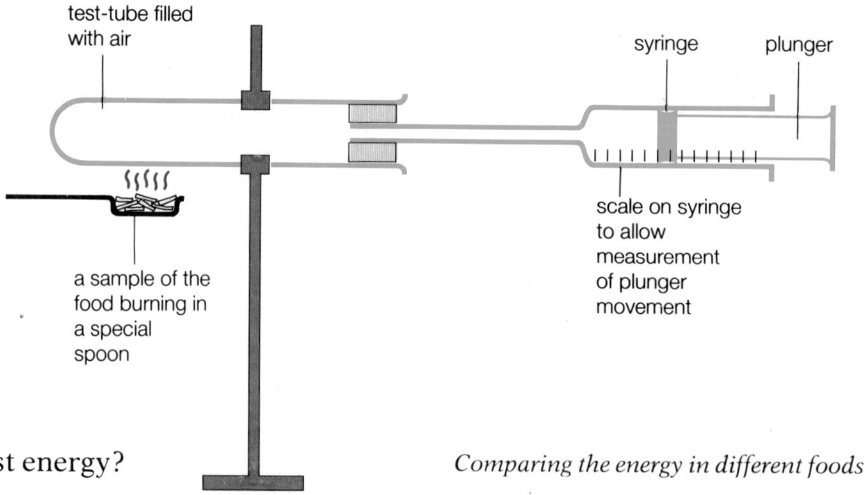

Comparing the energy in different foods

1 Which food contains the most energy?

2 Which food contains the least energy?

3 Explain how you would use the information in the table to compare the energy contained in the different foods.

4 Why were the experiments done 3 times?

5 Calculate the *average* distance moved by the plunger for each food sample.

6 What steps should you take to make sure this is a fair experiment?

7 Draw a bar chart to compare the average distances moved by the plunger for each food.

food	**1st try**	**2nd try**	**3rd try**
peanut	4	3	5
bread	1	1½	½
biscuit	1	3	2

Distance the plunger moved

Investigating heat loss

Finding out about losing heat

A science class did two different experiments to find out about heat loss. In both experiments 2 identical test-tubes were filled with equal amounts of hot water at 60 °C. The two tubes were then left to cool under different conditions. The temperatures of each were measured after 10 minutes. The diagram shows how one pupil recorded the results in her notebook.

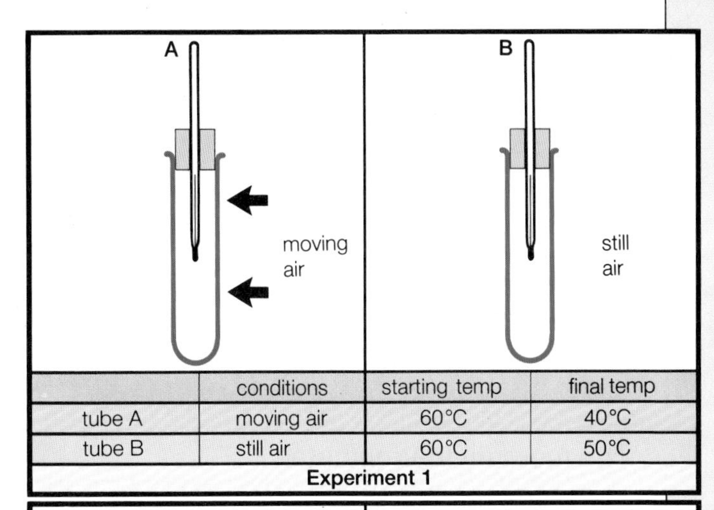

	conditions	starting temp	final temp
tube A	moving air	60°C	40°C
tube B	still air	60°C	50°C

Experiment 1

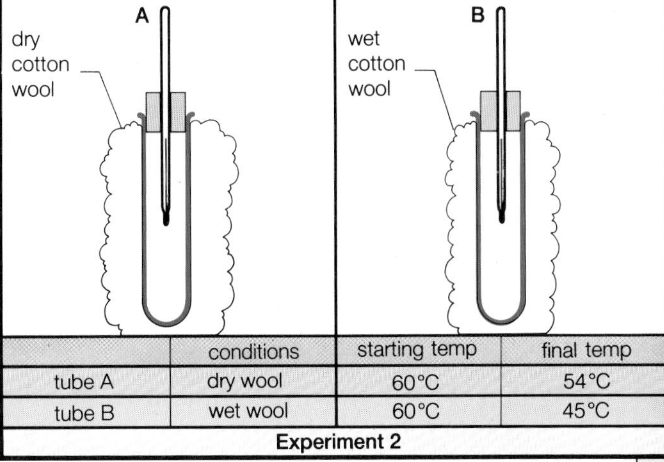

	conditions	starting temp	final temp
tube A	dry wool	60°C	54°C
tube B	wet wool	60°C	45°C

Experiment 2

1 Which has the greater cooling effect, still air or moving air?

2 Which tube cooled most during the experiment, the one covered in wet cotton wool or the one covered in dry cotton wool?

3 Use drawings to show how you would set up experiments to test:
  a Whether wool or nylon was better at keeping in the heat.
  b Whether a warm object cooled faster in a warm place or in a cold place.

DRAMA IN THE CAIRNGORMS

TWO HILL WALKERS who had been lost overnight were found dead today by the Cairngorm Mountain Rescue Team.

Mountain survival expert Chris Armstrong told our reporter: 'All the conditions were against them. It was a very cold rainy night and blowing a gale. Both walkers wore gym shoes and jeans, neither of which are windproof, waterproof or warm. Although their nylon cagoules gave them some protection from the wind and rain, they would have felt extreme cold due to the thin jumpers they wore under their cagoules. On the hills it is essential to be warm and dry underneath and protected from the chilling effect of the wind. I'm afraid that these lads were just not equipped for the weather and they paid for their mistake with their lives'.

4 Why is it more dangerous to be on the hills at night than during the day?

5 In what way were the walkers not suitably dressed?

6 Suggest suitable clothing which would have prevented the tragedy in the newspaper report.

7 What did the unfortunate walkers die of in the newspaper report?

8 If the walkers had been found sooner how might they have been saved?

9 Explain what part the rain and gale played in this tragedy.

Measuring temperature

Measuring temperature

Heat is a form of energy. When heat energy flows into an object the object gets hotter. The temperature of the object is a measure of how hot the object is. This can be measured by using a **thermometer**. There are many different types of thermometers but they all have something in common — they all change in some way when the temperature changes.

Heat is a form of energy

The mercury thermometer

Mercury thermometers are made of glass. A fine glass tube runs up the centre of the thermometer and this is connected at the bottom to a glass bulb filled with mercury. Heat energy makes the mercury expand (get bigger). The mercury has nowhere to go but up the tube. A *rise* in temperature makes the mercury go *up* the tube while a *fall* in temperature makes the mercury go *down* the tube. The tube has numbers marked on it to tell you the temperature. These numbers are called a **scale**. Mercury thermometers are cheap but they are easily broken. They are not able to measure temperatures much below 0 °C or much above 250 °C.

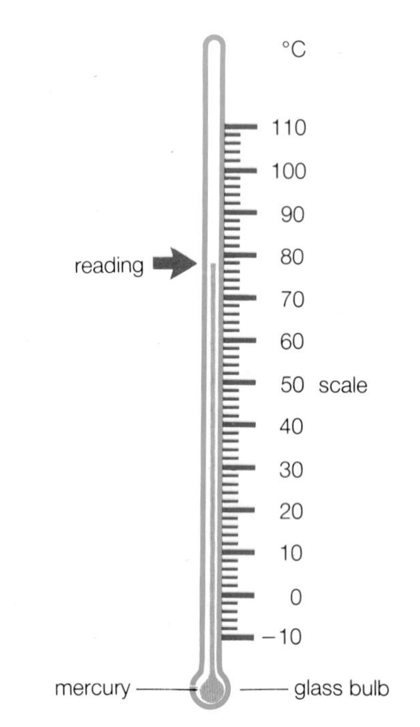

A mercury thermometer

1 Which of the following temperatures could be measured with a mercury thermometer:
- **a** The temperature of a furnace?
- **b** Room temperature?
- **c** The temperature of the North Pole?

The thermocouple

A thermocouple is made by joining together two different metal wires and connecting them to an ammeter (a meter for measuring electric current.) When the join is heated or cooled a small electric current flows and this can be measured on the meter. The reading on the meter shows how hot or cold the join is. A thermocouple is more expensive than a mercury thermometer but it can be used to measure temperatures as low as −250 °C and as high as 3000 °C. The ammeter can be some distance from the join so the thermocouple can be used to measure the temperature of places which are difficult or dangerous to get to. An example of this is the inside of a furnace.

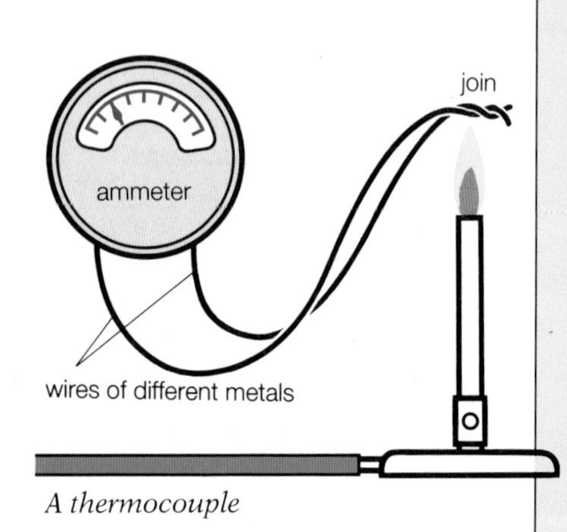

A thermocouple

2 Write down one advantage and one disadvantage of a thermocouple.

3 Where would a thermocouple be more useful than a mercury thermometer?

4 Where would a mercury thermometer be more useful than a thermocouple?

Changed by heat

The bi-metallic strip thermometer

When a piece of metal is heated it gets bigger or expands. Two different pieces of metal such as copper and iron when fixed together make a bi-metallic strip which bends when it is heated and this is shown in the diagram. The strip bends because the two metals expand by different amounts. If a bi-metallic strip is shaped into a spiral as shown it can be used to make a thermometer. As the strip gets hotter it curves more, and moves the pointer round the dial. The numbers on the dial show the temperature.

1 Look at the diagram of a bi-metallic strip bending when heated. Which metal expands more, copper or iron?

A bi-metallic strip bends on heating

A bi-metallic strip thermometer

A gas thermometer

The gas thermometer

In a **gas thermometer** a small quantity of liquid is trapped in a long thin tube which is connected to a bulb filled with air.

2 **a** Explain how this thermometer works.
b In this thermometer what changes with temperature?

3 Describe other types of thermometer you have seen, saying in each case how the thermometer shows a change of temperature.

The higher it goes the faster it flows

Cooling fast

Curious Kate likes a cup of hot milk at bedtime. She pours it out at 76 °C but does not drink it until it has cooled to 60 °C. It usually takes 8 minutes to cool if she leaves it standing in the kitchen. One evening Kate discovers that putting her cup of hot milk in the freezer makes it cool enough to drink in 6 minutes.

Next day at school Kate asks her science teacher why milk cools faster in a cold place. Her teacher gives Kate an experiment to perform.

In the experiment Kate heats the metal cylinder until its temperature is 60 °C. She then quickly places it in a large tank filled with cold water. The cold water is kept at 20 °C during the experiment. Kate takes the temperature of the cylinder every minute as the cylinder cools.

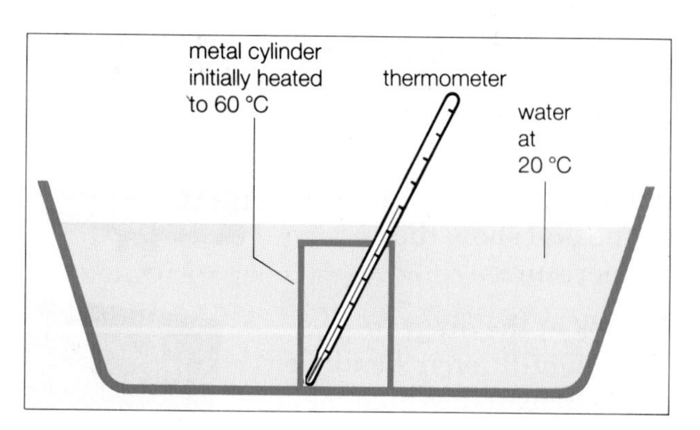

The temperature is taken every minute as the cylinder cools down

The graph shows what Kate draws from the results.

1 Copy and complete the table

	At Start	After 4 min	After 8 min
Temperature of cylinder			

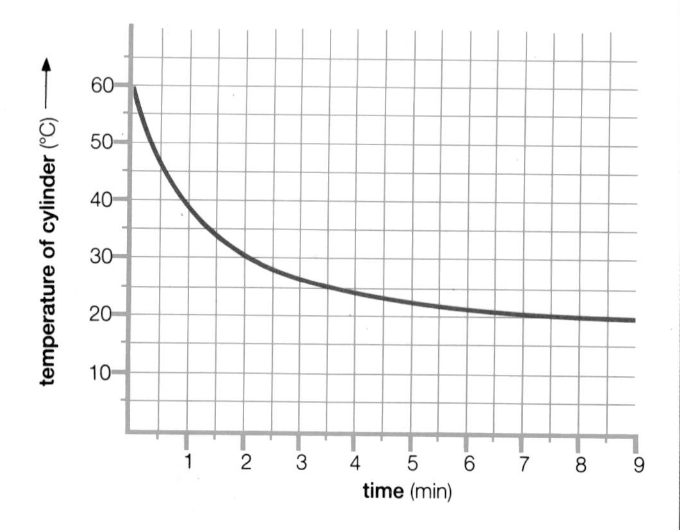

A graph like this is called a cooling curve

2 During which time did the temperature fall most:
  a The first 4 minutes?
  b The second 4 minutes?

3 Does the temperature fall faster when the temperature difference between the cylinder and the water is big or small?

4 Why is Kate's graph steep at the beginning but flatter towards the end?

Deep heat

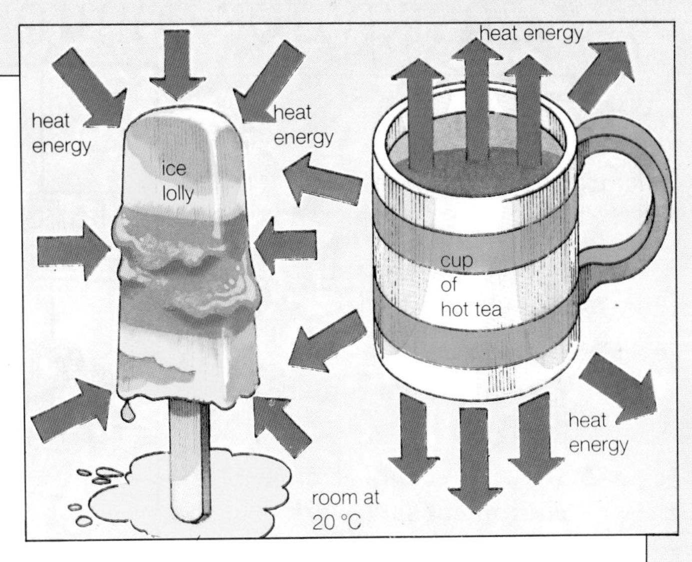

Left in the same room the tea gets cold but the ice lolly melts

Cooling down and heating up

Heat energy always flows from hot to cold. The bigger the temperature difference the faster the flow. Cool objects in warm places *take in* energy from their surroundings. That's why your ice cream melts quickly on a hot day. Warm objects in cool places *lose* heat energy to their surroundings as you saw in Kate's experiment.

Keeping warm under water

Water carries away heat faster than air. For this reason, a person surrounded by water at a temperature of less than 37 °C, loses heat energy very quickly. The colder the water, the faster the person cools down and becomes hypothermic.

Professional divers often work in extremely low temperatures. To protect them from hypothermia they wear special suits heated either by electricity or by hot water pumped down to them.

However, sport divers do not have special heating systems. They rely on their suits slowing down the flow of heat energy from their bodies to the water. One popular type of suit is the **wet-suit**. This is shown in the photograph. The wet-suit works by trapping some water close to the skin. The water gets heated by the body and the heat energy is kept in by the special material of the suit.

A hot-water suit

Sports divers wear wet suits

The graph shows the longest time people can usually survive in seawater with and without wet-suits. Use the graph to answer the following questions.

1 Would you survive longer in sea water in a wet suit or naked?

2 How long could a naked person last in:
a A Summer sea temperature of 18°C?
b A Winter sea temperature of 4°C:

3 How long could an average person in a wet-suit last in a winter sea temperature of 4°C?

4 At what temperature can an average person in a wet-suit survive for up to 30 hours?

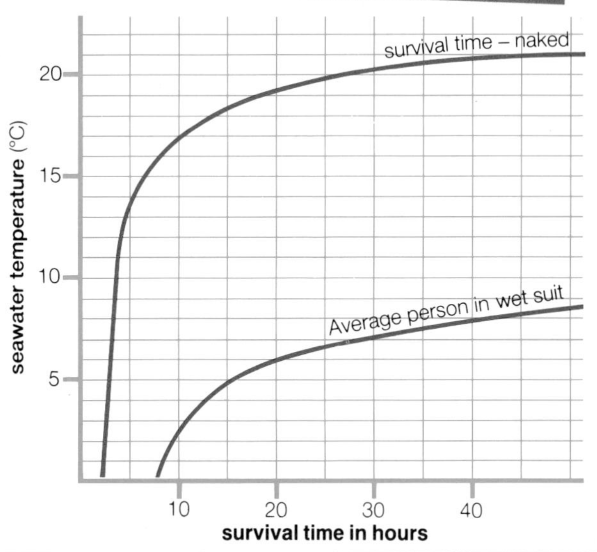

Energy for comfort

Energy in the home

At home we use energy for warmth and light and to make our lives easier.

1 In what ways does energy used in the home make life easier?

2 Which pieces of electrical equipment save work in the kitchen?

3 The diagram shows a modern kitchen. Find **13** objects which use energy then copy and complete the table.

Heating equipment	Lighting equipment	Other electrical equipment
electric kettle		

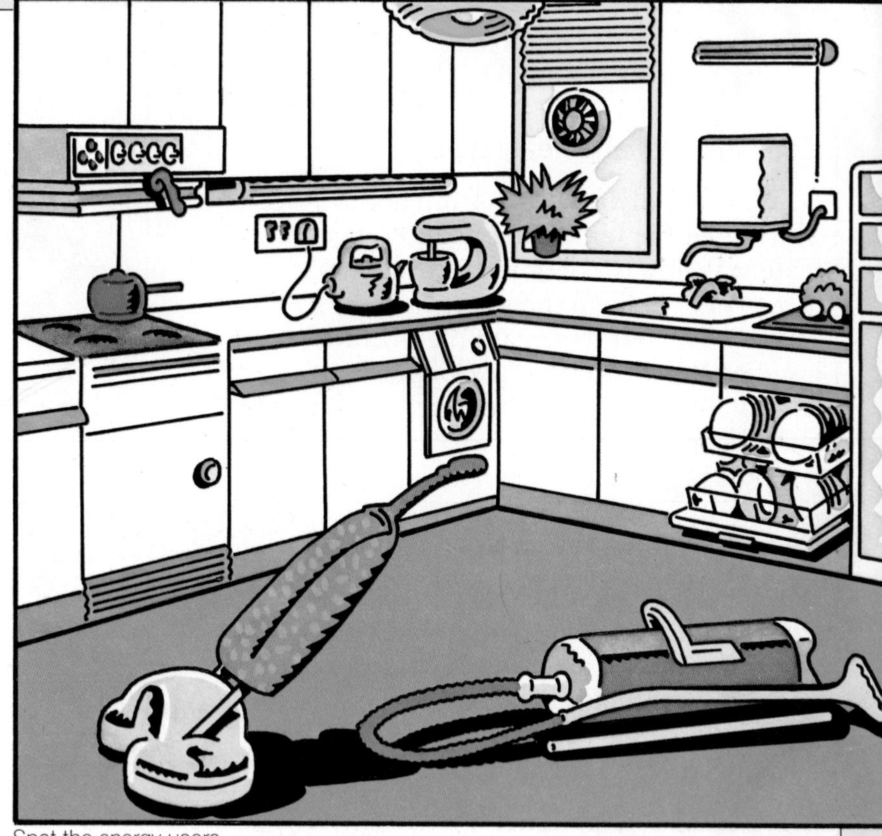
Spot the energy users

Electrical appliances

Hair dryers, vacuum cleaners, and food mixers are all examples of electrical appliances. An electrical appliance uses electrical energy to produce heat, light or some useful movement.

Just as vegetables are sold by the kg, electricity is sold by the **unit**. A unit of electricity is an amount of electrical energy.

Some appliances use up energy at a greater rate than others and so cost more to run. The running costs of appliances can be compared by finding out how many hours they run for on one unit of electricity.

4 What do you notice about the energy used by the appliances which produce a lot of heat?

5 What type of appliances are the most expensive to run?

6 Which is more expensive: running a fan heater for twelve hours or a fridge-freezer for a week?

7 Construct a bar chart to compare the energy requirements of the appliances shown.

Counting the cost

The electricity meter

The electricity meter keeps a record of the number of units of electricity you have used. Two types of meter are shown, the digital meter and the older dial meter. In both cases the dial on the right-hand side showing tenths of a unit is usually ignored when taking a reading.

A dial meter

A digital meter

Reading the meter

To find out how many units have been used in three months you read the meter at the beginning and at the end of the three-month period. You then subtract the smaller of the two numbers from the larger. An example of this is shown.

How to work out the units you have used on a digital meter

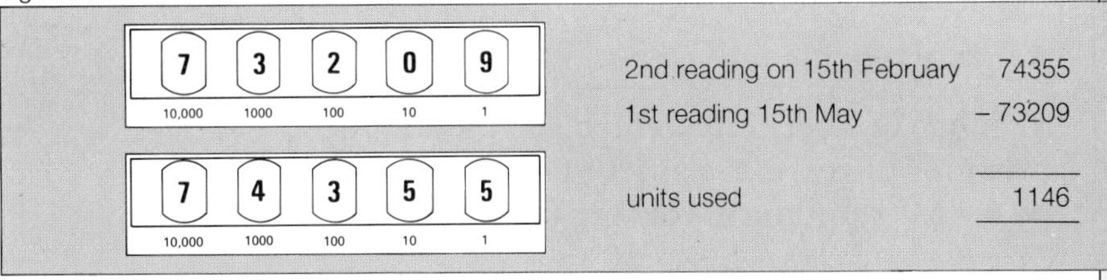

Calculating units used on a digital meter

Paying the bill

The diagram shows an electricity bill. The total has been left blank. The first 34 units are charged at 17 pence per unit. This high price is known as the **standing charge**.

1 How many units have been used altogether?

2 Use a calculator to find:
   a The total standing charge.
   b The total cost of the cheaper units at 5.6 pence each.
   c The total amount to be paid.

3 Two sets of readings are shown for Graham and Morag. Calculate the totals for both bills using the prices shown in the bill above.

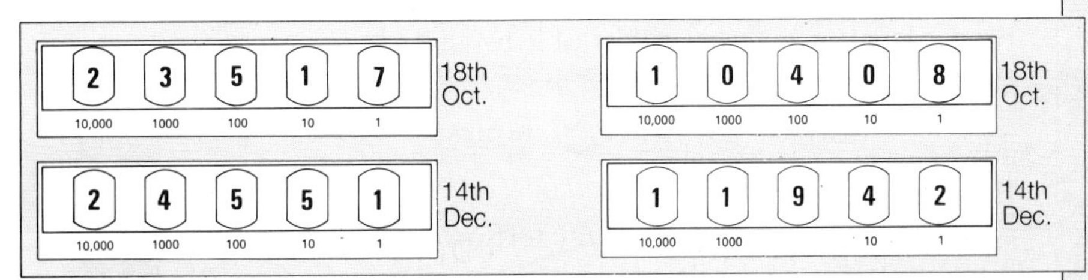

Electricity used by Graham

Electricity used by Morag

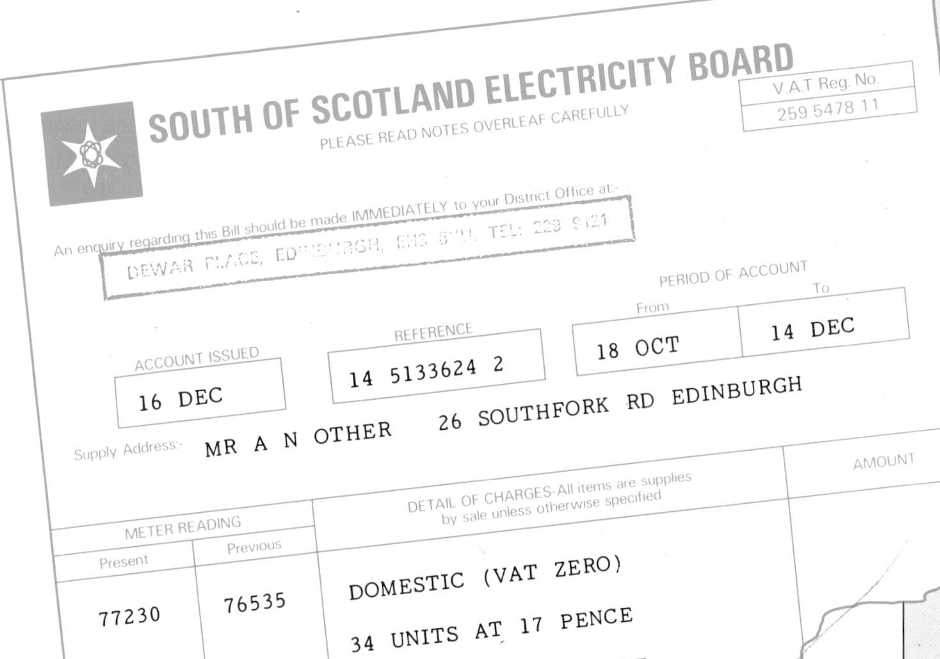

SOUTH OF SCOTLAND ELECTRICITY BOARD

PLEASE READ NOTES OVERLEAF CAREFULLY

V.A.T Reg. No. 259 5478 11

An enquiry regarding this Bill should be made IMMEDIATELY to your District Office at:-

DEWAR PLACE, EDINBURGH, EH3 8TL TEL: 229 9121

ACCOUNT ISSUED	REFERENCE	PERIOD OF ACCOUNT From	To
16 DEC	14 5133624 2	18 OCT	14 DEC

Supply Address: MR A N OTHER 26 SOUTHFORK RD EDINBURGH

METER READING Present	Previous	DETAIL OF CHARGES-All items are supplies by sale unless otherwise specified	AMOUNT
77230	76535	DOMESTIC (VAT ZERO)	
		34 UNITS AT 17 PENCE	
		661 UNITS AT 5.6 PENCE	

What's Watt?

Household appliances

Most household appliances carry information about the rate at which they use energy. The information is usually on a small plate behind or beneath the appliance. An example of this is shown in the photograph.

Watts

The number of watts (W for short) is a measure of how quickly an appliance uses up energy. When large amounts of energy are used up quickly it is more useful to talk about **kilowatts** (kW for short).

$$1 \text{ kW} = 1000 \text{ W}$$

A unit of electricity

The unit of electricity, which you met on the previous pages, is **the amount of energy used by a 1 kW appliance working for 1 hour**.

The unit is also called the **kilowatt hour** as you can work out the number of units used by multiplying the number of kilowatts by the number of hours:

$$\text{units} = \text{kilowatts} \times \text{hours}$$

Example 1

A 3 kW immersion heater left on for 2 hours uses 6 units of electricity.

Example 2

How much does it cost to heat a room for 5 hours with a 2000 W electric fire? Electricity costs 5.6 pence per unit.

$$2000 \text{ W} = 2 \text{ kW}$$

$$2 \text{ kW} \times 5 \text{ hours} = 10 \text{ units}$$

$$10 \text{ units at } 5.6 \text{ p} = 56 \text{ p}$$

The cost would be 56 p

1 An immersion heater is rated at 3000 W. What is its rating in kW?

2 How many units of electricity are used by the immersion heater when it is switched on for 3 hours?

3 If electricity costs 5.6 pence per unit what does it cost to run the immersion heater for 3 hours?

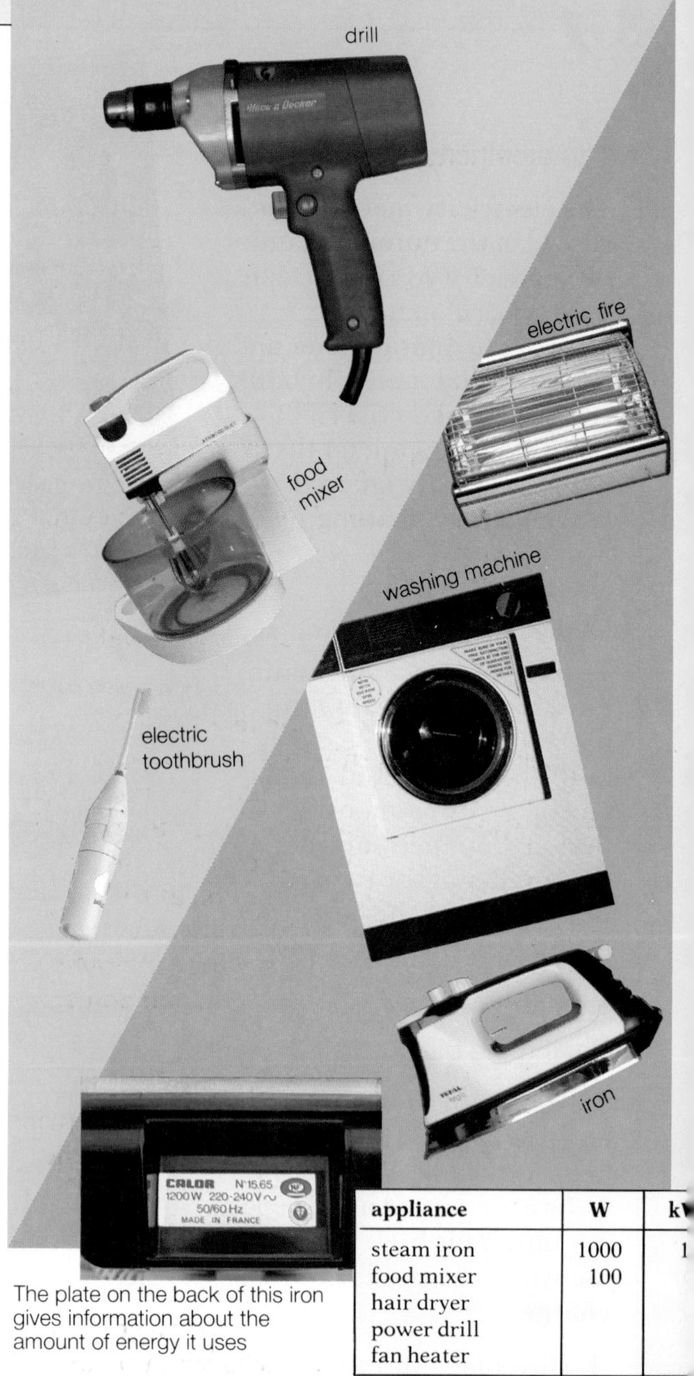

The plate on the back of this iron gives information about the amount of energy it uses

appliance	W	k
steam iron	1000	1
food mixer	100	
hair dryer		
power drill		
fan heater		

4 Redraw and complete the table using information from the appliance survey on page **42**.

5 Meadowbank Stadium in Edinburgh is floodlit by 4 lighting towers. Each tower contains 38 lights. Each light is rated at 2000 W. What does it cost to light a football match for 2 hours at the rate of 5.6 pence per unit of electricity?

6 Which needs more energy?

a Heating a room with a 2000 W fire for 1 evening (say 6 hours)?

b Lighting a room with a 100 W bulb for a week (say 40 hours)?

Tariffs

The cost of heating a home

The energy needed to keep a house warm costs money. How much money depends on the type of house, the fuel used to supply the heat and how quickly heat energy escapes from the house.

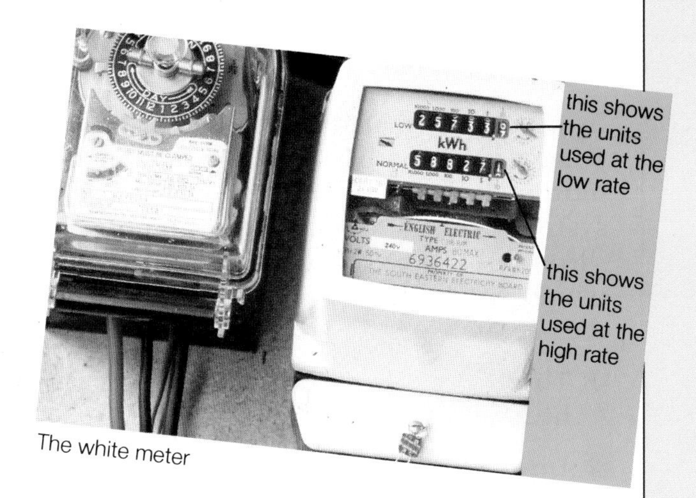

The white meter

Off-peak heating and the white meter

If your house is heated by electricity you may pay in 3 different ways. These ways of paying are called tariffs.

The domestic tariff. This is the normal rate of payment.

A mixture of the domestic tariff and the off-peak tariff. In this case you will have 2 separate meters. A normal meter and a special off-peak meter connected to special radiators called storage radiators. The off-peak meter only switches on at times when the electricity is cheap and the radiators store up the heat which is slowly released during the day, even if you don't want it!

The white meter tariff. If you are on this tariff you get electricity at less than half price for $8\frac{1}{2}$ hours during the night. However, the day-time electricity costs slightly more than the domestic rate.

A storage heater stores heart during the night when electricity is cheap and releases the heat slowly during the day when it is needed

The 3 tariffs are shown in the diagram.

1 Storage heaters are filled with a special type of brick. These bricks heat up during the times when electricity is cheap. As they cool down they slowly give off heat. What disadvantage does this type of heating have?

2 Suggest why electricity can be sold cheaply at certain times of the day and night.

3 Suppose that a storage radiator rated at 2.625 kW stores heat from 11.30 pm until 07.30 am.

a How many units are used during this time?

b Compare the cost of this on each of the 3 tariffs.

DOMESTIC
17p for first 34 units
5.6p for additional units

OFF-PEAK
Not less than 8 hours between 7.30pm and 8.30am
Not more than 4 hours between 8.30am and 5pm
5.6p for first 92 units
3.5p for each additional unit

WHITE METER
17p for each of the first 52 units taken between 7.30am and 11pm
6p for each additional unit taken between 7.30am and 11pm
2.4p for each unit taken between 11pm and 7.30pm

ELECTRICITY TARIFFS

These prices are approximate

Heat loss – causes and cures

A waste of money

In an average modern house, no special precautions have been taken to save heat, so most of the heat produced by the heating system disappears almost immediately through walls, roof, floor, doors, and windows. The diagram shows an estimate of the percentage losses.

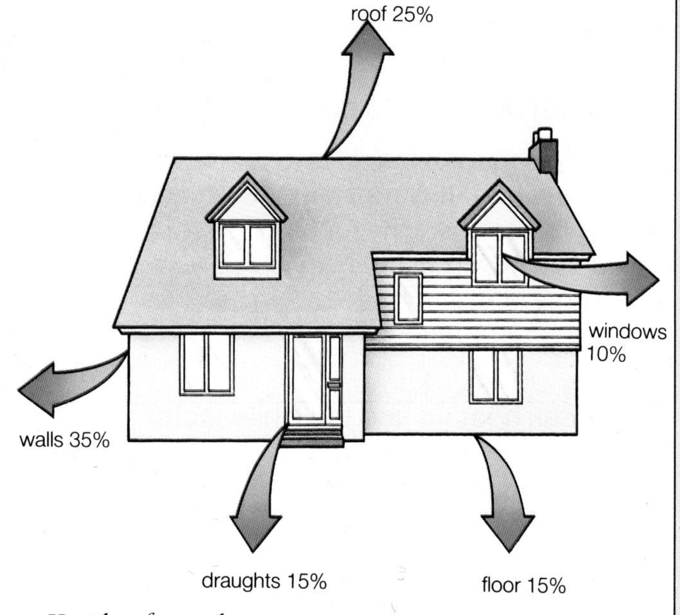

Heat lost from a house

1 Through which parts of a house does most heat escape?

2 Draw a pie-chart to compare the heat lost through the different parts of the house.

3 During the Winter, an average house uses 80 units a day for heating. Taking the cost of a unit to be 5.6 pence:
- **a** Calculate the cost of heat lost per week through the roof, walls, floor, doors, and windows.
- **b** Draw a bar chart to show these weekly losses.

Insulate

Reducing heat loss saves money. Heat loss from the roof, walls, hot water cylinder, and floors can all be reduced by **insulating**, that is, using a material which is difficult for heat to get through.

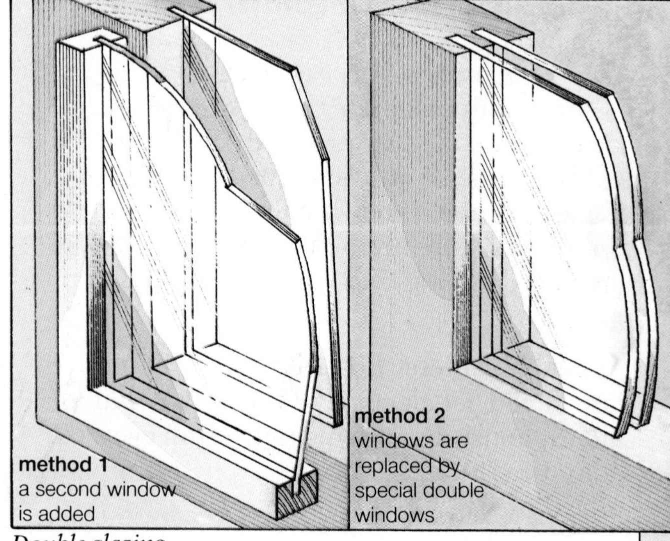

Double glazing

Heat loss through windows can be cut down by **double glazing**. Some double glazing systems add a second window to the windows which are there already. The layer of air trapped between the two glass panes is a good insulator and so slows down the rate at which heat can escape through the windows.

Other double glazing systems use special factory-made units in which the space between the two panes of glass contains a vacuum. This type is even more effective in slowing down heat loss.

Warm air can also escape through narrow openings in the house such as the gap under a door or round the edges of windows. This can be stopped by filling in the gaps with strips of material, such a rubber or plastic. This is called **draught-proofing**.

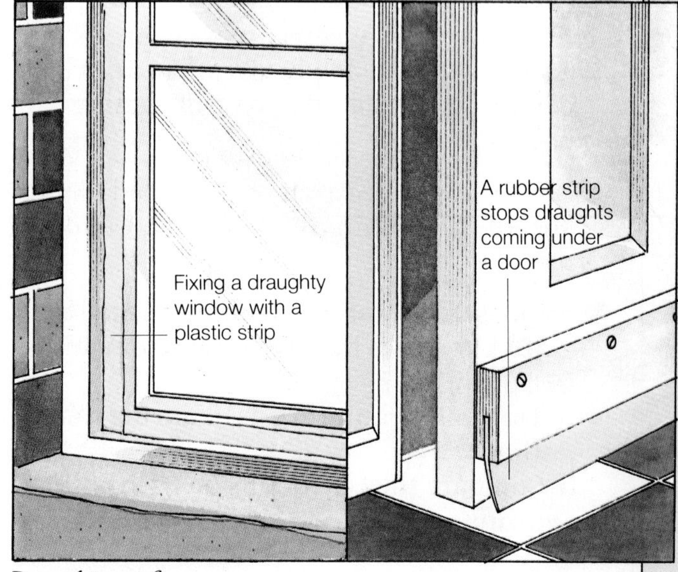

Draught proofing

Air for insulation

Air keeps in the heat

Usually the material used to insulate a house contains a great deal of air. As air is a good insulator the material slows down the heat loss.

A ceiling can be insulated by placing thick layers of fibre-glass wool between the wooden beams in the loft. This is called **loft insulation** and is shown on the right.

Many houses have double walls separated by an air space called a cavity. The air in the cavity helps to prevent heat escaping from the house. The cavity works even better if it is filled with special insulating material. This is usually pumped in through holes in the walls after the house is built. This is called **cavity-wall insulation**.

Floors can be insulated by filling the space under the floorboards with fibre insulation as shown.

Insulating a hot water cylinder by wrapping it in a special jacket can cut the heat lost by the cylinder by 75%.

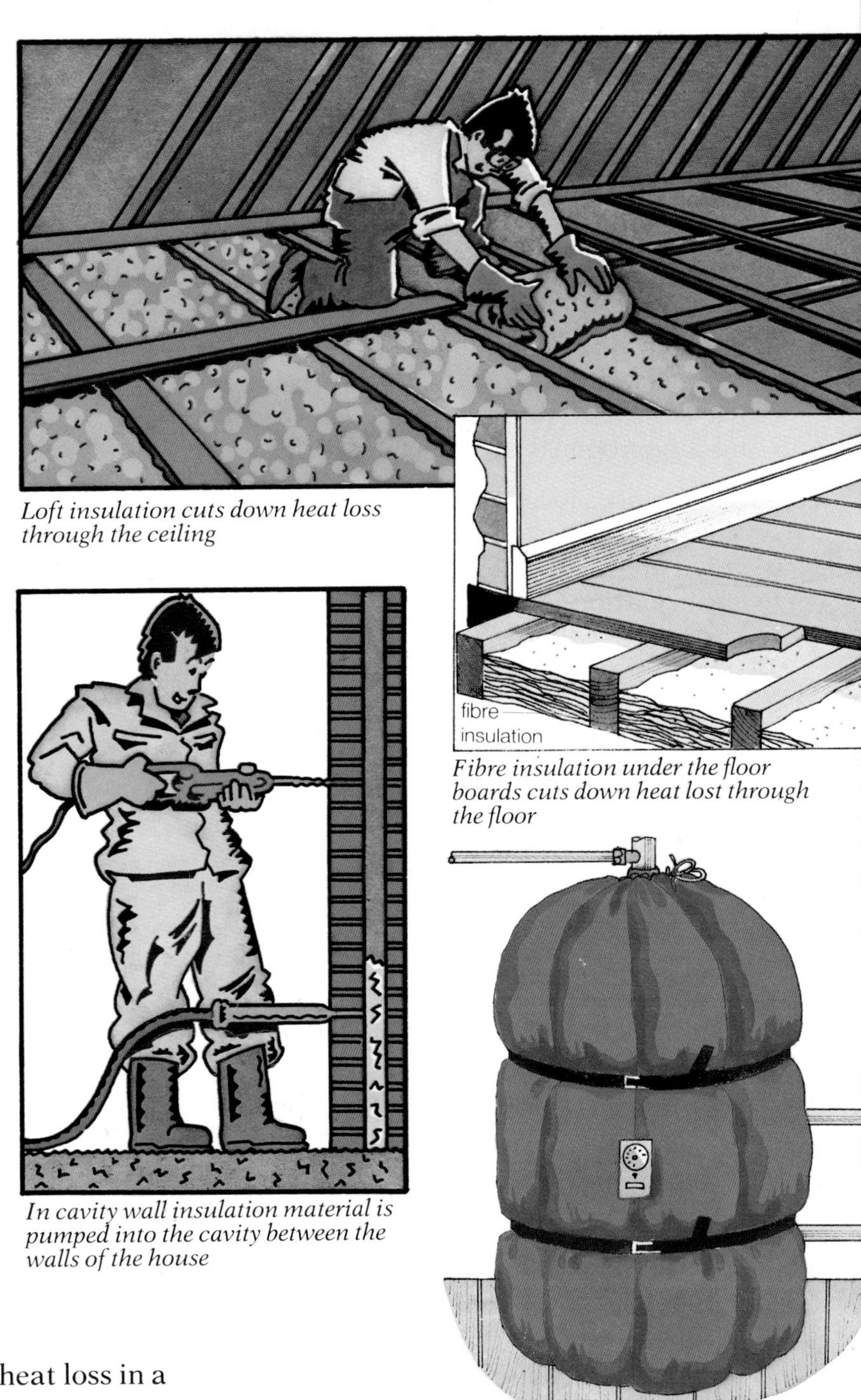

Loft insulation cuts down heat loss through the ceiling

Fibre insulation under the floor boards cuts down heat lost through the floor

In cavity wall insulation material is pumped into the cavity between the walls of the house

Covering the hot water cylinder with an insulating jacket saves a lot of energy

1. List 6 ways of cutting down heat loss in a house.
2. David insulated his hot water cylinder and his electricity bill for the next year was £56 less. If the cost of a unit is 5.6 pence how many units did he save in the year?
3. If you insulate your loft why is it advisable to insulate the cold-water tank in your loft as well?

Insulating a cold-water tank

Making comparisons

Which fuel?

Electricity, solid fuel, and gas can all be used for heating. The tables give the information needed to compare 3 different fuels.

1 Which is cheaper, installing solid fuel heating:
   a in a detached house
   b in a 2-bedroomed flat?

2 How much does it cost to run gas heating in a detached house with no cavity insulation?

heating system	what you pay for a new system: for the system alone	what you pay for a new system: for the system including the cost of cavity insulation	what you pay each year to run the system: without cavity insulation	what you pay each year to run the system: with cavity insulation
Solid fuel smokeless fuel roomheater with back boiler, 6 radiators, Electric immersion heater for summer hot water	£1400	£1600	£300	£280
Mains gas wall mounted boiler, 6 radiators	£1200	£1300	£240	£220
Electricity 2 storage heaters, 4 panel heaters, 1 downflow heater for bathroom, immersion heater for hot water	£880	£1000	£210	£165

Heating a 2-bedroomed flat

3 Which home has the cheaper running costs for all fuels and why do you think this is?

4 Which is the cheapest fuel:
   a For the detached house?
   b For the flat?

5 In which house does insulation work best?

6 Which is the cheapest house to insulate?

7 For which house is there the largest range of prices for installing a new heating system?

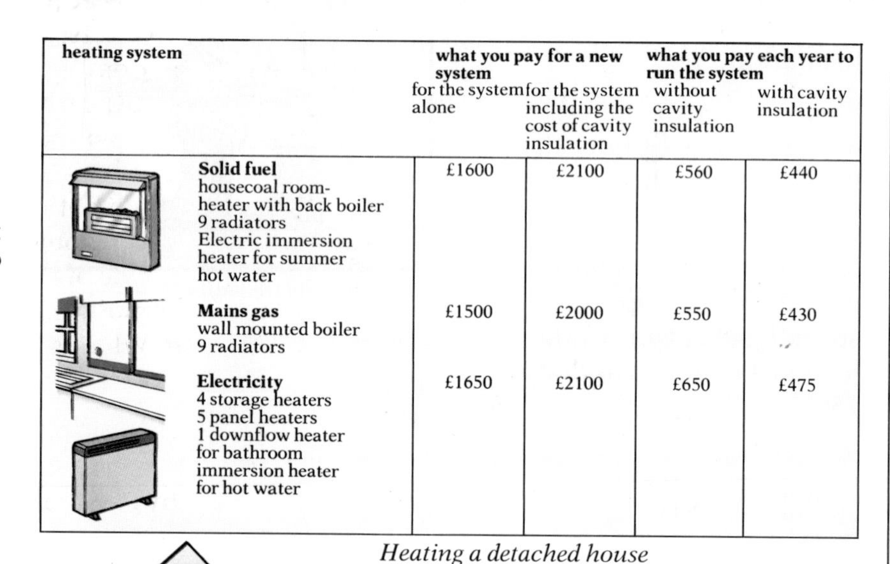

heating system	what you pay for a new system: for the system alone	what you pay for a new system: for the system including the cost of cavity insulation	what you pay each year to run the system: without cavity insulation	what you pay each year to run the system: with cavity insulation
Solid fuel housecoal room-heater with back boiler, 9 radiators, Electric immersion heater for summer hot water	£1600	£2100	£560	£440
Mains gas wall mounted boiler, 9 radiators	£1500	£2000	£550	£430
Electricity 4 storage heaters, 5 panel heaters, 1 downflow heater for bathroom, immersion heater for hot water	£1650	£2100	£650	£475

Heating a detached house

Save it

Controlling the temperature

Most heating systems use a **thermostat** to keep the temperature of the house or room steady. A thermostat does this by automatically turning the heating off when the room gets hotter than the chosen temperature and turning it on again when it gets colder.

You can choose the temperature you want by adjusting the dial on the thermostat. Turning it to a lower temperature saves money.

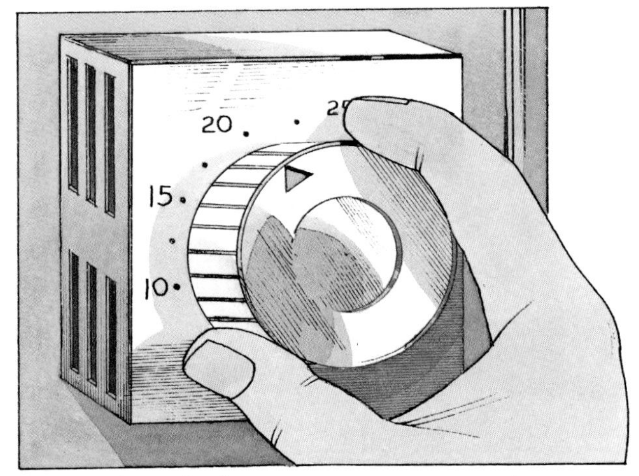

Turning down the thermostat saves money

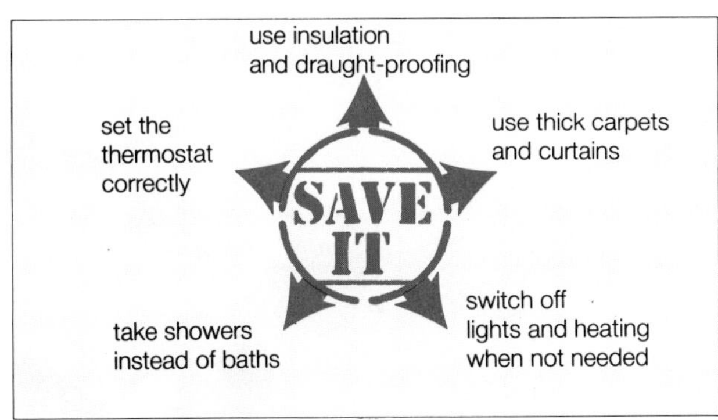

Five ways of saving energy in a house

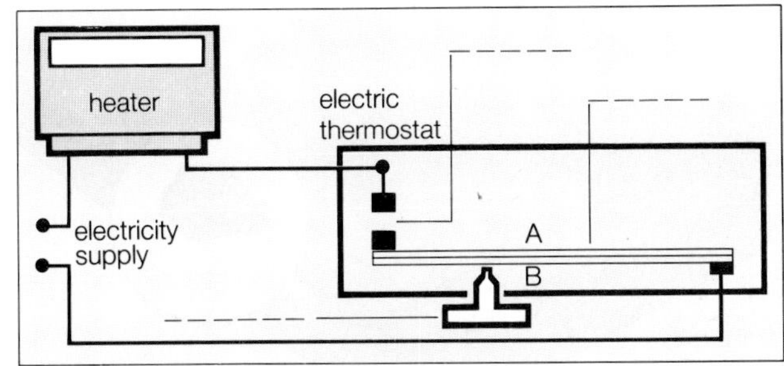

A thermostat used with electricity

1 Using thick curtains and carpets in a house helps to save energy. Explain why.

2 A 3 kW immersion heater heats enough water for a bath in one hour. Taking a shower uses up only about one fifth of the water needed for a bath. A unit of electricity costs 5.6 pence.
- **a** How much does it cost to heat the water for a bath?
- **b** How much does it cost to heat the water for a shower?

3 Two 100 W lights are left switched on unnecessarily in a house for an hour a day on average. A unit of electricity costs 5.6 pence and a 100 watt lamp uses 1/10 unit of electricity per hour. Estimate how much money is wasted in a year.

4 A thermostat for controlling an electric heater is shown in the diagram. When the temperature falls a bi-metallic strip bends and closes two electrical contacts. This switches on the heater. The adjusting screw adjusts the distance between the contacts.
- **a** Copy the diagram and label: **i** the adjusting screw **ii** the bi-metallic strip **iii** the electrical contacts.
- **b** Which way does the strip move if it gets too hot?
- **c** Use your answer to **b** to decide which side of the bi-metallic strip expands most on heating, A or B?
- **d** What is the purpose of the adjusting screw?

5 Claus Clod put in a new central heating system. The whole system was controlled by one thermostat. To check that it was working Claus measured the temperature of the air in his living room every half hour. His results are shown in the table.
- **a** Plot a graph of temperature (on the y-axis) and time (on the x-axis).
- **b** At what temperature did the thermostat switch on?
- **c** At what temperature did it switch off?
- **d** Mark on your graph when the thermostat was on.

The results of Claus Clod's experiment

temperature (°C)	16	17	18	19	20	20	19	18	17	16	17	18	19	20	20	19	18
time (hours)	0	½	1	1½	2	2½	3	3½	4	4½	5	5½	6	6½	7	7½	8

Fuels from the past

Fossil fuels

Electricity is very useful. It gives us heat, light, and power to make things work. It can also be sent easily from one part of the country to another. However, it has to be made by electricity generators. The energy needed to drive the generators comes from fuels.

The most common fuels used in Britain are **coal**, **oil**, and **natural gas**. These are called **fossil fuels** because they are all dug out of the ground.

1 The diagram shows the amount of energy used by a country in 1980 and an estimate for the year 2000.

a In 1980 coal supplied roughly a quarter of the total energy needs. What fraction was supplied by oil?

b Which fuel will supply a smaller fraction of the country's needs in the future?

c Suggest what might be meant on the diagram by 'other sources of energy'.

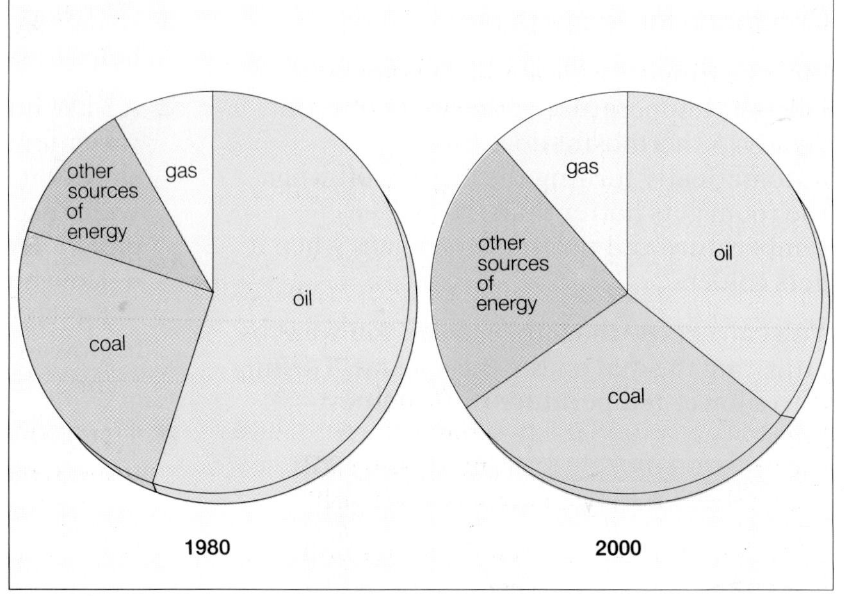

Energy balance present and future

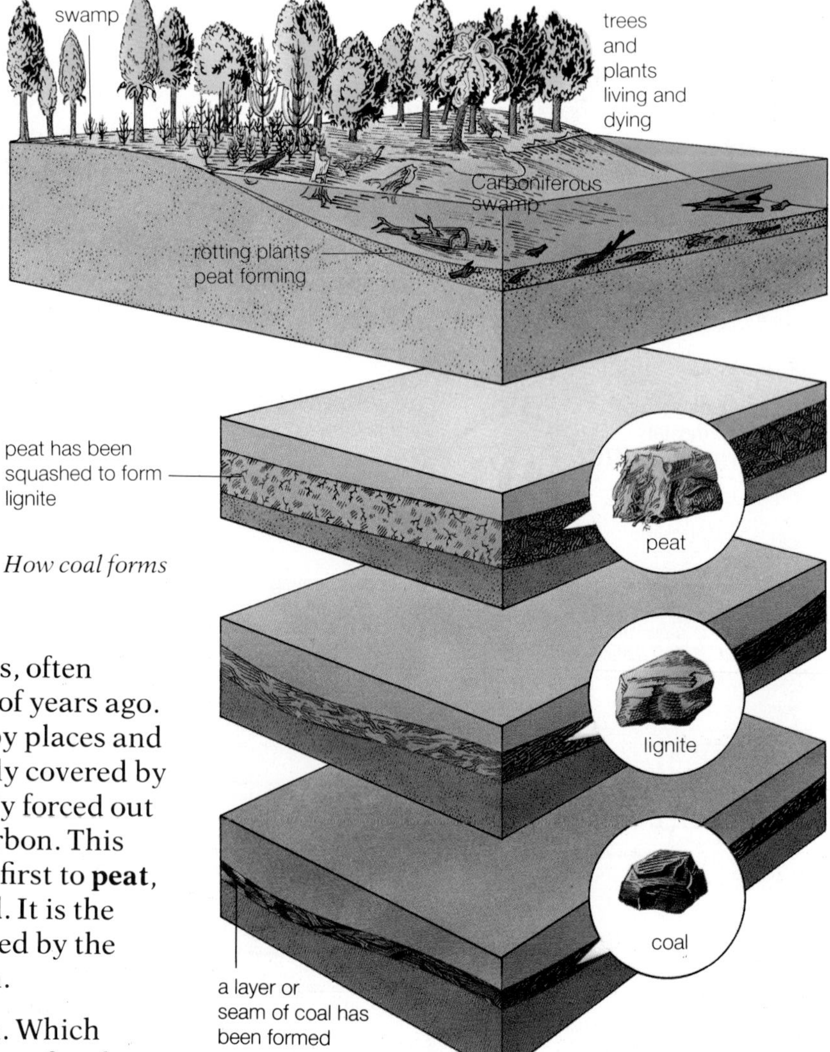

How coal forms

Coal

Coal is the remains of dead plants, often trees, which died many millions of years ago. They fell to the ground in swampy places and as they rotted they were gradually covered by mud. The weight on top gradually forced out oxygen and hydrogen leaving carbon. This changed the partly rotted plants first to **peat**, then to **lignite**, and finally to **coal**. It is the carbon in coal which burns, helped by the remaining oxygen, and hydrogen.

2 Peat, lignite, and coal all burn. Which contains the highest percentage of carbon and which contains the lowest?

Oil and gas

Oil

While coal was forming millions of years ago in fresh-water swamps, oil was being made in the seas.

Oil is the remains of tiny plants and animals, called **plankton** which lived in the sea. When they died they sank to the bottom and were covered by layers of mud, and sand. As there was no oxygen they could not rot and so their energy remained trapped inside them. As many years went by and the remains were buried deeper and deeper, bacteria, heat, and the pressure of the water, mud, and sand above them slowly changed them to oil.

Oil is found under the bed of the sea or under land which was once covered by sea.

Oil is formed from dead plankton

Natural gas

Natural gas, the gas you burn in your cooker, is usually found with oil and coal. Sometimes it seeps out of oil to form a **gas cap**. This is shown to the right. Sometimes the gas is dissolved in the oil and has to be removed later. It is also possible for gas to seep out of coal buried deep in the ground and to gather in large pockets.

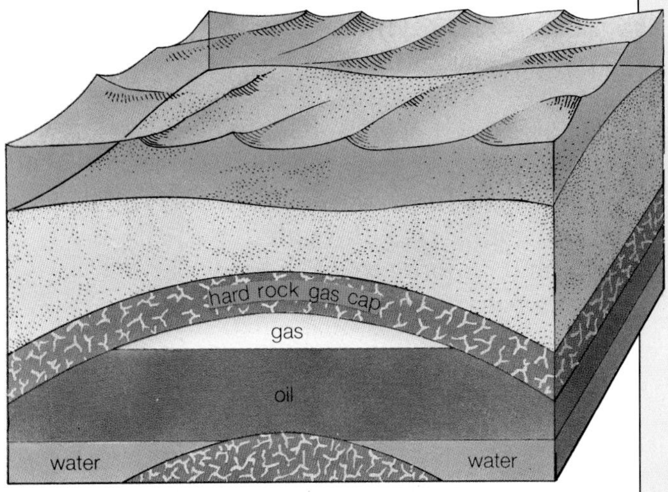

Natural gas is often found trapped between rock and oil. This is called a gas cap

country	% produced	% used
America	36	38
Russia	29	25
Britain	2	3
Romania	2	2
Others	31	32

Natural gas production and use

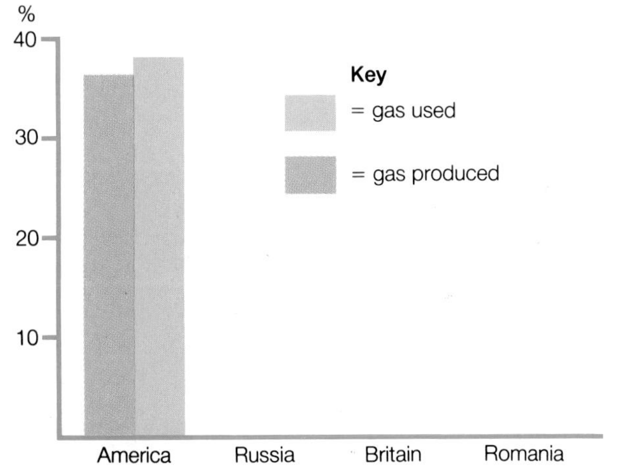

A comparison of gas produced and gas used in 1980

1 From the information given in the table, say which country used most natural gas.

2 Copy and complete the bar graph in the diagram using the information in the table.

3 From your bar graph say which country produced:

a the most gas
b the least gas
c more than it uses
d less than it uses
e just enough.

How oil forms

Oil on the move

As dead plankton was being turned to oil on the sea-bed the layers on top were turning into **sedimentary rock**. For example, sand became **sandstone**, mud became **mudstone** or **shale**, and the skeletons of shellfish became **limestone** and sometimes fossils.

Sedimentary rocks have thousands of small spaces or **pores** in them and it is in these spaces that the oil collects, rather like water in a sponge. Sometimes it reaches the surface and seeps out but often it gets stopped by meeting **impermeable rock**, that is, rock through which it cannot move. There are two main ways in which oil can be trapped underground:

An anticline. Here the oil is trapped by a dome of impermeable rock.

A fault trap. A fault in the earth is where the layers of different rocks have slipped sideways. Oil which was slowly moving through permeable rock may reach a fault and find itself trapped by a barrier of impermeable rock.

1 What is the main idea you have been reading about above:
a sedimentary rock
b drilling for oil
c how oil reservoirs form
d a fault trap?

2 Explain in your own words how oil gets trapped underground.

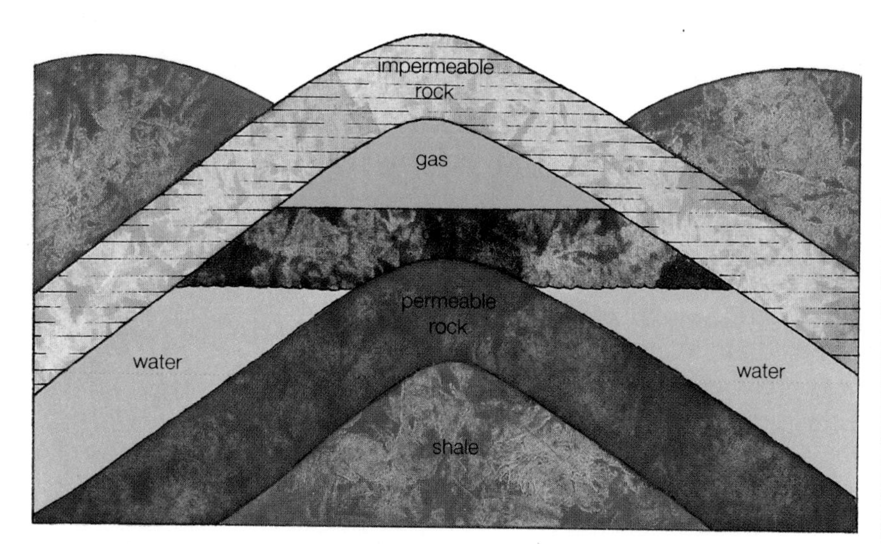

An anticline

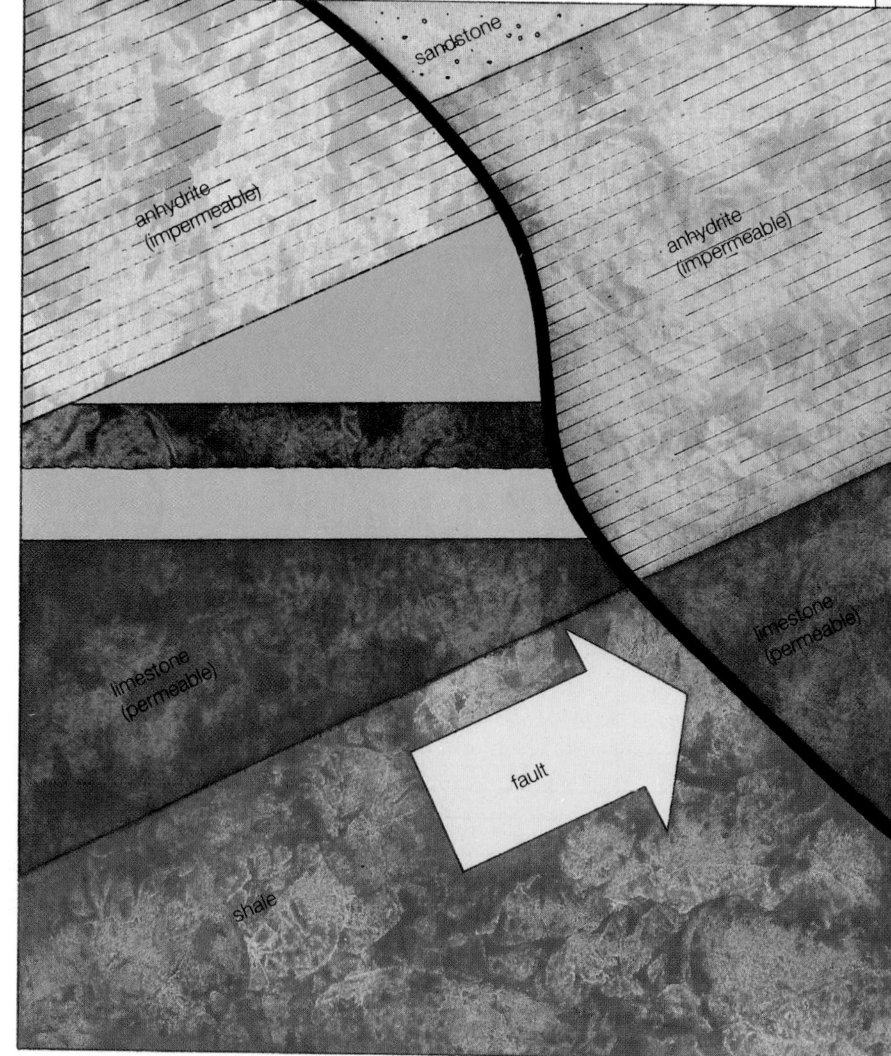

A fault trap

Finding oil

Geological survey

Oil geologists try to find anticlines or fault traps by looking at **geological maps** to find the type of rocks which usually hold oil. They also examine rock samples. This method is no good when searching for oil beneath the sea.

Drilling for rock samples

Aerial surveying

In **aerial photography** an aeroplane flies over an area of land taking photographs. Later the photographs are put together to map out the land and allow the geologist to search for shapes which could indicate oil.

Aircraft can also be used to carry special instruments called **gravimeters** which measure changes in the Earth's gravity and in this way give scientists information about the rocks under the surface.

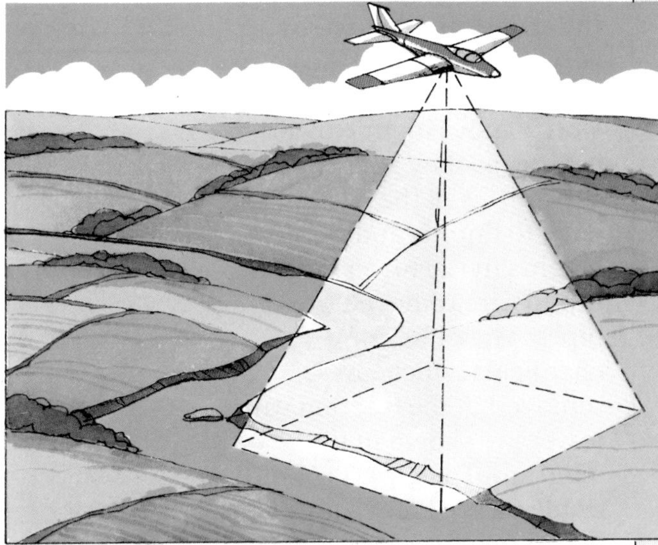
Photographing the land

Seismic survey

An explosion is set off and the underground echoes are picked up by special microphones. The pattern of echoes tells the geologist about the type of rocks underground.

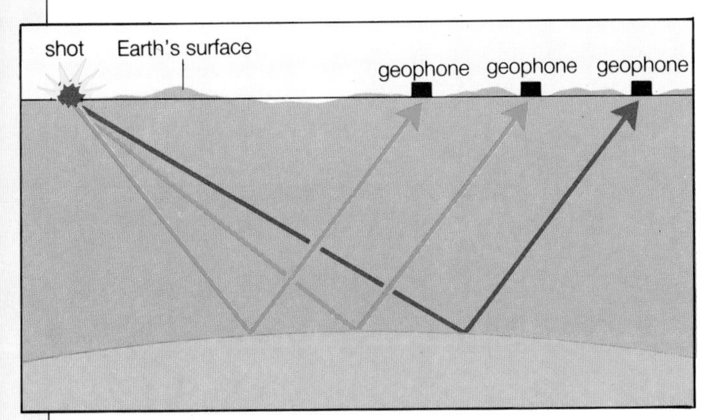

The sound from the explosion bounces off layers of rock and the echoes are picked up by special microphones called geophones

Drilling

After all the surveys are done the final test is to drill a hole. This first test hole is called a **wildcat**.

1 List 4 different ways of searching for oil.

The final test is to drill a hole — a wildcat

Sorting out the fractions

Refining oil

Oil straight from the ground is called **crude oil**. It is a mixture of many different substances. Crude oil is not very useful on its own. It must first be treated to separate the many useful substances it contains. This treatment is called **refining** and it takes place in an **oil refinery**. The oil first goes to very tall towers called **fractionating towers**. There the crude oil is heated by very hot steam and the gases which come from the oil slowly move up the tower, cooling as they go. Different substances in the gases turn back to liquids at different heights in the tower. These liquids are removed through pipes. The different chemicals which are removed in the fractionating tower are shown in the diagram. These parts of the crude oil are known as its **fractions**.

1 Explain in your own words what takes place in an oil refinery.

A single barrel of oil contains approximately 150 litres. The percentage amounts of different substances which can be made from the oil are shown in the diagram.

2 What is the largest part of the oil used for?

3 How many litres of petrol come from a single barrel of oil?

4 How many litres of diesel fuel come from a single barrel of oil?

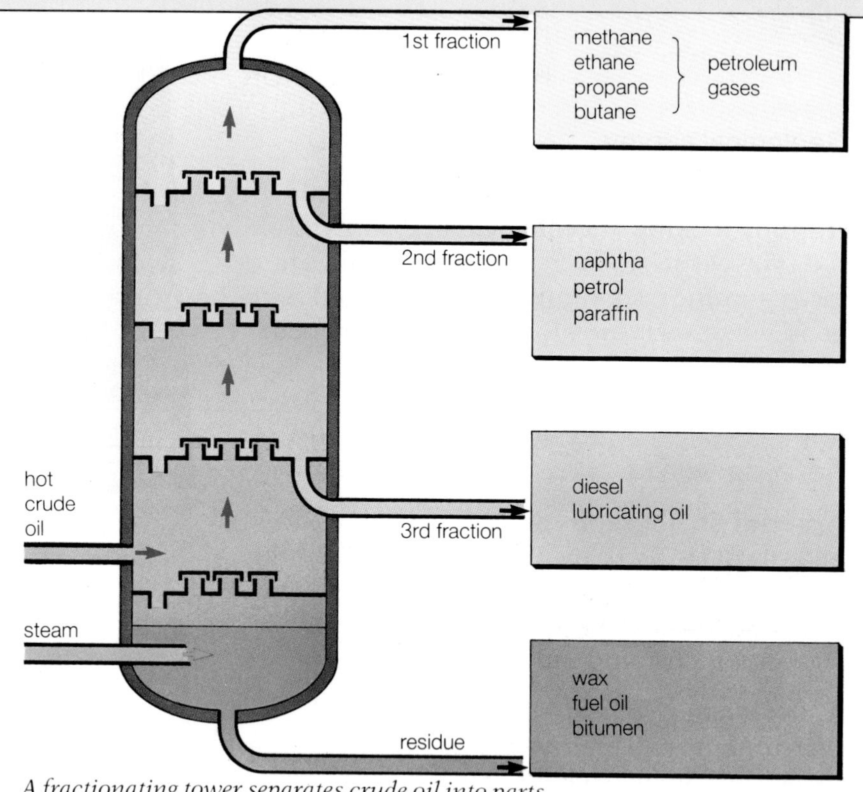

A fractionating tower separates crude oil into parts

Pie chart showing what can be produced from one barrel of oil

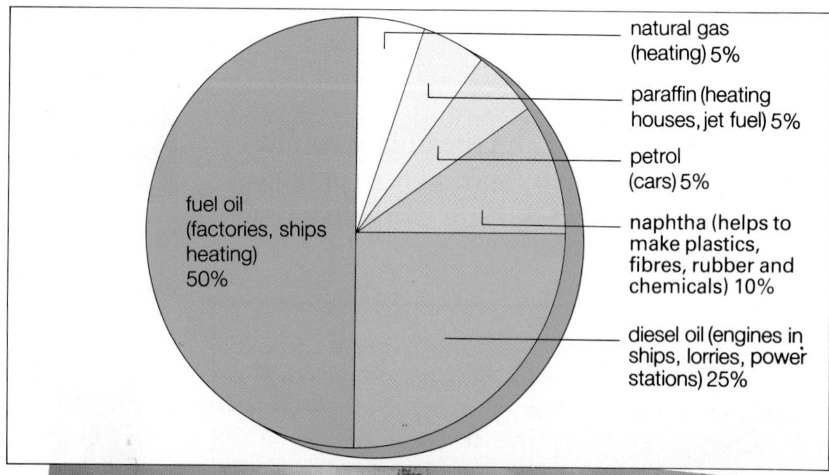

Crude oil is broken up into different parts in fractionating towers

Using the fractions

Petrol

Petrol is used to make motor cars work. In the engine the petrol is turned into a fine mist and mixed with air. The mixture of petrol and air is exploded by a spark plug. The force of the explosion moves the parts which make the wheels turn.

Paraffin

Paraffin was the first substance to be separated from crude oil. Before electricity and gas came along people used paraffin to heat and light their homes. Nowadays paraffin is not used much in the home. A special sort of paraffin called JETAI is used as fuel for jet planes.

Bitumen

Bitumen is a dark waterproof substance. It is hard at room temperature but it goes soft when it is strongly heated. It is often mixed with small stones and used to surface roads.

Paraffin wax

Paraffin wax is used to make candles. It is also used to make the waxy paper used to hold food and liquids.

Lubricating oil

Lubricating oil is used to make moving parts of machines run smoothly.

Liquified petroleum gas (LPG)

Camping gas is a handy way to heat and light your tent when you are camping. Inside the cylinder is liquid butane, one of the petroleum gases found in crude oil.

Fuel oils

Fuel oils are thick and heavy and are used to heat large boilers in factories, power stations, and ships. Fuel oils are also used in oil-fired central heating systems.

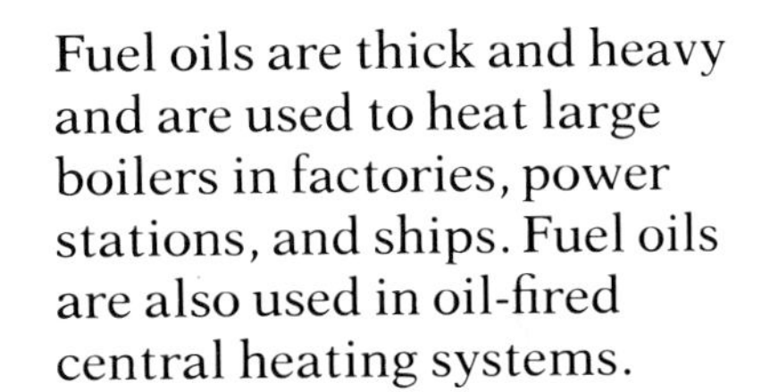

Diesel

Diesel oil is known in Britain as DERV (diesel engine road vehicle). It is used as a fuel for certain types of engine often found in ships, lorries, and buses.

1 Name the part of crude oil which is used for:
- **a** Central heating systems.
- **b** Fuelling motor cars.
- **c** Making candles.

2 What name is given to the type of paraffin used in jet planes?

3 What do the letters DERV stand for?

4 What is DERV used for?

5 What do the letters LPG stand for?

6 Give an example of LPG.

7 Why is bitumen a good material to use on roads?

Energy from the atom

It won't last long

We live in a world hungry for energy. Most of our energy comes from fossil fuels but we are fast using them up. Compared with the millions of years it took to make these fuels we will have used them up in a short time. Oil, for example will have supplied us with energy for less than 200 years. The amount of fossil fuel left in the world is known as the **reserves**. An estimate of these reserves is shown. Every effort should be made to save our supply of fossil fuels.

1 Which fossil fuel do we have most of?

2 Which fossil fuels will probably run out in your own lifetime?

100
75
50
25
years

Reserves of gas, oil and coal

The advantages of nuclear fuel

One way of saving our fossil fuels might be to use another fuel. Uranium is a fuel which is also dug out of the ground but it is not burnt like fossil fuels. Uranium is a **nuclear fuel**. Under special conditions the centre or **nucleus** of the uranium atom can be made to split or **fission**. When this happens the nucleus releases several small particles called **neutrons**. Each neutron can then make another uranium atom split up and so on. This is called a **chain reaction** and when it happens a large amount of heat is produced.

1 kg is a lot less than 60 tonnes!

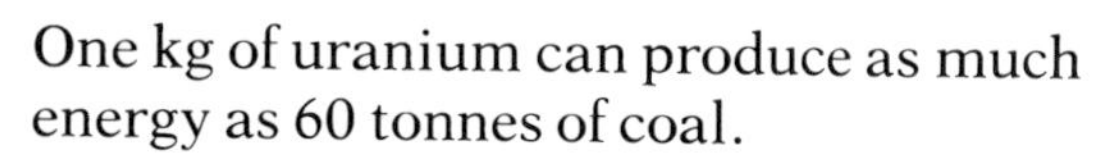

One kg of uranium can produce as much energy as 60 tonnes of coal.

3 How many kg of coal produce the same amount of energy as 1 kg of uranium (1 tonne = 1000 kg).

4 Longannet power station, working full out, can use 5 million tonnes of coal a year.

a How many 25 tonne wagon-loads of coal are needed a year?

b How many 25 tonne wagon-loads of uranium would be needed to produce the same amount of energy?

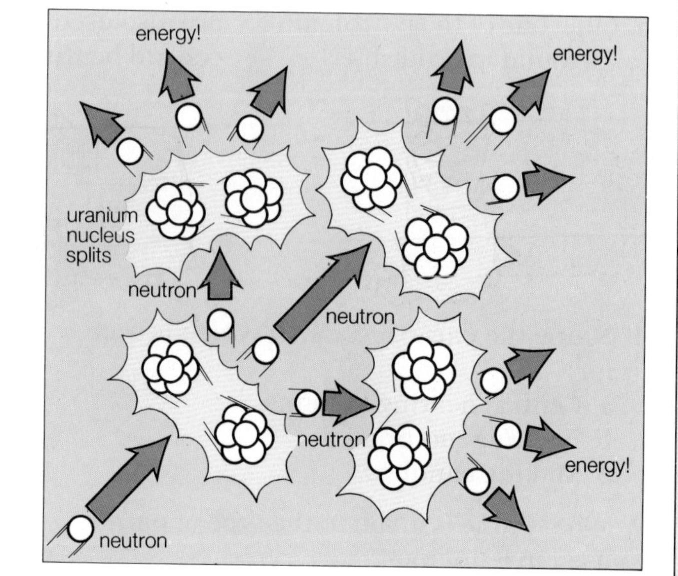

Nuclear fission
A neutron splits a uranium nucleus and more neutrons are released along with a lot of heat energy. Each new neutron splits another uranium nucleus. This is a chain reaction. The heat produced is used to make steam

Nuclear problems

turbine
generator
condenser
steam
coal-fired boiler
cooling tower
water

A coal-fired power station
Heat from the burning coal turns the water into steam in the boiler. The steam turns the turbine blades and the turbine drives the generator to make electricity

Nuclear fuel and electricity

In a coal-fired power station the heat energy from burning coal is used to heat a boiler and change water into steam. The steam is then used to drive the turbine which turns the electricity generator. In the condenser the steam is changed back to water and returned to the boiler. In a nuclear station electricity is made in exactly the same way. However, the heat to make the steam is released from the chain-reactions taking place in the uranium contained in the nuclear reactor.

Testing a nuclear flask at 100 mph

1 Describe in your own words the similarities between a coal-fired and a nuclear power station.

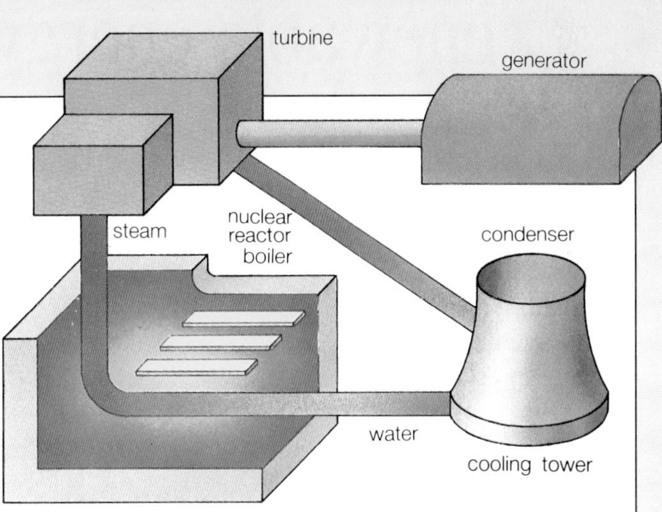

A nuclear power station
A chain reaction in the uranium produces lots of heat. In the boiler hot gases transfer the heat from the reactor to the water which turns into stream. The steam drives the turbine which turns the generator to make electricity

The problems with nuclear fuels

During a chain reaction harmful types of radiation are given off. Some of these can travel right through objects. A nuclear reactor has to be surrounded by thick concrete to protect people from the radiation and even then some people worry about the danger of radiation escaping from a nuclear power station.

Used nuclear fuel or **nuclear waste** is dangerous as it is very **radioactive**, that is, it gives off lots of harmful radiation. Transporting it about the country is risky and special flasks have been designed to prevent the radiation escaping in the event of an accident. To show the public how safe it could be to transport nuclear waste by rail the Central Electricity Generating Board deliberately crashed a train into a nuclear flask at 100 mph. The flask was left intact which is more than can be said for the Electricity Board's bank account. The test cost £1.6m!

Nuclear waste has to be stored for many years before it becomes safe.

To make it less likely to escape radioactive waste can be made into solid blocks of glass or a type of artificial rock. There are plans to get rid of these blocks by burying them deep underground or dumping them on the bed of the ocean.

2 Why do you think many people are worried about the plans for getting rid of nuclear waste?

Renewable energy

Renewable and non-renewable energy

Fossil fuels will not last forever. When they have been used up we will never be able to replace or **renew** them. They are said to be **non-renewable**. Some non-renewable sources of energy are practically ever-lasting because we use so little. An example of this is nuclear fuel.

Geothermal energy, heat from the Earth's centre, is another type of long-lasting but non-renewable energy.

Renewable energy continues to flow whether we use it or not. It comes from the sun, wind, waves, tides, running water, and plants.

1 Copy and complete the chart.

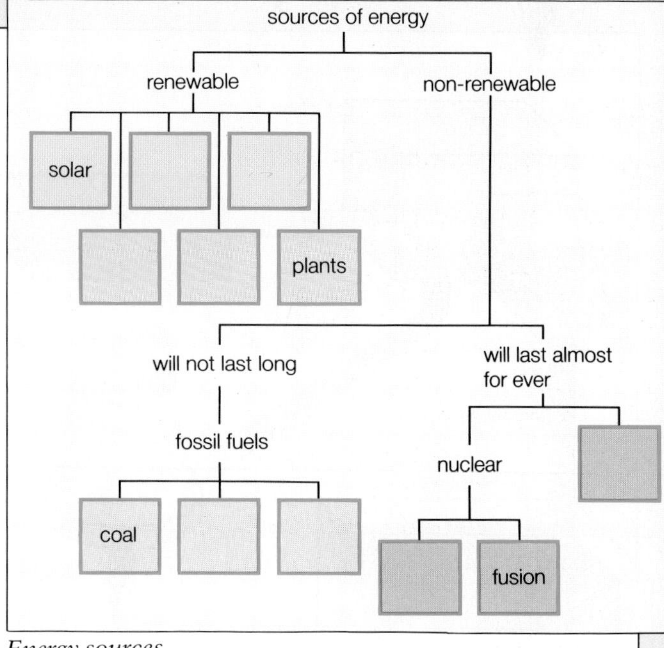

Energy sources

Renewable energy

Four examples of how renewable energy sources can be used to make electricity are shown.

Wind energy can be used to turn a wind-turbine connected to an electricity generator.

Sea waves can be used to move special 'nodding ducks' up and down to generate electricity.

A solar cell changes the Sun's energy directly to electricity.

In a hydro-electric scheme falling water is used to operate the electricity generators.

2 Explain how wind, wave, and hydro-electric power are also examples of energy from the sun.

3 List the advantages and disadvantages of using the energy sources shown.

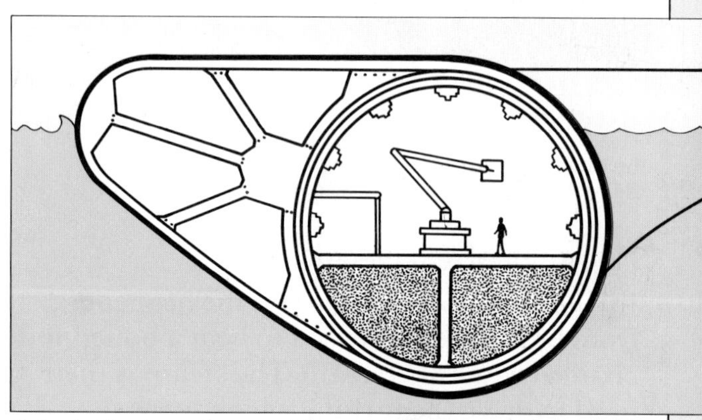
Salter's Ducks nod up and down in the sea and change wave energy to electricity

A wind turbine

Solar panels

A hydro-electric dam

Something for nothing

Annoying your neighbours

Energy from renewable sources can be used at home. A suitable windmill and **solar panels** can provide all the energy a well-insulated house needs. However, if you relied on a windmill you would probably not be too popular with your neighbours and you might find yourself in trouble on windless days!

The following three questions refer to the diagram.

1 How many kW of renewable energy are being used to run the house?

2 What steps have been taken to cut down heat loss from the house?

3 What advantages and disadvantages would such a system have?

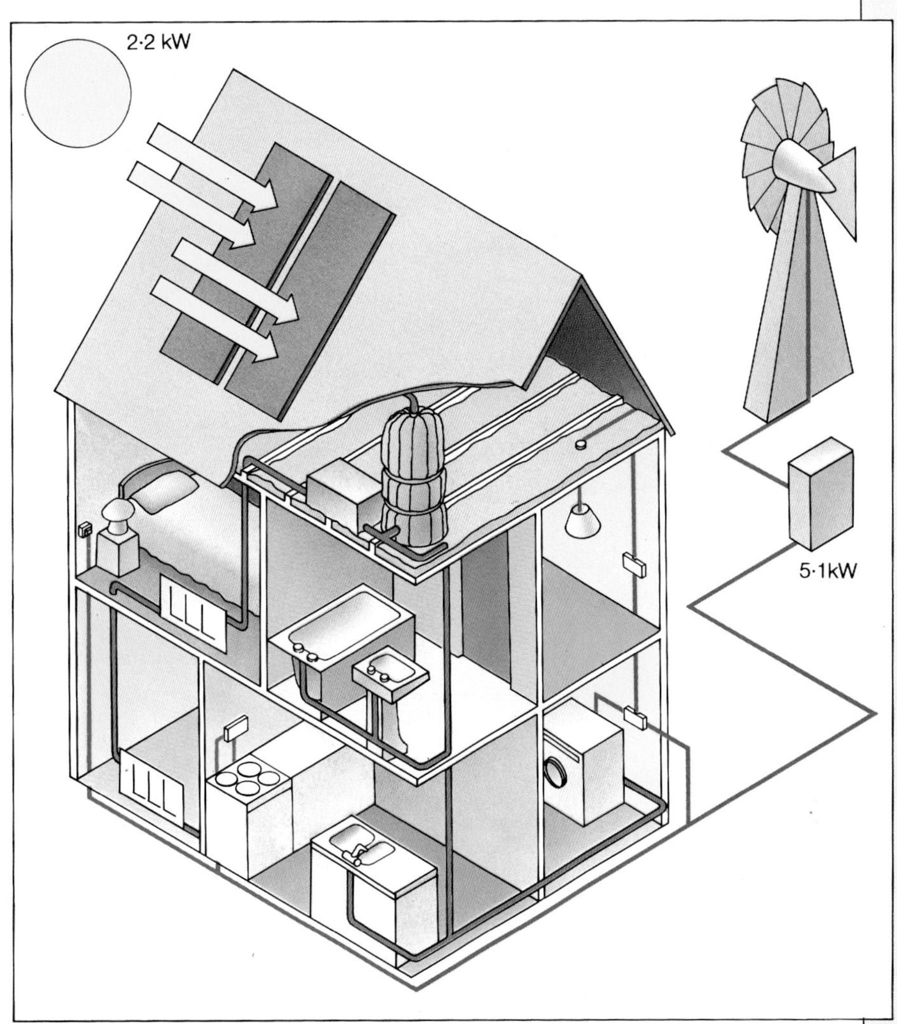

Running a house on renewable energy

Details of a solar panel are shown in the diagram. As water flows through the panel it absorbs energy from the Sun's rays. In time the water in the storage tank warms up but it usually needs to be further heated by an immersion heater before it is really hot.

4 Is the water hottest at A or at B?

5 Explain what effect the following would have on how well a solar panel worked:
position of panel on roof, angle to sun, length of pipe in panel, speed of water flow, colour of panel.

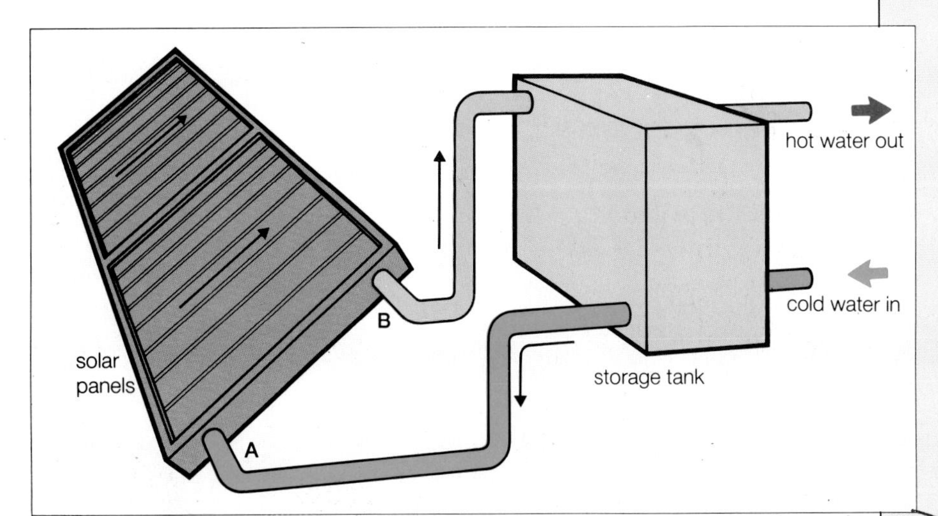

Heat energy from the Sun passes into the water as it flows through the solar panel

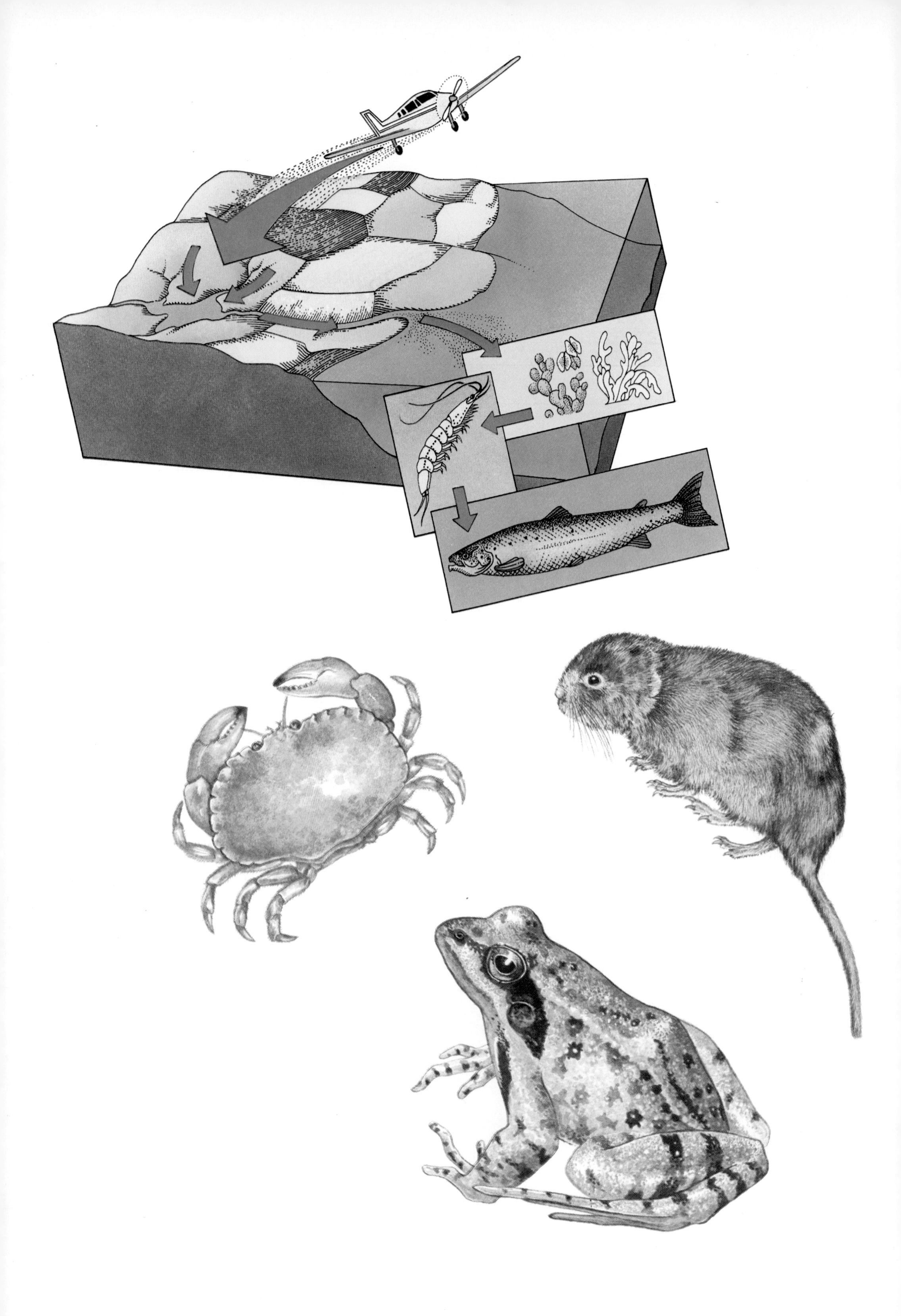

THE ENVIRONMENT

This section is about your environment and the factors influencing it. In it you will learn about the ways in which living things depend on one another for their survival, the problem of waste and the ways in which human beings affect their environment for good, and for bad.

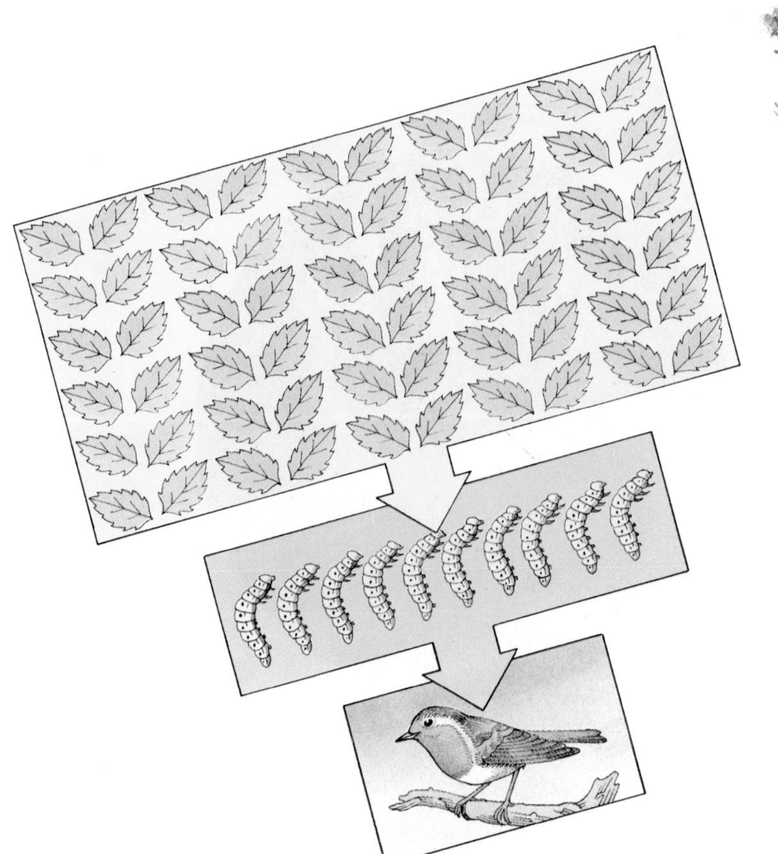

Be it ever so humble . . .

A place to live

Look around you. What do you see?

You are probably sitting in a room with some other people. The room and the people make up your surroundings. The word which is used in science for your surroundings is **environment**.

The environment of any living thing (animal or plant) is the place where it lives together with the other living things which live there.

A town environment

Living on land

Most British people live in towns or cities. They live in a **town environment** like the one shown in the top photograph.

A town environment is one kind of **land environment**. Another kind of land environment is a **woodland** like the one shown in the photograph opposite.

1 Give five examples of living things which live in a town environment.

2 Give five examples of living things which live in a woodland environment.

3 Name two other kinds of land environment.

A woodland environment

... There's no place like home!

Living in water

All living things need water to stay alive. Some living things can only live in water. The photographs show two different kinds of water environment. The **seashore** is one kind of **saltwater environment**. A **stream** is one kind of **freshwater environment**.

1 Give five examples of living things which live in a seashore environment.

2 Give five examples of living things which live in a stream environment.

3 Name two other water environments.

A saltwater environment

Something in common

Different environments have different kind of animals and plants living in them. But all environments have some things in common:

- a supply of energy and food, and
- living things which depend on each other.

In this part we will be looking at these things in more detail. You may get a chance to go out and look at an environment for yourself.

A freshwater environment

You can't know everything

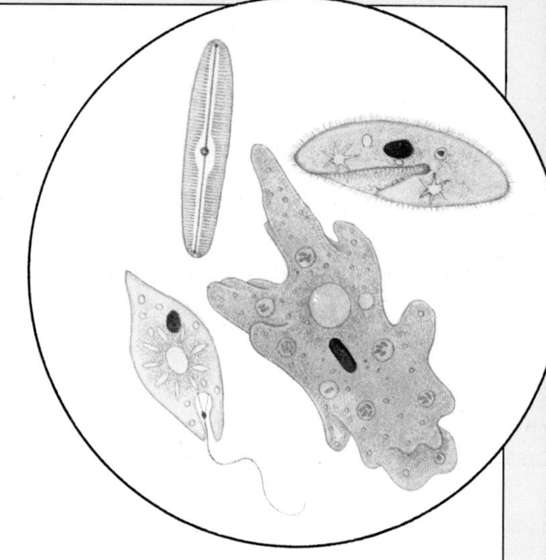
Pond life seen through a microscope

A different sort of key

The living things which you named on pages **62** and **63** were fairly well-known ones. Many other living things are not so well-known. These other animals and plants may be hidden away (for example, in the soil or under leaves and stones), or they may be so small that you cannot see them without a microscope.

There are thousands of different kinds of living things in Britain. It is impossible for any one person to name them all at a glance. But it is possible to name them all by using **keys**.

How a key works

The diagrams show four different kinds of bird which may be seen at the coast. Below the diagrams is a key which you can use to name the four birds. For example, you can see that **Bird A** has a straight beak (la) so go to part 2 of the key. It has no crest of feathers on its head (2b). So, of the four kinds of bird named in this key it must be the **oystercatcher**.

1 Describe one difference between bird B and bird D.

2 Use the key to identify birds B, C, and D.

3 The common tern is also found at the coast. It has a short, straight beak, and no crest of feathers. Make another key to include the common tern as well as the other birds.

Four birds of the sea coast

A key to four *birds of the Coast*

1	a	Straight beak	2
	b	Curved beak	3
2	a	Crest of feathers on head	*Lapwing*
	b	No crest of feathers	*Oystercatcher*
3	a	Beak curved downwards	*Curlew*
	b	Beak curved upwards	*Avocet*

Using a key

Freshwater life

The photograph shows some students looking for animals and plants in a freshwater pond. The drawings show living things they found.

1 How many living things are named in the key below?

2 Use the key to name the living things A–M.

A key to freshwater plants and animals

1	**a**	Plant	2
	b	Animal	4
2	**a**	Floating plant with single leaf	*Duckweed*
	b	Submerged plant with many leaves	3
3	**a**	Overlapping leaves	*Elodea*
	b	Leaves not overlapping	*Stonewort*
4	**a**	Soft bodied. No protective cover	5
	b	Shell or other protective cover	7
5	**a**	Body divided into many sections	*Tubifex*
	b	Body not divided into many sections	6
6	**a**	Flattened body	*Flatworm*
	b	Thread-like body	*Roundworm*
7	**a**	Shell. No limbs	8
	b	No shell. Limbs	10
8	**a**	Double shell	*Mussel*
	b	Single shell	9
9	**a**	Spiral shell	*Snail*
	b	Shell not a spiral	*Limpet*
10	**a**	Four pairs of legs	*Mite*
	b	Three pairs of legs	11
11	**a**	Two tail prongs	*Young stonefly*
	b	Three tail prongs	12
12	**a**	Long tail prongs	*Young mayfly*
	b	Short tail prongs	*Young dragonfly*

A B C D E F G H I J K L M

Freshwater finds

Here, there – but not everywhere

Even shrimps can be choosy

If you look carefully, you can usually find freshwater shrimps in a stream. But they are not found everywhere. They seem to prefer living in some parts of a stream rather than others.

All parts of a stream are not the same. For example, in some parts the water will flow quickly, in other parts it will flow slowly. Some parts of a stream are shallow, others are deep. Some parts have mud at the bottom and others have pebbles.

1 Suggest three things which might decide which parts of a stream freshwater shrimps prefer.

2 You can find out how fast a stream is flowing by dropping in a piece of wood and timing how long it takes to be carried a fixed distance. The table shows the results of doing this three times for the same part of a stream.

Freshwater shrimp

	first time	**second time**	**third time**
distance travelled (metres)	36	36	36
time taken (seconds)	36	18	20

Steam speed results

a At what speed (in metres per second) does each result suggest that the stream is flowing?
b Why do you think that the three results were not all the same?
c What was the average speed of the stream?

Shellfish decisions

The diagram shows the apparatus used to try to find out if freshwater shrimps prefer a particular sort of surface. Twenty shrimps were put into the water at the centre of the dish. The apparatus was left for an hour and then the number of shrimps that had settled on each surface was counted. The results are shown in the table.

3 Which surface did the shrimps seem to prefer?

4 Draw a bar chart to show the results.

5 Suggest two things which would have to be kept the same for all parts of the dish during the experiment.

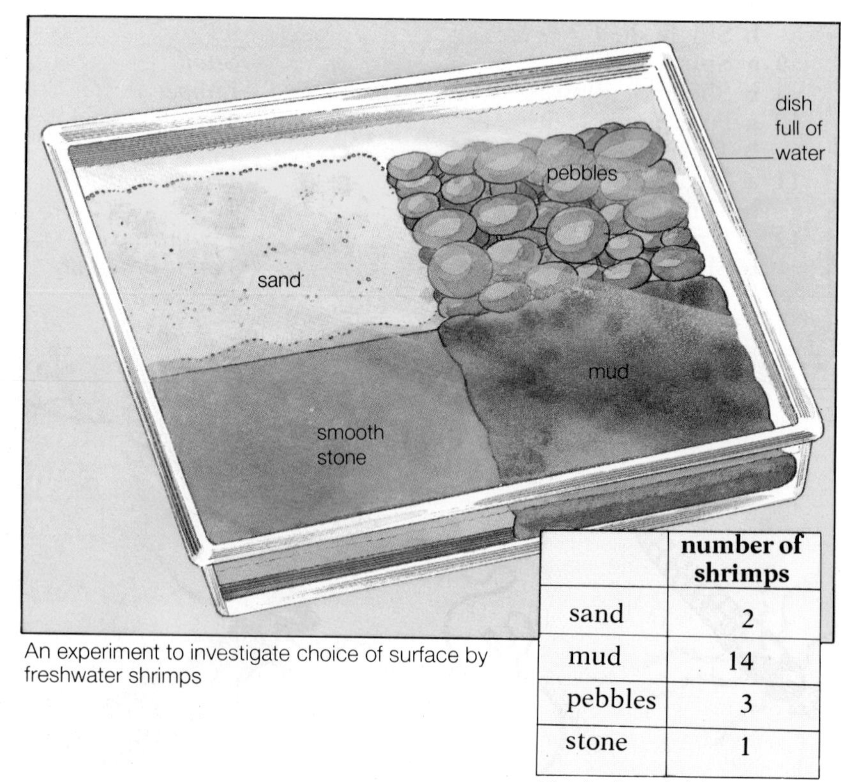

An experiment to investigate choice of surface by freshwater shrimps

	number of shrimps
sand	2
mud	14
pebbles	3
stone	1

Distribution of shrimps

Dark doings

Shady customers

Ferns are common plants of the land environment. But they prefer damp and shady conditions, so they are not found everywhere. They are often found in woodlands. All parts of a wood are not the same. For example, in some parts more light will get through than in others. Some parts of a wood will be more sheltered than others. In some parts the soil will be very wet, in others it will be dry.

1 Suggest three things which might decide where in a wood ferns will be most likely to grow.

2 You can find out how wet a soil is by measuring how much weight it loses when it is dried out. (The loss of weight is the weight of water which was in the soil.) The results opposite show what was found for one sample of soil.
  a What *weight* of water did the soil have in it?
  b What was the *percentage* of water in the soil?

Woodland ferns

soil drying experiment	
weight of wet soil	= 60 g
weight of dry soil	= 45 g

Water content of a soil

Helen was tired. For three hours they had been exploring the dark unknown. They had entered the cave system at 8.00 am. First came the steep descent using fixed ladders and ropes. Then came the passages, lower and lower, narrower and narrower, until progress was only possible at a crawl. She was totally dependent on her long experience of caving, her carefully selected equipment and her companion, Anna, close behind her.
At last they reached their destination – Cathedral Cavern opened out before them. They seemed all alone. And then their torches picked out a stream and pool at their feet. In the water swam strange yet familiar creatures. Small, blind fish, their skin a ghostly white, darted here and there.

A tight squeeze

A strange environment

3 What was 'strange' about the environment Helen was exploring?

4 In what way did the environment seem to have influenced the animals living there?

Cave life

Seasonal changes

Prickly customers

Hedgehogs live in woodland and hedgerow environments throughout Britain. In Spring they wake from their long Winter sleep. They start to hunt around for food — small insects, worms, and slugs. The mild Spring weather means that there will be plenty of these around.

Once they are well fed, hedgehogs mate. Their young are usually born in the warmer days of July or August. Once again plenty of food is available. The young spend their early days in a nest of grass and leaves, usually well protected in a thick hedge.

In early Autumn, as the temperature gets cooler, the hedgehogs roof their nests in preparation for the Winter. The hedgehog is a **hibernating** animal. As soon as the weather gets cold the family retire to their nest, curl up together and go to sleep. Unless there is a spell of really mild weather the hedgehogs remain in hibernation from the end of October until the end of March.

Adult hedgehog

Baby hedgehog

1 Why do you think hedgehogs got their name?

2 In what season of the year do hedgehogs mate?

3 What is meant by hibernation?

4 Why do you think hedgehogs need to hibernate during the winter?

5 A hedgerow environment is not the same all the year round. Describe how it will differ in Summer and Winter seasons of the year.

Hibernating hedgehog in nest

Life has its ups and downs

Rabbiting-on

Rabbits can breed *extremely* quickly. A pair may mate when only six-months old and their young will be born one month later. The pair may have eight lots of young in a year and each lot may be nine babies. So why aren't we knee-deep in rabbits?

Rabbits grazing

Fox eating rabbit

Any environment can only provide enough food to support a certain number of rabbits. If the rabbit **population** increases above this number then some rabbits must starve. Also, when animals are crowded together diseases spread rapidly. Rabbits have many enemies too. Foxes, badgers, weasels, and stoats hunt rabbits for food. Humans trap and shoot rabbits for their meat and fur, and also to stop crops being eaten.

1 List three different ways in which rabbit populations are prevented from increasing.

2 How many baby rabbits might be produced by a single pair in one year?

Can we control ourselves?

The line graph shows the way in which the world population of human beings has changed over the years. The recent '**population explosion**' is mainly due to our ability to control disease and produce more food and, therefore, live longer.

3 About how big was the human population in 1000 AD?

4 About how many times bigger than this is the population today?

5 About when did the population explosion begin?

If the population explosion continues then food supplies will eventually run short. In some countries, though, the population is being held steady (the birth rate is about the same as the death rate). Knowing about, and using, birth control methods such as the 'pill' means that couples can choose the size of their families. Rabbits don't have this choice but they have diseases and enemies!

World population growth over the past 2000 years

number of people (millions)

4000
3000
2000
1000

1000
2000
year (AD)

Graph showing growth of human population

country	birth rate per 1000/year	death rate per 1000/year
Kenya	51	12
Brazil	36	8
United Kingdom	12	12
West Germany	10	12
Russia	18	10

Population changes in different countries

6 Name 3 countries in which the birth rate is greater than the death rate.

7 Use the table to say in which countries the population is: **a** increasing, **b** steady, and **c** decreasing.

Energy for the environment

Available energy

You learned a lot about energy earlier in this book. Two important things to remember are:

- energy is the ability to do things, and
- energy can be changed from one form to another.

1 What four forms of energy are shown in the photographs?

2 Describe how you could change one of these forms into another.

All living things need food

Staying alive

All living things need a supply of energy to stay alive. You learned about the energy in food on pages **8** and **36**. It is fairly obvious how most animals get their food. Plants though don't look as if they are ever doing much. But appearances can be deceptive!

3 Why do living things need food?

4 Explain how animals get their food.

The Sun

Universal energy source

The Sun is the source of energy for living things. **Heat energy** and **light energy** from the Sun reach Earth after a journey of 150 million kilometres through space. Heat energy can't be captured by plants or by animals, but it warms-up all living things and their surroundings. Light energy *can* be captured — but only by **green plants**.

Making food

The energy capturers

Green plants are able to capture light energy because they contain an energy-capturing chemical called **chlorophyll**. Chlorophyll is green. This is why so many plants are green. Some plants which contain chlorophyll may not look green though because they also contain other coloured chemicals. For example, many seaweeds are brown but they do contain chlorophyll and they are able to capture light energy.

1 Some plants, like certain mushrooms and toadstools, have no coloured chemicals in them. They look whitish. Do you think that they are able to capture light energy? Explain your answer.

2 Construct a table which lists the plants shown opposite as either 'Able to capture light energy' or 'Not able to capture light energy'.

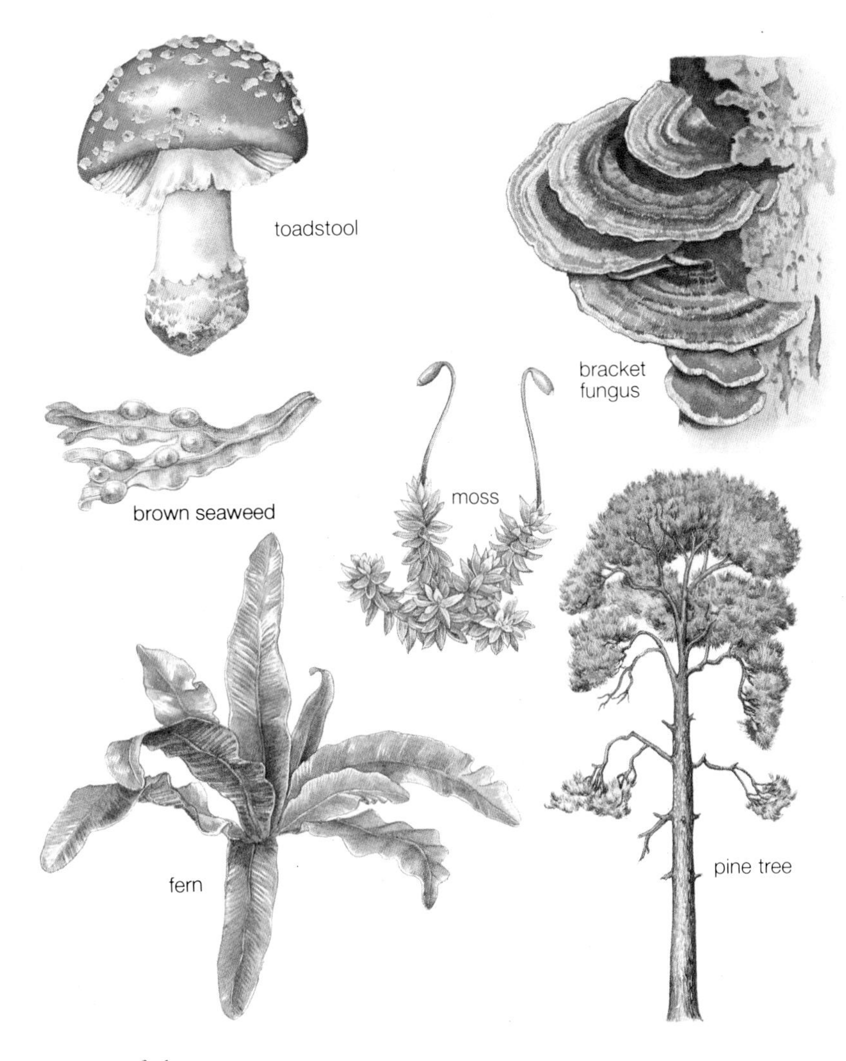

A variety of plants

Putting it together

Green plants use the energy that they capture to *make* food. Living things which can make food are called **producers** — so green plants are producers.

3 Why are green plants called producers?

The diagram shows what a green plant needs to be able to make food and how it gets what it needs.

Although green plants need a constant supply of carbon dioxide and water, their chlorophyll is used over and over again. Once it has passed on its captured energy it is ready to capture more.

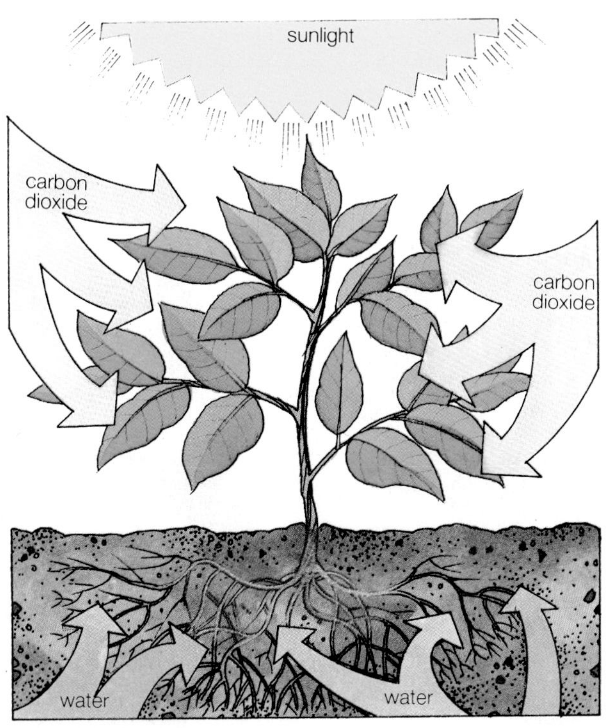

How green plants make food

Eat and be eaten

A woodland herbivore

Animal appetites

Animals get the food they need either by eating plants or by eating other animals. They have to feed in this way because they cannot make food for themselves. Living things which feed on other living things are called **consumers** — so animals are consumers.

Consumers which feed mainly on plants are called **herbivores**. The photograph shows a squirrel eating a nut. As well as nuts, squirrels eat buds and roots.

A woodland carnivore

Consumers which feed mainly on animals are called **carnivores**. The photograph shows an owl eating a woodmouse. As well as mice, owls eat other small mammals and birds.

Consumers which feed on both plants and animals are called **omnivores**. The diagram shows a badger eating a slug. As well as slugs, badgers eat frogs, worms, grass, and fruits.

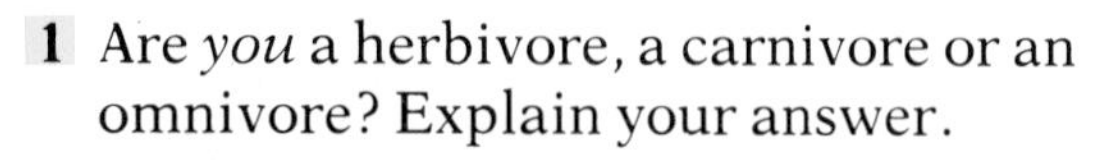

1 Are *you* a herbivore, a carnivore or an omnivore? Explain your answer.

2 Explain why it can be an advantage to an animal to be an omnivore.

A woodland omnivore

Let us prey

Carnivores are often called **predators** and the animals on which they feed are called their **prey**. For example, an owl is a predator and a mouse is its prey.

3 The diagram shows five predators and their prey. Match each predator to its prey.

4 What sort of consumer is most likely to be the prey of a predator?

Hunt the prey

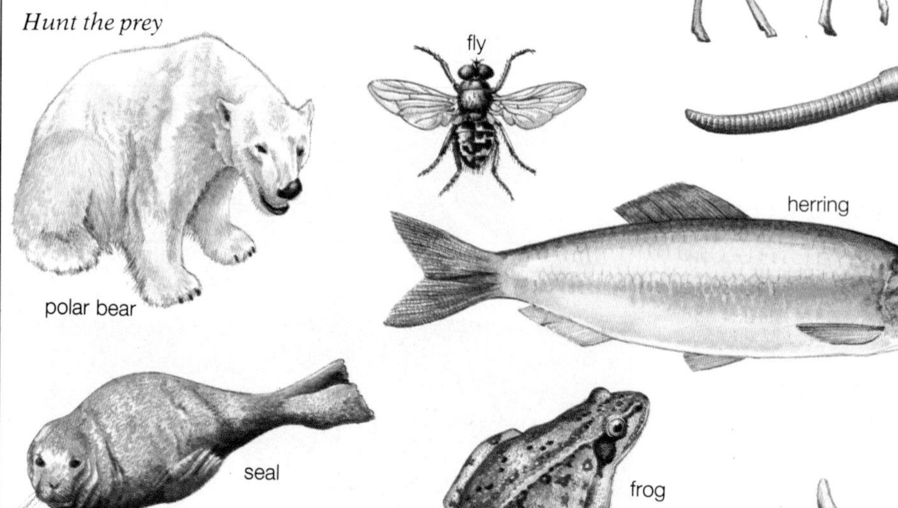

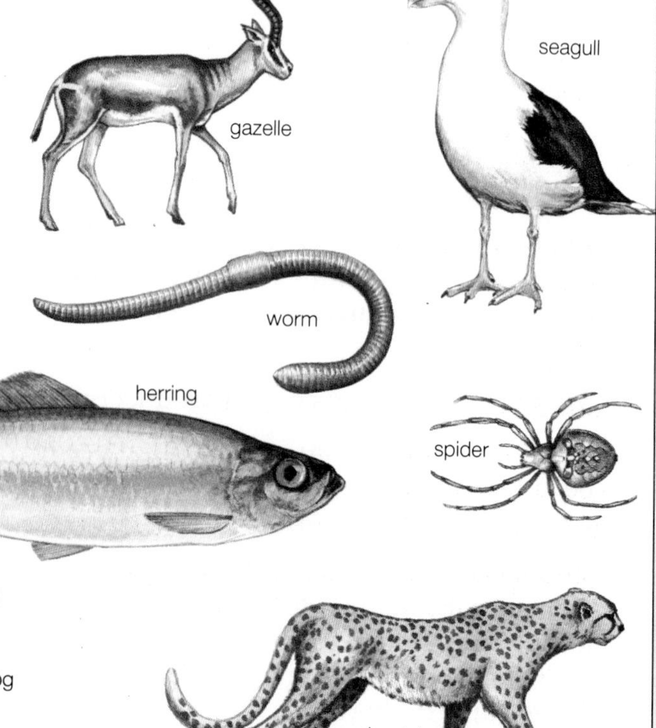

Getting it together

African lions

The sociable killer

Unlike other cats, African lions are sociable creatures. Twelve to fifteen lions may live together in a group or **pride**. The pride will contain more females than males. The lionesses do most of the hunting for the pride. Lions prefer living in areas with scattered trees and shrubs.

The lion's share

Like most large carnivores lions will hunt almost anything, although they seem to prefer wildebeeste and zebra. Lions will also rob other creatures, such as hyenas, of their kill.

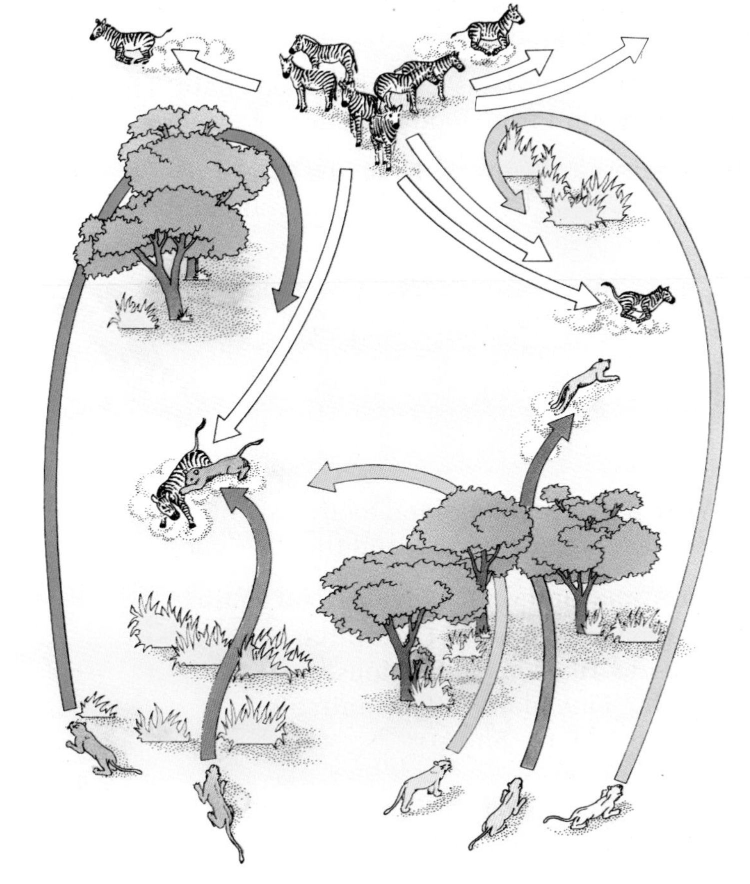
Hunting strategy of lionesses

The hunt

Most hunts take place at night. Although the lionesses can run at about 55 kilometres per hour they can only do so over short distances and must also rely on stealth. The diagram shows how a group of lionesses might hunt together. The prey are zebra and the movements of individual lionesses and zebra are shown by arrows.

1 What do we call:
  a A group of lions?
  b A female lion?

2 What two preferences are mentioned above and how do you explain them?

3 In the diagram, how many lionesses are shown hunting together and how many zebra are being hunted?

4 What was the result of the hunt shown in the diagram?

5 Explain, in your own words, how lionesses hunt zebra.

Lions eating

Food chains

Links in a chain

The diagram shows three living things which are found in a seashore environment.

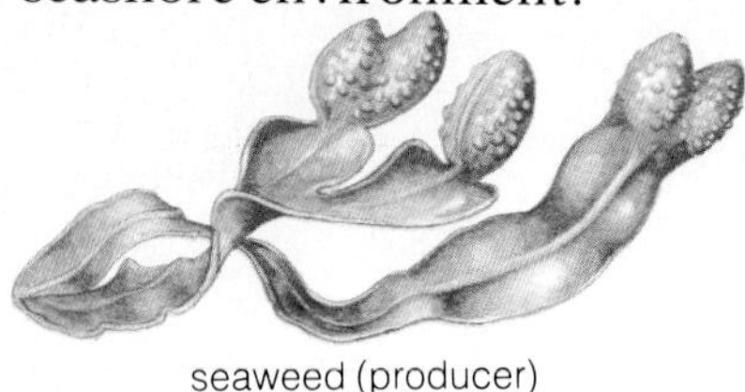

A three-link food chain

The seaweed is a producer. It is eaten by snails which in turn are eaten by seagulls.

Each plant or animal is a link in a **food chain**. The arrows in a food chain point from food to feeder.

Food chains don't always have just three links. The diagram shows a four link food chain from a woodland environment.

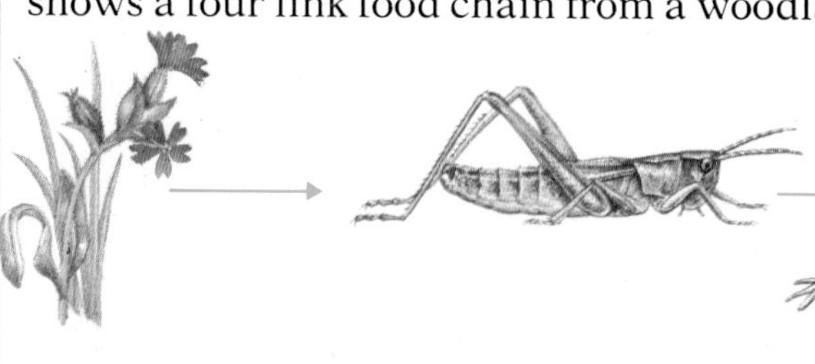

A four-link food chain

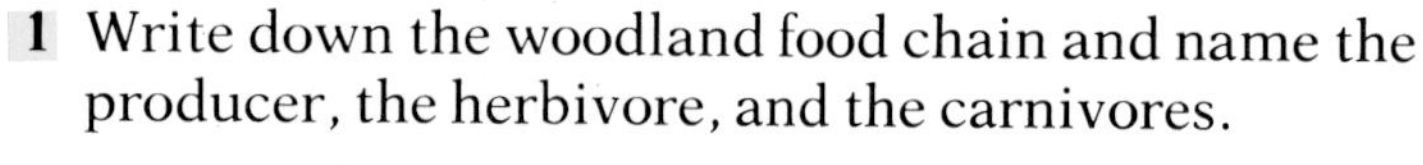

1 Write down the woodland food chain and name the producer, the herbivore, and the carnivores.

2 Rearrange and write down as food chains:

a Cabbage Thrush Caterpillar
b Stoat Blackberries Mouse
c Fish Tiny plants Tiny animals
d Grass Man Sheep

Prehistoric food chains

The diagrams shows one food chain from prehistoric times.

3 Name a prehistoric herbivore and carnivore.

4 Write down the food chain in the usual way.

Prehistoric food chain

Food webs

Life isn't quite so simple

On page **72** you learned that badgers eat slugs!

Plant → Slug → Badger

But you also learned that badgers eat frogs and worms as well.

Grass snakes also eat frogs, frogs eat slugs and worms, and. . .!

So, food chains are not isolated from each other. They are all connected together in the sort of way shown in the diagram. A set of interconnected food chains like this is called a **food web**.

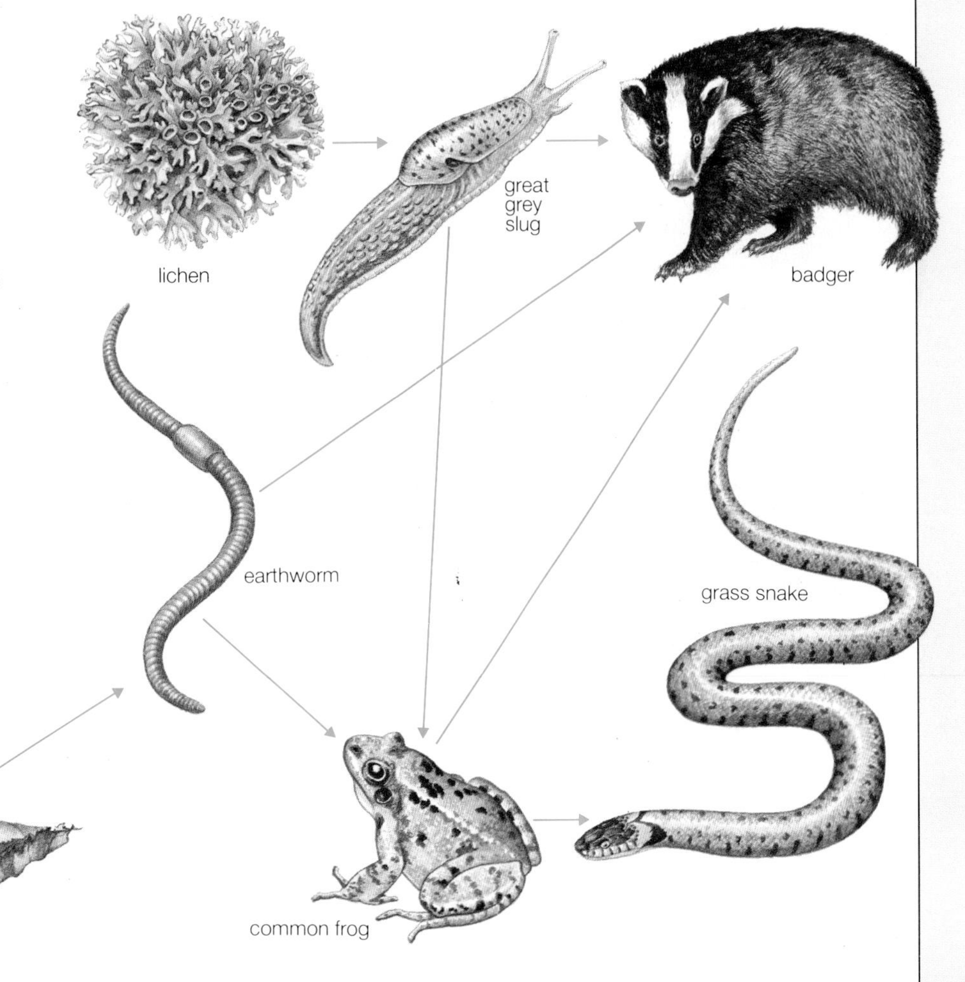

A woodland food web

A seashore food web

The diagram shows a partly completed food web from a seashore environment.

1 From this food web, name a:

a producer **b** herbivore **c** carnivore

2 **a** What do limpets eat?
b What feeds on prawns?

3 From this food web, write down a food chain with four links.

4 Copy out the seashore food web and add the following information. Herring gulls eat crabs, and limpets are sometimes eaten by human beings. Mussels eat tiny plants and tiny animals, and are eaten by crabs, herring gulls and humans. Starfish eat mussels and are eaten by gulls.

5 Draw a food web which shows the connections between grass, rabbits, sheep, foxes, and human beings.

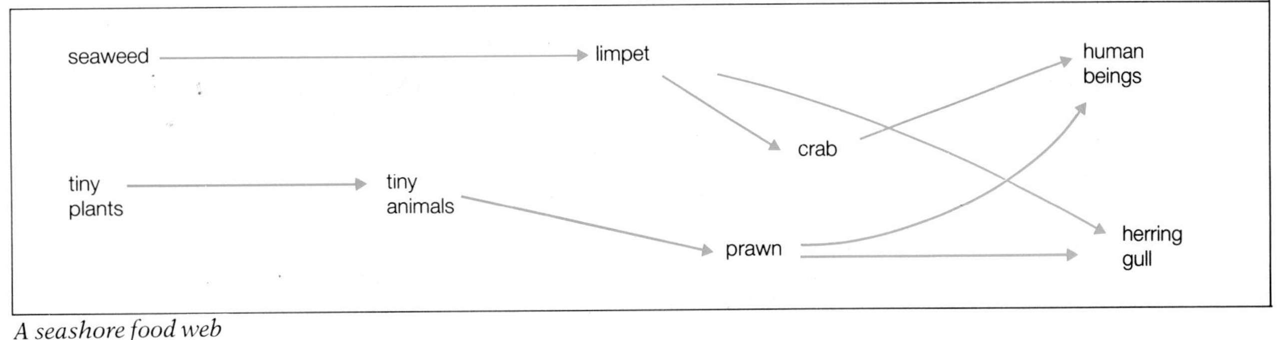

A seashore food web

The missing links

A garden food web

It is surprising what you can find by turning over stones!

Seeing what turns up

In one corner of their garden, Ian and Jennifer collected some woodlice, centipedes, dead leaves, and millipedes. They wondered if these were connected in a food web and decided to try to find out.

They set up the experiment shown in the diagrams. Each dish had a lid on it, and each lid had tiny holes. They put the dishes in a dark, cool place and left them for a few days. The table shows what they found when they looked at the dishes again.

1 Why did they put lids on the dishes and why did the lids have tiny holes?

2 Why did they keep the dishes in a *dark, cool* place?

3 What did their results tell them the different animals probably ate?

4 Draw a food web which shows your answers to question 3.

5 To get the most information they could from their experiment they should really have set up two other dishes. What should they have put in these dishes?

6 What results would you have expected from these two dishes? Explain your answers.

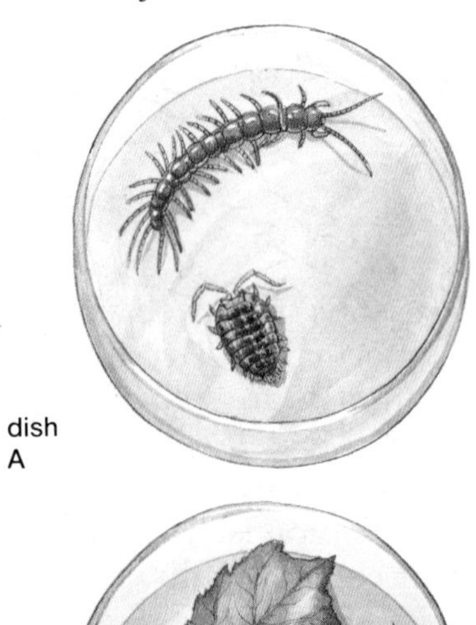

dish A

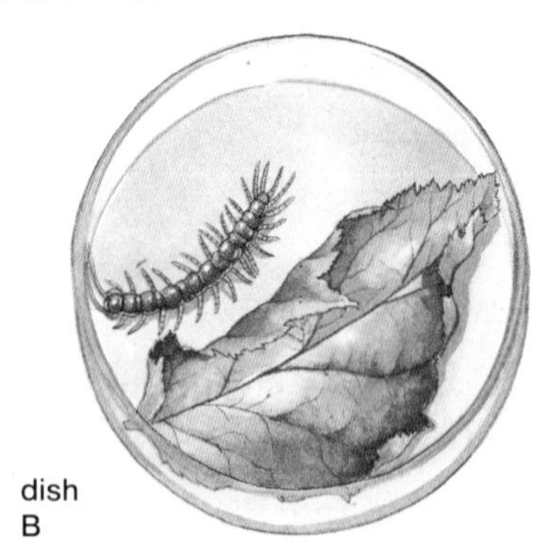

dish B

dish C

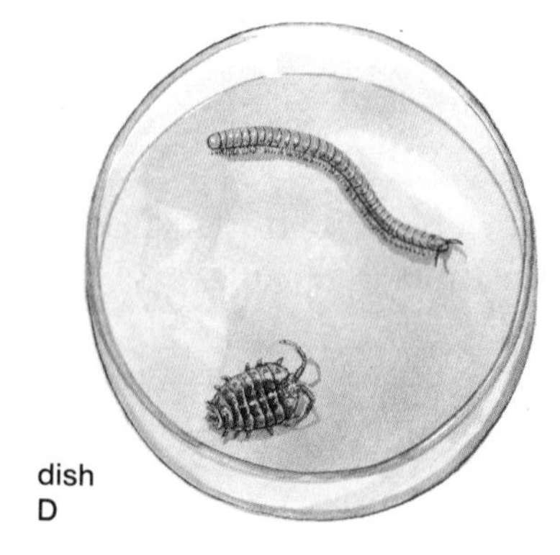

dish D

The experiment

The results

dish	what they found at the end of the experiment
A	a part eaten woodlouse and a living centipede
B	a dead centipede and dead leaves
C	dead leaves and a living millipede
D	a dead millipede and a dead woodlouse

A waste of energy?

Fewer but bigger

The diagram below shows a simple food chain. At the start there are enough leaves to feed a large number of caterpillars. But these caterpillars can only feed a small number of robins. This is partly because robins are much bigger than caterpillars and partly because energy is 'lost' from each link in the chain.

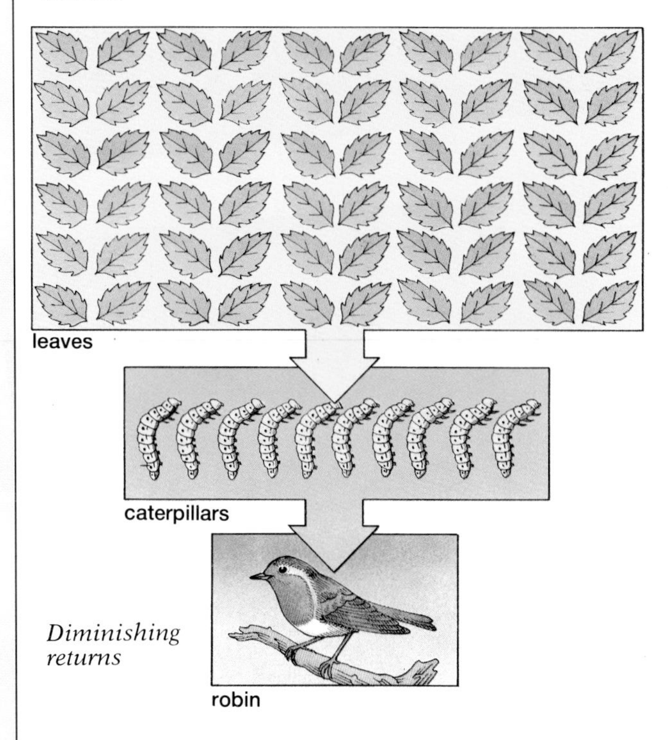

Diminishing returns

A close look at energy losses

The diagram opposite shows what happens to the light energy which reaches grassland used for grazing bullocks. The energy is measured in kilojoules (kJ). The figures are for an average year in Britain and for one square metre of grass.

1 How much energy is shown as:
   a Reaching the grass?
   b Being eaten by the bullock?
   c Adding meat to the bullock?

2 Give two ways in which energy is 'lost' from this food chain?

3 What percentage of the light energy from the Sun is captured by the grass?

4 What percentage of the energy in the grass is eaten by the bullock?

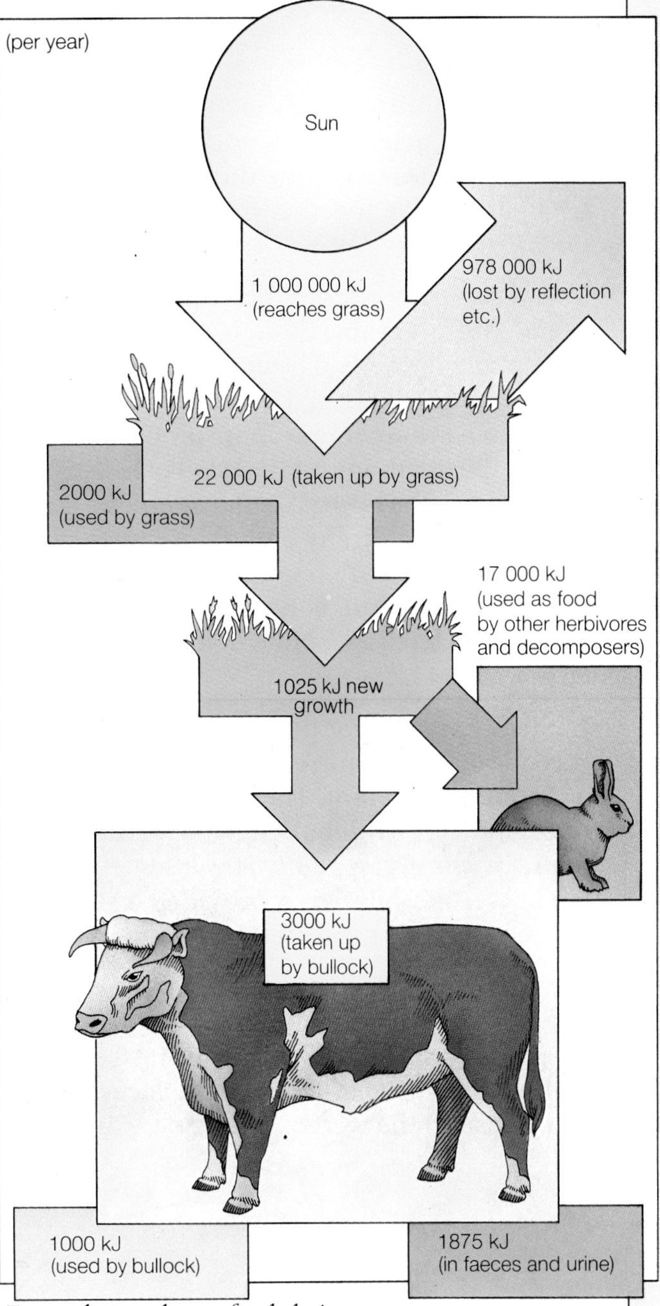

Energy losses along a food chain

5 What percentage of the light energy from the Sun eventually adds to the growth of the bullock?

In most food chains there is about a 90% loss of energy between links. This means that more energy is available to humans through short food chains such as:

Wheat → Human beings

than through longer chains such as:

Grass → Sheep → Human beings

Strange associations 1

You scratch my back and I'll scratch yours

Many living things live together in groups — lions live in prides and zebra live in herds. But sometimes two quite different kinds of living thing live together in a way that helps both.

Most crabs rely on their hard shells to protect them. **Hermit crabs**, though, take up home in empty whelk shells. The crab can retreat fully into the shell if it is in danger. The crab often picks up a **sea-anemone** in its pincers and places the anemone on the whelk shell. So, everywhere the crab goes the anemone goes too. The crab gains by being camouflaged. Also its enemies are scared off by the stinging tentacles of the anemone. The anemone benefits by feeding on bits of food that the crab leaves.

Hermit crab and sea anemone

Lichens are peculiar plants. They are made of threads of **fungus** mixed together with cells of a **simple green plant**. The fungus cannot make food for itself but benefits from the food made by the green plant. The green plant benefits from the shelter provided by the fungus, and it is protected from drying out.

Lichen

Lichens do not have roots. They simply take in water, dissolved chemicals and gases over their whole surface. They grow on trees, walls, rocks, and lots of other surfaces. They grow best on the wetter, west side of Britain.

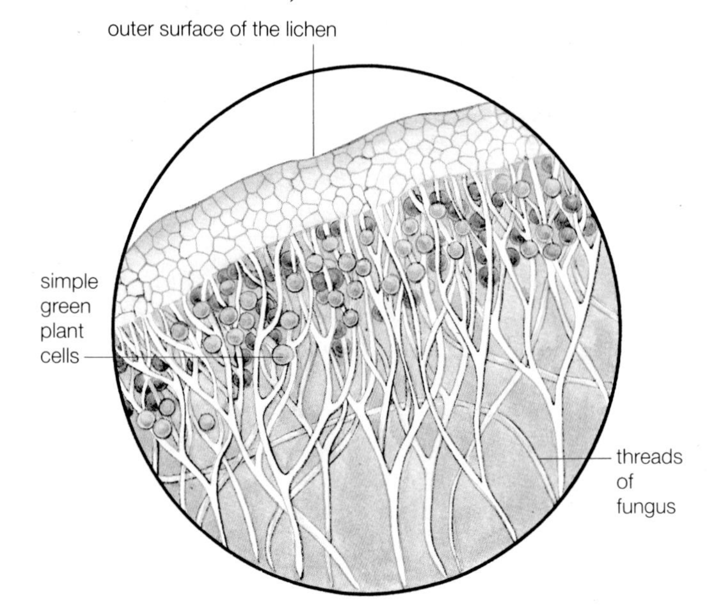

Structure of lichen seen through a microscope

1 What sort of environment would you expect to find hermit crabs in?

2 Why is this section called 'You scratch my back and I'll scratch yours'?
- **a** Because many living things live in groups together.
- **b** Because sea-anemones live on the backs of hermit crabs.
- **c** Because lichens grow best on rough surfaces.
- **d** Because different creatures can live together in a way that helps both.

Strange associations 2

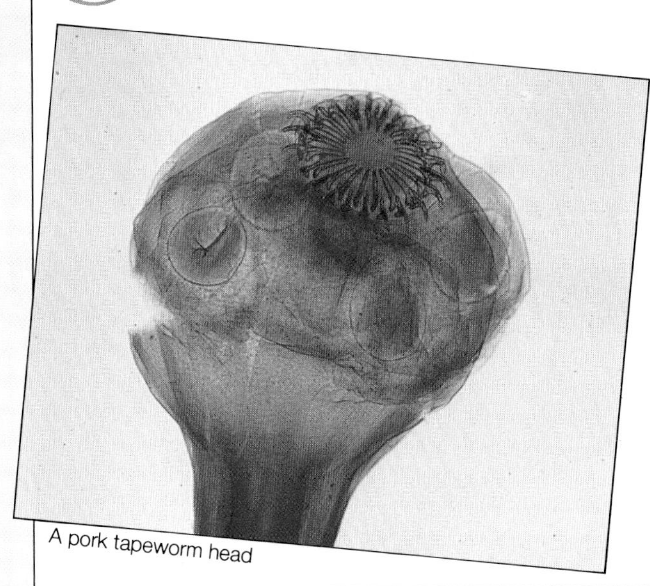
A pork tapeworm head

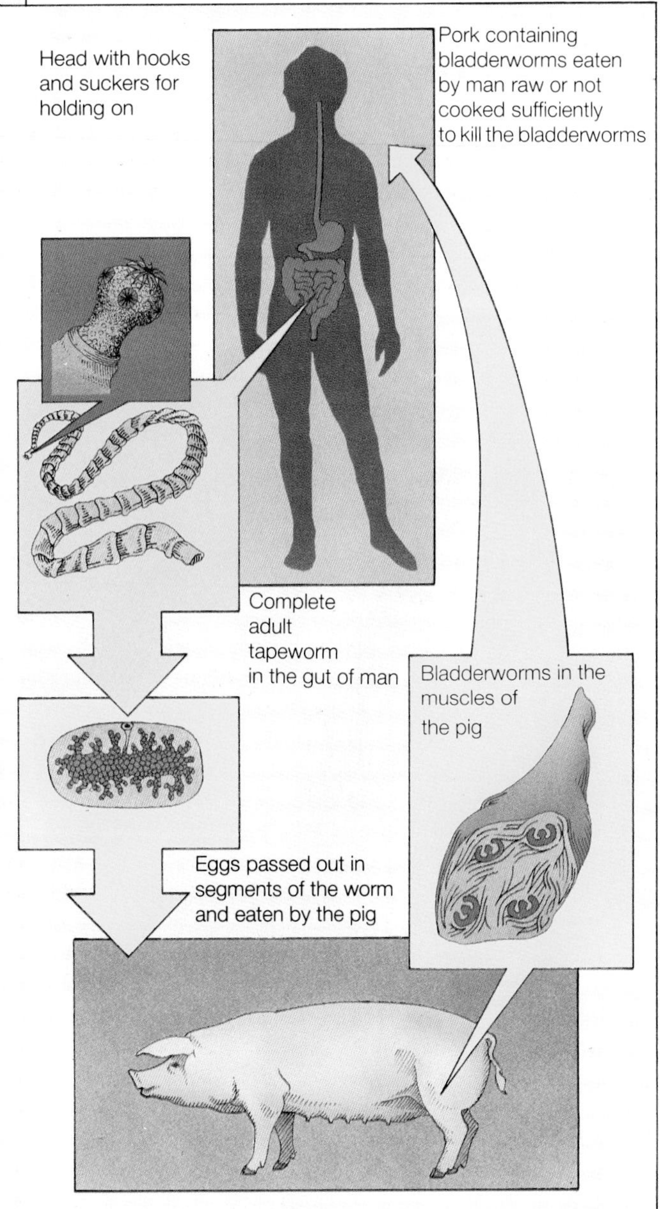

Life cycle of the pork tapeworm

Heads I win — tails you lose

Some living things live together in a way which benefits one but harms the other.

The adult **pork tapeworm** lives in the **human gut**, fixed in place by the hooks and suckers on its 'head'. This tapeworm may be as much as 8 metres long. It takes in digested food from the gut. It is protected from being digested itself by its tough 'skin'.

Tapeworms contain both male and female sex organs and so a single worm can produce lots of eggs. The complicated life-cycle of the pork tapeworm is shown in the diagram. Part of this life-cycle is in pigs and part in human beings.

Segments regularly drop off the end of the adult tapeworm. These segments are packed with tiny, hooked young worms. The segments pass out of the human being's body in the faeces. In places with poor sewage-disposal arrangements the segments may get eaten by pigs. (In some countries human faeces are used as a fertiliser on fields where crops are being grown.)

In a pig's gut the hooked young escape from the segments. They burrow into the gut lining. If they reach a blood vessel they may get carried in the blood to a muscle. Here they settle down to form structures called bladderworms. Pig muscle is pork. If pork containing bladderworms is not cooked properly and is then eaten by a human being then the bladderworms can hatch out. They attach themselves to the human's gut lining and grow into adult tapeworms, and the cycle can start again.

1 When a pork tapeworm is living in the human gut, how does the tapeworm benefit and how does the human being suffer?

2 List the main stages in the life-cycle of a pork tapeworm and say what the environment of each is.

3 Suggest some ways in which the infection of humans by pork tapeworms can be stopped.

re you a waster?

An increasing problem

We all produce **waste** at home, at work, and at play. The population of the world is increasing and so is the amount of rubbish.

Each person in Britain produces about 160 kg of household rubbish per year, on average. In some countries less is produced (e.g. U.S.S.R., 110 kg), in others more (e.g. America, 210 kg). Schools, factories, shops etc all add to this waste production too.

1 About how much household rubbish is produced in Britain each year? (Take the population to be 50 million.)

2 Draw a bar chart to compare the production of household rubbish in Britain, Russia, and America.

After the match

What's in the bin?

The table lists the kinds of things found in a family rubbish bin and gives the weight of each kind of rubbish.

kinds of rubbish	**weight** (kg)
food remains	4
paper	7
plastics	4
metals	2
glass	2
other items	1

Household rubbish

3 Give an example of one thing which might be found in each of the kinds of rubbish listed.

4 What is the total weight of the rubbish?

5 Calculate the percentage of the total rubbish for each of the kinds of rubbish.

6 Draw a pie chart to show your answer to question 5.

7 Fifty years ago a large part of the rubbish in a family rubbish bin would have been ashes. Explain this and suggest other possible differences between the kinds of rubbish then and today.

An environment spoiled by dumping

Don't foul it up!

The contents of your rubbish bin will be regularly removed for you. But some items of rubbish won't fit into a bin. It is usually quite easy to arrange to have things like old cars, beds, furniture, and TV sets removed separately. It is certainly better to take the trouble to do this than to dump them.

To keep the environment tidy and safe, waste must be either:

- removed, or
- treated in some way (e.g. burned or buried), or
- recycled (this is explained on pages **82** and **83**)

Nature's roundabout

The links in a decomposer food chain

Keeping the place tidy

When an animal or a plant dies its remains are used as food by **decomposers**. Many decomposers, such as **bacteria** and **fungi**, are microscopic and are only noticed because of the decay they cause. Decomposers also decay the waste materials produced by animals (urine and faeces).

1 The diagram shows some plants and animals which are involved in a decomposer food chain. Write down this chain and name the decomposer.

Going round in circles

Decomposers are very important. By decaying dead remains and waste they set free materials which can be used again by living things.

So, the materials which make up the bodies of living things can be used time and time again by being **cycled** in this way. But the energy that living things need is passed through food chains and can't be cycled and used time and time again.

The diagram shows how energy and materials are passed on in nature. The yellow arrows show the passing on of energy. The orange arrows show the passing on of materials.

Use the diagram to answer the following questions.

2 What eventually happens to the energy from the Sun?

3 Which living things are able to reuse materials from the environment?

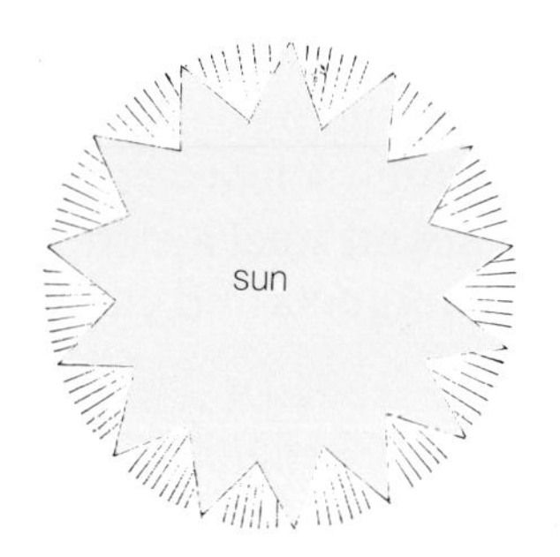

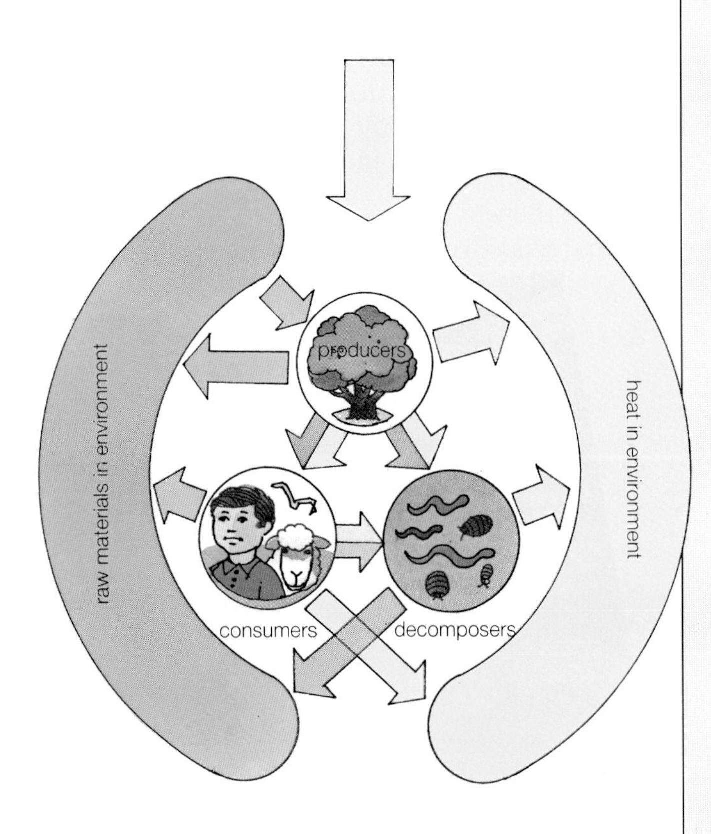

The movement of energy and materials in nature

Waste-not . . .

Quite a mixture

What a load of rubbish!

Rubbish from households and factories is quite a mixture. It may look a mess but it contains valuable materials such as **metals**, **glass**, and **paper**. These three groups of waste can all be **recycled**, that is they can be treated in some way and used over again. But to do this they must be separated from the rest of the rubbish. One way to do this is to get people to keep them separate from the start. Some towns have **waste-paper collections**. People may be asked to put old glass bottles into big containers called **bottle-banks**. But making separate collections costs money and people have to be persuaded that it is worth the effort.

Removing materials from mixed rubbish after collection can be a messy job. But there are ways in which science can help. For example, iron and steel are metals which are attracted by **magnets** and can be picked out by these.

A bottle bank

1 Why are you asked *not* to put plastic bottles into a bottle-bank?

2 What is the above writing mainly about?
- **a** The mess made by rubbish.
- **b** Separating waste for recycling.
- **c** Waste paper collections.
- **d** Persuading people not to waste.

3 List the ways described of separating materials from waste.

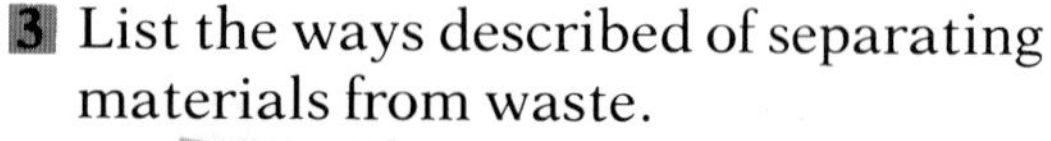

Hand sorting rubbish

Electromagnet lifting scrap iron

Economy measures

Paper is made from the pulped wood. Steel is made from iron ore which is dug out of the ground.

People are using more and more paper and more and more steel. More trees can be grown to replace those used up — but only up to a limit. Also there is a limited amount of iron ore in the ground. So recycling of paper and iron makes good sense.

1 List five uses each for paper and steel.

Warmth from waste

A **district heating plant** uses household rubbish as fuel. The diagram shows how the plant produces heat which could be used, for example, to heat water supplies to houses and flats. Although this way of providing central heating is a good idea it has not been used much in Britain. It costs a lot to build the system and supply the housing.

2 What sorts of household rubbish will be most use for a district heat plant?

3 Whereabouts in the plant is heat from the burning rubbish used to heat water?

4 Use the diagram to write a description of what happens in a district heating plant.

A district heating plant

Fouling it up

A country car wash

A day in the country

Most Sundays the Fowlers take a trip to the country. It is handy that Bob has a car — even if it is an old banger with a smoky exhaust. At least it gets them to their picnic spot. Their favourite place is by the side of a stream. This gives them a chance to wash the car and get some of that filthy oil off it. Then they have lunch. There are plenty of places where they can hide away the empty cans and other rubbish so that you hardly notice them. After lunch the Fowlers just sit and rest, and marvel at the beauty of the scenery.

The Fowlers say that their Sunday out does them a power of good — but what does it do for the country?

A picnic 'sight'

Pollution is all the things that we put into our environment which make it unpleasant or dangerous for us or for other living things.

1 Describe the ways in which the Fowlers pollute:
a the land,
b the air,
c the water.

2 Explain what the Fowlers should do to stop polluting their environment in these ways.

Only one Earth

The Earth doesn't seem quite so big when seen from space. The view makes you realise that Earth can only take a limited amount of pollution. More than this and the land, the water, and the air may be poisoned beyond recovery and that will be bad news for human beings.

The Earth seen from space

3 Why can Earth only take a limited amount of pollution?

4 List ways in which we pollute the land, water, and air.

5 Give reasons why pollution is a bigger problem today than it was a hundred years ago.

6 Design a poster to persuade people to avoid polluting their environment.

Pollution . . . why worry?

Stonework damaged by air pollution

A victim of mercury poisoning

Acid rain

When coal is burned the sulphur in it is released as **sulphur dioxide**. This dissolves in moisture in the air and eventually produces sulphuric acid. This acid can gradually eat away stone — so think what it can do to your lungs! The acid can also fall as rain and pollute streams and lakes causing the death of fish and other living things. Smoke from factories can be cleaned up a lot before being released into the air, but it costs a lot of money to do this.

A Japanese tragedy

About thirty years ago fishermen in the Minamata Bay area of Japan began to show signs of a nervous illness. They suffered from headaches, numbness, and fatigue, and so did their families. Doctors were baffled when they noticed that the local cats showed the same symptoms. It was discovered that the fish from the area were polluted with **mercury** — but the discovery came too late. Over 100 people died or suffered serious nervous damage as a result of eating the fish. What had happened was that a local factory had dumped mercury into the bay. This had been taken up by food chains leading to the local people.

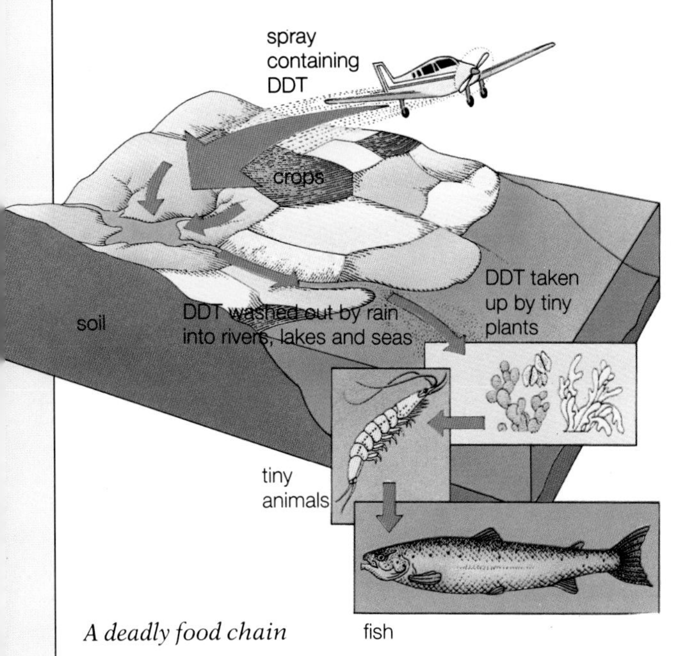

A deadly food chain

Not only pests get poisoned

Farmers spray their crops with all sorts of **pesticides**. These pesticides are chemicals which kill insect pests which would damage the crops. One pesticide which used to be very popular was **DDT** — but now its use is banned. Rain washes DDT off plants into the soil and then out of the soil into rivers. From the rivers DDT gets into the sea. So DDT gets into a wide range of living things through food chains. It is stored in their bodies and may eventually reach a dangerous level.

1 Name two chemicals which can cause pollution.

2 Which types of pollution (land, air, or water) does each passage describe?

Living indicators of water pollution

A polluted river

One sort of water pollution

Many industries such as breweries and paper manufacturers use rivers as a way of getting rid of their waste. Bacteria in the water can use some of this waste for food. In doing so they produce chemicals such as nitrates which encourage plant growth. This provides food for animals. *But* the bacteria use up oxygen from the water. In small numbers they are no problem. But when there is a lot of pollution there are a lot of bacteria and they may use up so much oxygen that it becomes difficult for animals and plants to live.

Checking the level of pollution

One measure of the level of pollution of a river is the amount of oxygen dissolved in it. A quicker indication may be to look at the sort of animals which are living in it. The results of both these methods are shown in the diagrams.

1 Which animals would you expect to find in the most polluted water?

2 Which animals would you expect to find in clean, unpolluted water?

3 How much pollution would be suggested by the presence in it of caddis fly larvae and freshwater shrimps?

4 What oxygen content might you expect to find for heavily polluted water at 5 °C?

5 How much pollution would be suggested by an oxygen content of 3.5 cm^3 per litre of water at 20°C?

amount of pollution	animals present	volume of oxygen (cm^3)/ litre of water	
		at 5 °C	at 20 °C
clean unpolluted water	stonefly nymph, mayfly nmyph, salmon, trout, grayling, good coarse fishing	6·5–9·0	4·5–6
little pollution	caddis fly larvae, freshwater shrimp good coarse fishing — trout rarely	6·0–6·5	4·0–4·5
some pollution	water louse, blood worm midge larvae, leech, roach, gudgeon moderate to poor fishing	3·5–6·0	2·5–4·0
heavy pollution	sludge worm rag-tailed maggot no fish life	0–3·5	0–2·5

Indicators of water pollution

Living indicators of air pollution

Plants and pollution

You have probably noticed that the trees in industrial areas often seem stunted, as if they are not growing so well as trees in the country. This is partly due to air pollution. Gases like sulphur dioxide slowly poison the plants in towns.

You heard about those curious plants, the **lichens**, on page **78**. They are *very* sensitive to sulphur dioxide.

The centre of a town is likely to have no lichens at all. All you will find on the damper parts of tree trunks will be powdery green patches of a simple plant called ***Pleurococcus***. As you work your way out of town first you will see grey-green **crusty lichens**, next **leafy lichens**, and eventually **shrubby lichens**. An easy rule to remember is that the more the lichen sticks out, the cleaner the air. Where shrubby lichens are abundant you have really pure air.

A stunted city tree

Tree bark with *Pleurococcus*

A crusty lichen

A leafy lichen

Shrubby lichens

Variety is the spice of life

The graph compares the number of kinds of lichens, and plants like them, found growing on different surfaces at different distances from the centre of a big city.

1 On which surface does the biggest variety of plants grow?

2 How does distance from the city centre seem to affect the number of kinds of plants? Explain your answer.

3 On which surface does the number of types go down quickest as you work your way into the city?

4 On which surface is the number of types least affected by distance from the city centre?

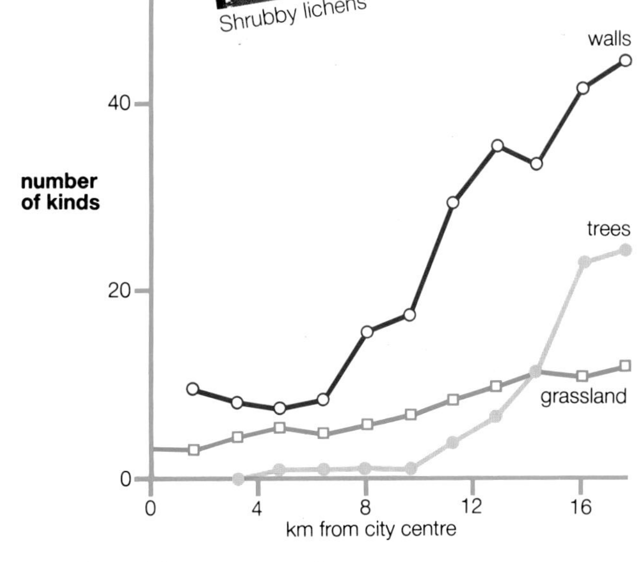

The effect of distance from city centre on variety of lichens and plants like them

Human needs

Bushman

Innuit

Desert dwellers

The **Bushmen** live in the Kalahari Desert of South-West Africa. This is a land of little rain and almost no vegetation. The Bushmen live by hunting animals such as antelope. The women collect roots and grubs for food. Each Bushman family makes a temporary shelter of branches and grass. They are very skilled at finding water. They may suck it up from underground by using long straws or they may collect fruits which contain a lot of water.

A home in the snow

Innuit live in Greenland and North Canada. They have learned to live among ice and snow. Civilisation has brought modern comforts to many, but some still live in the old ways. They are expert fishers and hunters of animals such as seal. In the winter they make snow homes, but in the summer they live in skin tents. Wood is scarce so the Innuit use the fat from seals (blubber) as a fuel.

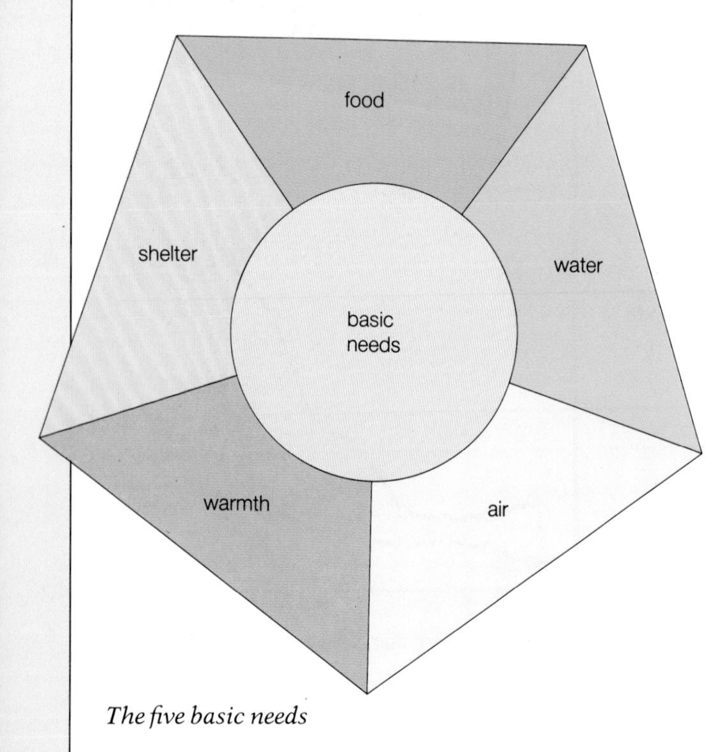

The five basic needs

Basic needs

People often imagine that they need all sorts of things. For example, you might believe that you need a car — but you know that you will still keep living if you don't have one. **Basic needs** are the things that people must have if they are to stay alive.

Human beings have five basic needs. They need **food, water, air, warmth, and shelter**. Some people, such as the Bushmen and the Innuit meet these basic needs in quite simple ways.

1 What 5 things do you need to keep alive?

2 Compare the ways in which Bushmen and Innuit meet their basic needs.

Meeting those needs

Land use

It is hard to believe that Britain was once a land covered in trees. The growing human population cleared the forests. This made room for farming and provided wood for building and for use as a fuel. The appearance of the country-side was changed gradually to give the pattern of land use shown in the pie chart.

1 What percentage of the land is now given over to growing trees?

2 Which of our basic needs is the land mostly used for?

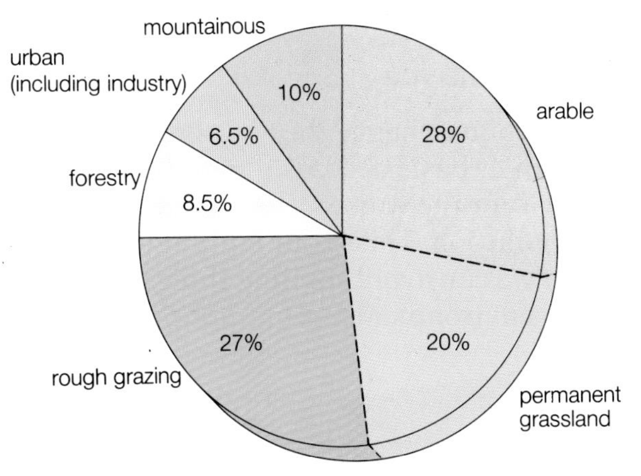

Pie chart showing land use in Britain

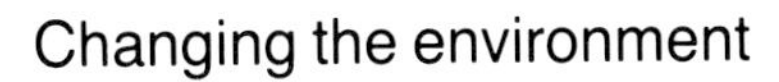

Changing the environment

The photographs show some of the ways in which we have changed our environment to meet our basic needs.

3 Say what change is shown by each of the photographs and which basic need is being met.

4 Write a description of other ways in which we change our environment to try to meet our basic needs.

5 Explain how your basic needs are met in the place that you now are.

Farm

Modern housing

Power station

Reservoir

What on earth are we doing?

This concerns you

Human beings change the environment to supply their basic needs. But often the change is for the worse — for example, it may cause pollution. This is our fault. If we care enough we can avoid spoiling things. After all it is *our* environment.

The osprey — a protected animal

A limestone-pavement nature reserve

The sundew — a protected plant

Conservation

Caring for environments, and the plants and animals in them, in a way that stops things being spoiled is called **conservation**.

The protection of rare kinds of plants and animals is a form of conservation that most people are familiar with. Without such protection, often by law, many types of living thing might become extinct.

Another form of conservation protects different sorts of environment of special interest. For example, woodland, moorland, etc. may be protected and cared for as **nature reserves**.

Nature reserves are usually small areas of land of a particular sort. Large areas of land may be conserved too. In the **National Parks** of England and Wales there is a balanced use of land for farming, industry, forestry, sport, etc. No single use is allowed to grow at the expense of the others and to the disadvantage of the environment.

1 What three forms of conservation are described above?

2 How many National Parks are shown on the map? Which of these is nearest to where you live?

3 Find out about nature reserves near where you live. Make a list of their names, where they are and what is special about them. You may be able to visit one of them and write about what you see.

4 Find out about 'The Countryside Code' and write a description of what this asks you to do and why.

Change and conservation

Conservation, not preservation

Conservation doesn't just mean keeping things as they are. It can involve big changes to improve environments that have been spoiled in some way. Open-cast coal mining makes a mess of the environment, but it doesn't have to be left that way. The photographs show that big improvements are possible.

Open-cast coal mining

Restored mining area

Conservation doesn't just mean making sure that animals are not killed. It can involve killing some animals to make sure that the population doesn't get too big. Red deer are lovely animals, but if their numbers increased too much there might be a food shortage. This could cause many to die from starvation. If the deer are **culled**, by shooting the weaker animals, then the danger is avoided and the population remains healthy. But the culling has to be carefully controlled.

Red deer

What's in it for us?

Humans are part of the web of life on Earth. Careful conservation will ensure that our basic needs are met without upsetting the basic needs of other living things. As a bonus we will have an environment that we can all enjoy.

1 Why is conservation important?

2 Find out about the work of conservation groups in your part of the country. Write an account of what they are trying to do. You might even want to help in such a group.

Conservation group at work

MATERIALS

This section is about different materials. Steel, copper, nylon, polystyrene, and wool are some of the materials you will meet. When you have read this section you will have a better understanding of why a material is used for a particular job and how materials can be protected from wear and tear.

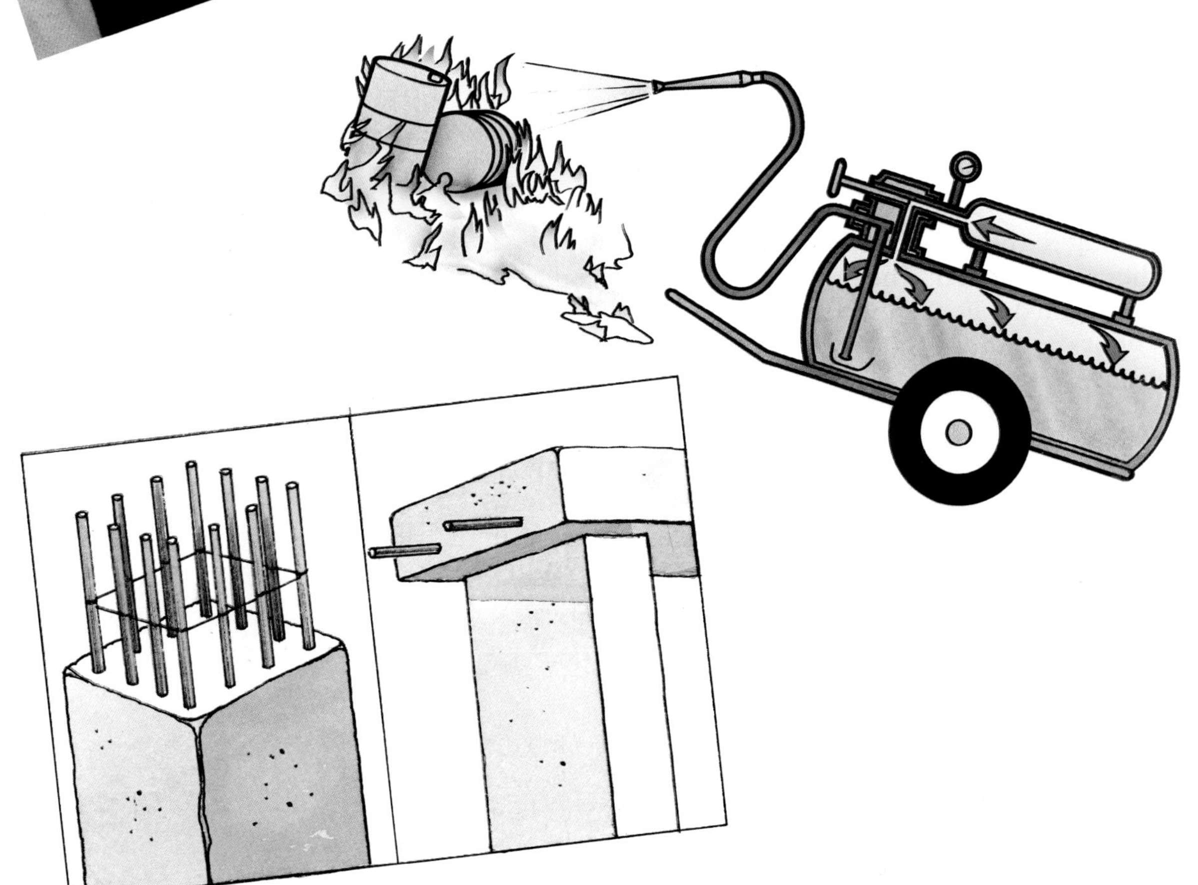

Looking at materials

Sorting out materials

Human beings are very good at making use of their surroundings. Early people used natural materials like stone and wood for making tools and weapons. They used caves for shelter and protection, and used animal skins for clothing. As time went by people learnt to make weapons and tools from metals. They built houses from stone, brick, and wood and wove cloth to make clothes. Today we can even make and use totally new materials such as nylon. These new materials are called **man-made materials**

1 In the diagram you can see a variety of objects made from different materials. Arrange them into two lists according to whether they are made from natural or man-made materials.

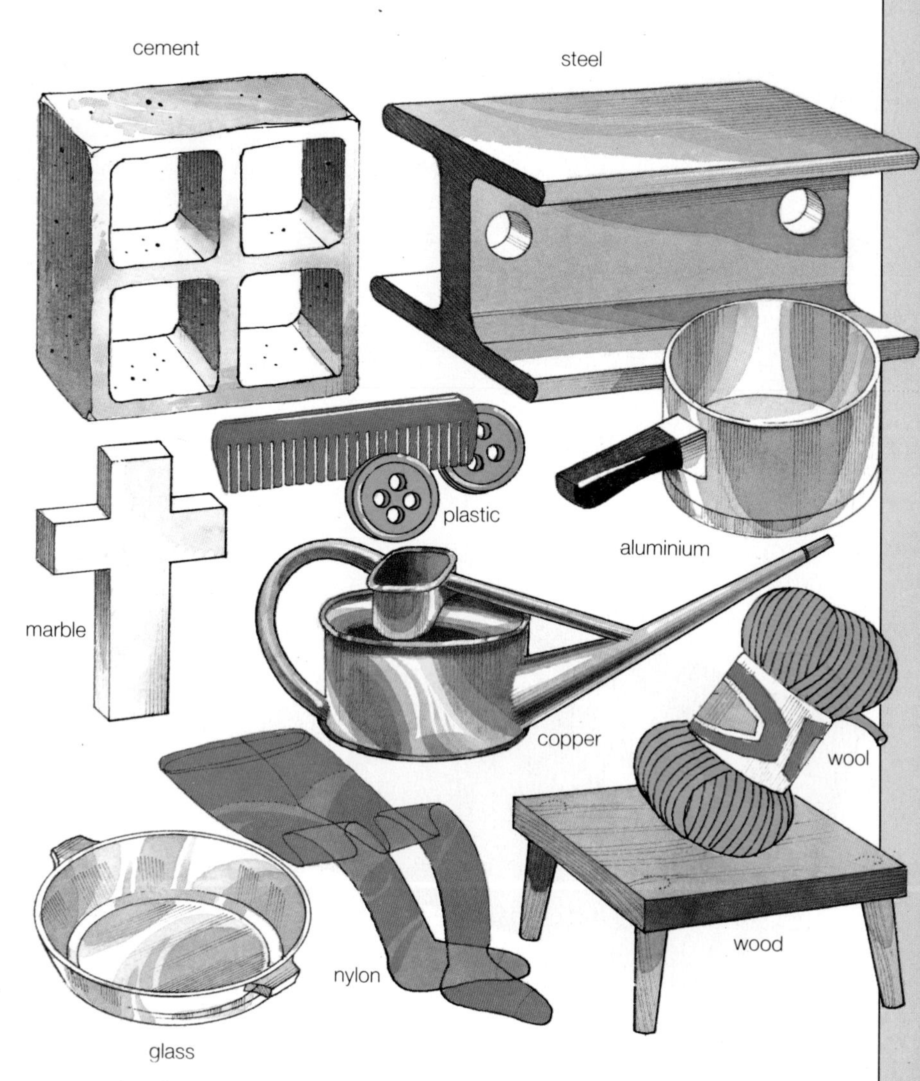

Natural and man-made materials

Why classify?

There are many ways of grouping materials. One way is according to their use. For example, materials can be used for **clothes** or for **shelter**. The **properties** of a material are the things it can do. For example, one property of glass is that it lets light through. Materials are often grouped according to their properties.

Knowing what group a material belongs to can tell us what to expect about its properties. For example, if an unknown material can be placed in the group 'metals' because of its hardness and appearance, then we would expect it to conduct electricity because all metals conduct electricity.

2 Copy the two lists of materials (on the right) and complete them by adding a heading to each group.

3 A mystery material is found on the moon. It is hard and rough and conducts electricity. Use the table shown to identify which group the material belongs to and list its properties.

copper	plastic
aluminium	nylon
iron	wood
zinc	paper
steel	stone

Supply the missing headings

property	group A	group B	group C
lets light through	yes	no	yes
hardness	very hard	hard	soft
appearance	smooth	rough	smooth
conducts electricity	no	yes	no
dissolves in water	no	yes	no

Which group does the mystery material belong to?

The variety of uses

Uses of steel

Uses of copper

Uses of nylon

Uses of polystyrene

Many uses for the same material

Materials can be used to make lots of different things.

Strong, tough steel probably has the largest number of uses ranging from small objects such as paper clips to large steel beams used in building.

Copper is a beautiful and a useful metal. It is an excellent conductor of electricity and so is used for making wires, cables, and other electrical parts. Copper can also conduct heat well. This explains why pipes, boilers, and cooking pots are often made of copper.

When nylon was first manufactured in the mid-1930s it was used mainly to make ladies stockings which came to be called 'nylons'. Nowadays it has many more uses.

Polystyrene is a type of plastic. Its uses include model kits, disposable cups, and various types of packaging.

1 Use the photographs to list some uses of steel, copper, nylon, and polystyrene.

2 List as many different materials as you can which are used for:
a cooking pots
b clothing
c building houses
d packaging.

3 Suggest why steel frying pans often have copper bottoms.

The magic of mixing

Metal magic

Copper has been used by man for almost 10 000 years. At first people probably found lumps of copper lying on the ground and hammered them into the shape they wanted. However, we don't usually find pure copper. It is usually found in the ground joined with other substances. This is called a copper **ore**.

About 7000 years ago man discovered how to separate pure copper from its ores by using heat. Separating a metal from its ore in this way is called **smelting**. People were able to use pure copper to make tools, ornaments, and vessels but there was one big snag! Copper, like many pure metals is soft. It *pulls* apart if you stretch it and, what is more important, it can't be used to make a cutting edge. A copper knife is useless!

A food vessel, chinese bronze, 800 BC

A remarkable discovery was made in the Middle East about 6000 years ago. By mixing a little tin with the molten copper a new substance called **bronze** could be made. Bronze was much harder than copper and could be used for making cutting edges. A metal mixed with another substance is called an **alloy**. Bronze is an alloy of tin and copper.

This discovery must have astonished those who made it since tin is even softer than copper. Yet mixed together they made this new hard substance. Nowadays we know that the tin acts as a sort of grit, getting between the copper particles and stopping them from sliding apart when pulled.

The history of steel (an alloy of iron and carbon) is more recent than copper because it is more difficult to extract iron from its ores. It is thought that iron was widely used near the Black Sea about 3500 years ago and 500 years later people in India could make steel. Nowadays man has learnt to make a large number of different alloys. Some of them are shown in the table.

1 What is meant by an alloy?

2 What name is given to an alloy of:
- **a** copper and tin,
- **b** iron and carbon?

3 What is the main idea you have been reading about above?
- **a** Copper
- **b** Iron
- **c** Bronze
- **d** Steel
- **e** Alloys

4 Explain in your own words why mixing two soft metals together can produce a hard alloy.

5 Use books to find out all you can about alloys then copy and complete the table.

Alloy	Made from	Uses
Steel	——	——
——	copper and tin	——
solder	——	electrical joints joining metals
——	magnesium and aluminium	atomic reactor fuel cans engine blocks
stainless steel	——	cutlery, sinks medical equipment
——	copper and zinc	——
pewter	tin and lead	——
cupro-nickel	——	copper coins

Alloys and their uses

Hard facts

Concrete, a modern material?

Crushed stone — a coarse aggregate

Concrete is another good example of how a hard wearing material can be made by mixing the right things together. Although concrete is often thought of as a modern material it was discovered by the Romans about 2000 years ago.

Concrete is a mixture of three things, cement, water, and aggregate. Aggregate is a gritty material like sand or small stones. Cement when mixed with water forms a stone-like 'glue' which binds together the particles of aggregate to make them strong.

The strength of concrete depends on several things. One important thing is the amount of water added to the mixture. Only a small amount is needed to harden the cement. Any extra water has to evaporate (dry up). This leaves small holes in the concrete and makes it weak.

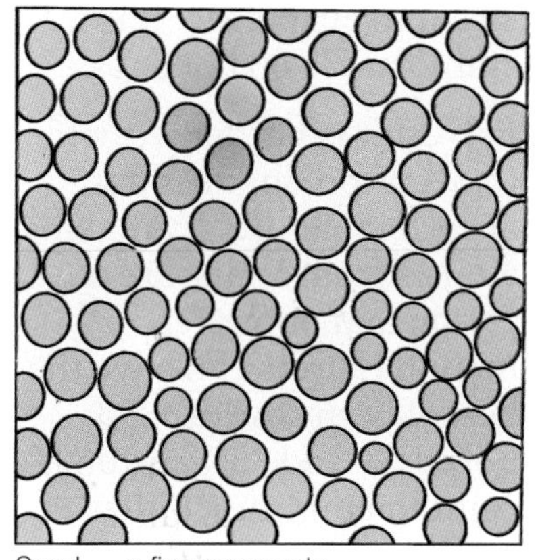
Sand — a fine aggregate

The strength of concrete also depends on which aggregate is used. A coarse aggregate such as crushed stone has sharp particles. This produces a strong concrete but is hard to mix. A fine aggregate such as sand has smooth round particles. This produces a weak concrete, usually called mortar, which is easy to mix and can be used for brick laying. Usually the aggregate used for concrete is a mixture of sand and stone. The *right* mixture of sand and stone makes a very strong concrete.

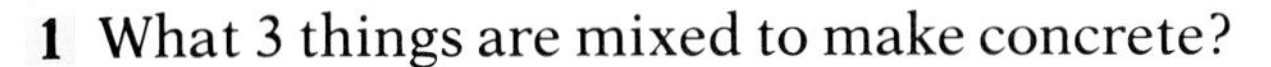

1 What 3 things are mixed to make concrete?

2 Name two things which decide the strength of concrete.

3 How is mortar made and what is it used for?

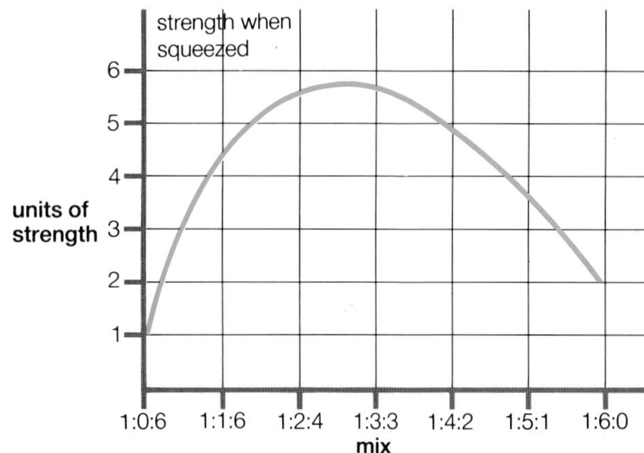

A graph showing how the strength of concrete depends on the mixture

In an experiment 7 samples of concrete were made by mixing different amounts of cement, fine aggregate, and coarse aggregate. The samples were then tested for strength on a special machine. The results are given in the graph. On this graph 1:1:6 means 1 part of cement mixed with 1 part fine aggregate and 6 parts of coarse aggregate.

4 Which mixture is the weakest?

5 Which mixture is the strongest?

6 If you had 2 bags of cement and you wished to use them both to mix up some of the strongest mixture how many bags of sand and how many bags of coarse aggregate would you need?

Dressing up

The best of both worlds

Clothes can be made from a wide variety of materials: **natural fibres** such as cotton or wool, **man-made fibres**, such as nylon or polyester, or a mixture of fibres. A **fibre** is a long thin thread of material, like a hair. The label on a piece of clothing usually tells you about the material used. Cotton absorbs moisture and allows sweat to evaporate. It is comfortable on hot days.

Polyester is harder wearing than cotton but does not absorb moisture. By making clothes from a mixture of cotton and polyester manufacturers can have the best of both worlds. 65% polyester and 35% cotton is a common mixture. Shirts made from this are hard wearing, comfortable in Summer and drip-dry.

A man-made fibre or mixture may be made by many different companies and sold under different **trade** or **brand names**.

1 Which of the following are natural fibres: wool, cotton, nylon, polyester?

2 Name a natural fibre which comes from a plant.

3 Give a brand name for a wool/cotton mixture.

4 Give the brand name of one man-made fibre which is made from chemicals coming from oil.

5 How does a pure cotton shirt differ from one made from 65% polyester: 35% cotton?

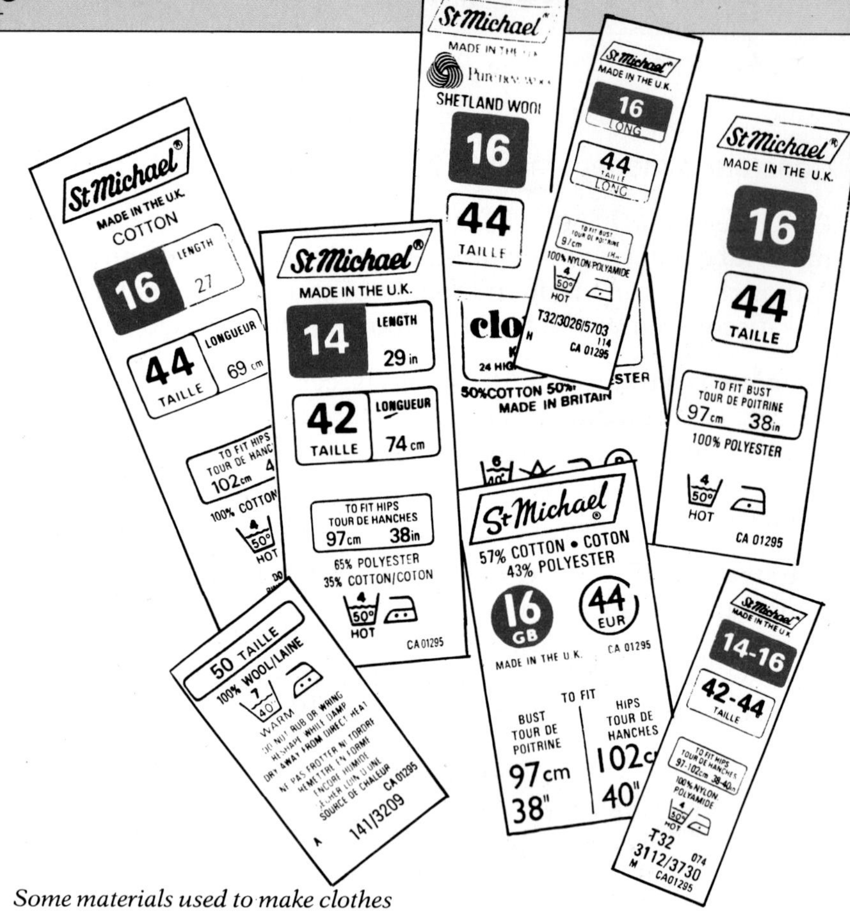

Some materials used to make clothes

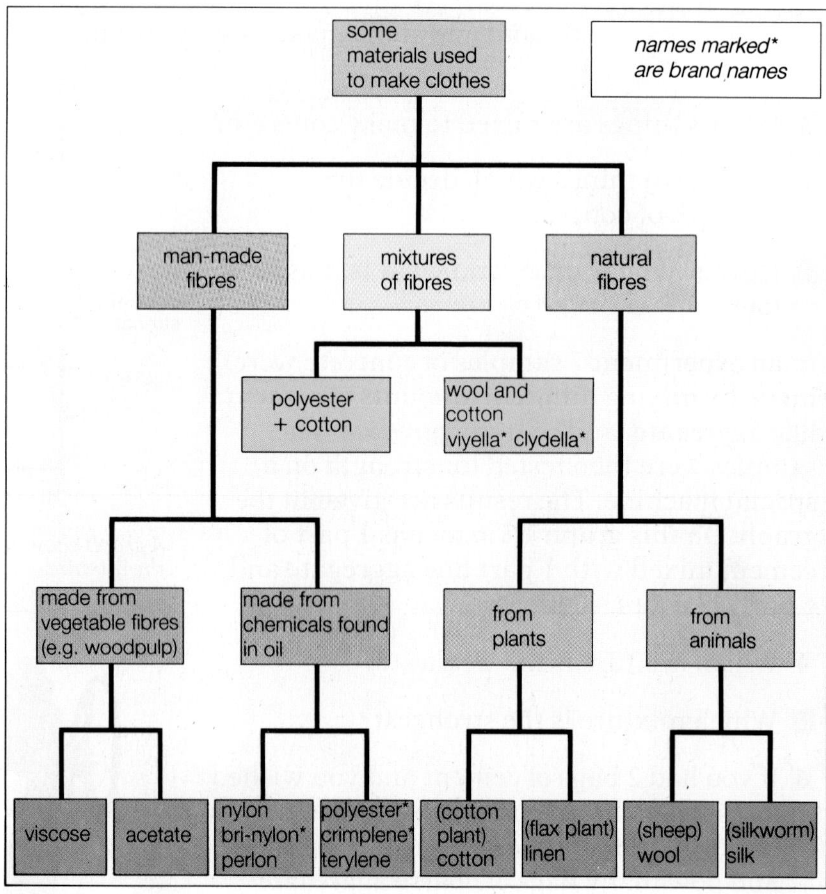

A key showing some of the fibres used to make clothes and their brand names

Properties of materials

Useful properties

The properties of a material may include the way a material looks, feels, or behaves.

Strength is the ability not to change its shape when pulled, squeezed, or twisted. Steel and concrete are strong materials and are often used to support buildings.

Hardness is the ability to stand up to wear and scratches. Materials with this property are often needed to cut other less hard materials. Diamond is the hardest of all natural materials.

Resisting water or being **waterproof** is a useful property of materials like rubber and PVC.

Materials which are **heat-resistant** can often be found on kitchen work surfaces where hot objects are placed. However, pots and pans are made from metals having exactly the opposite property. These are chosen to let heat through easily. This is the property of being a **good conductor** of heat.

1 Make a list of as many materials as you can used in the home and opposite each write two of its properties.

2 Give as many examples as you can of a hard materials being used to cut a softer material.

3 What properties are shown in the photographs?

Checking out materials

Flame testing a fabric

A **flammable** fabric continues to burn after the flame which set it alight has been removed. A **flameproof** fabric does not catch fire or goes out very quickly.

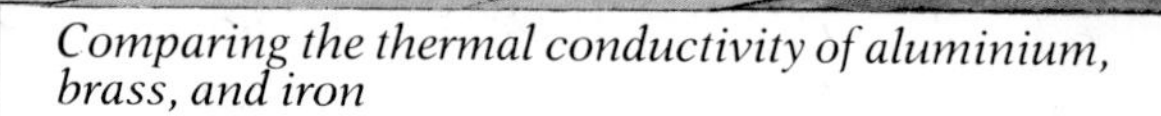

Comparing the thermal conductivity of aluminium, brass, and iron

Thermal conductivity

The **thermal conductivity** of a material is a measure of how easily it allows heat to pass through it. This apparatus is comparing the thermal conductivity of bars of iron, brass, and aluminium.

Mystery test

In this test wire made from different metals is being compared. In each case the number of weights needed to snap the wire is recorded.

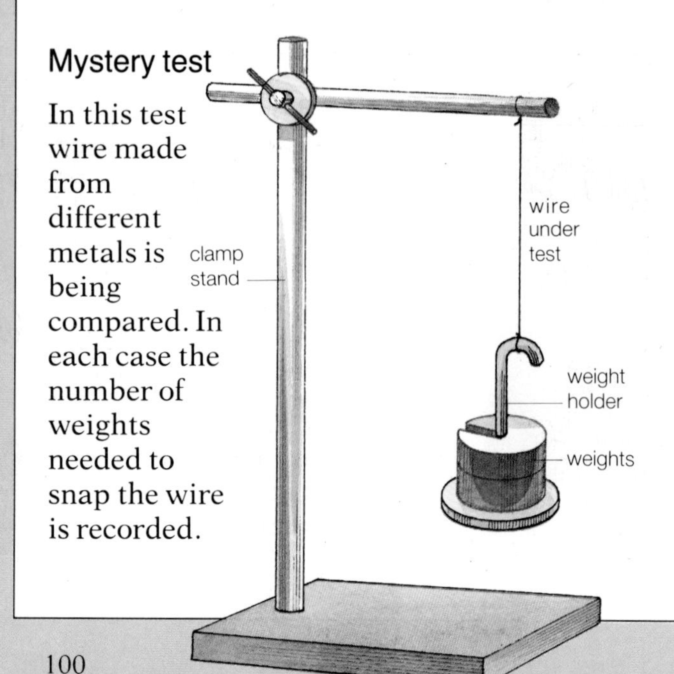

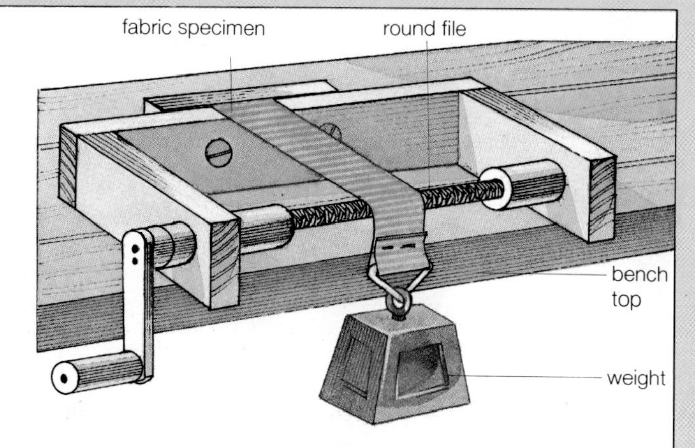

Wear resistance of a fabric

The handle in the diagram is turned until a hole is worn in the fabric. Using such an apparatus it is possible to compare the **wear resistance** of different fabrics.

Electrical conductivity

A material with good **electrical conductivity** allows electricity to pass through it easily. If the bulb in the diagram lights the material is a **good conductor** of electricity. If it does not light it is a bad conductor or **insulator**.

1 Give a reason for flame testing a fabric.

2 **a** Describe how to carry out an experiment to compare the wear resistance of nylon and cotton.
b How would you make sure it was a fair test?

3 Explain how the apparatus shown can be used to compare thermal conductivity.

4 What property is being compared in the mystery test? Describe the experimental procedure.

5 Why would it be difficult to *compare* the electrical conductivity of three different metals using the electrical conductivity apparatus.

Putting it into practice

Teapot trouble

J.G. Wood, a manufacturer of household goods, wants to make and sell a teapot mat designed to stop hot teapots burning table surfaces. Wood instructs D. Baker, his head of research, to test three different materials to see which is the most suitable. The research department uses the apparatus shown on the previous page but changes it slightly by adding three identical thermometers. After the tests Baker presents Wood with the results shown in the graph and table. However, due to the rush, one set of results has been missed out of the graph and none of the lines have been labelled. Can you sort out the confusion and save Baker's skin?

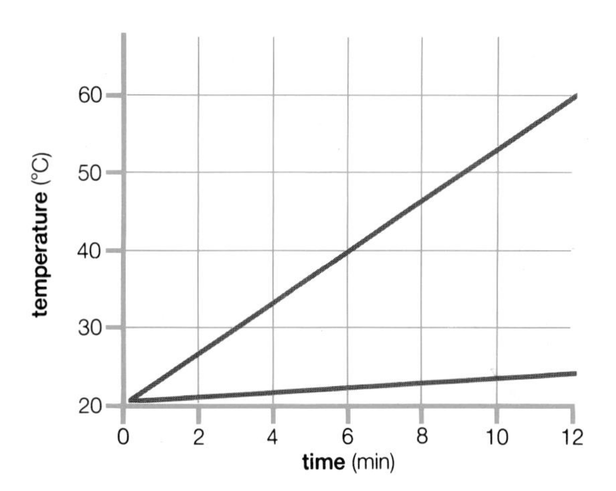

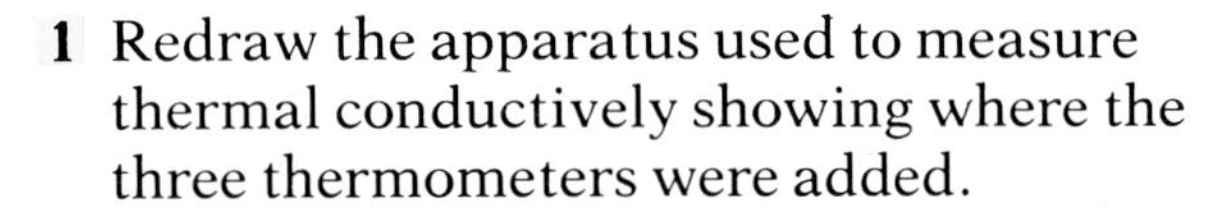

1 Redraw the apparatus used to measure thermal conductively showing where the three thermometers were added.

2 Which result did Baker miss out?

3 According to the results which material should Wood choose?

4 Copy the graph and complete it by adding the line showing the missing result.

time (min)	temperature (°C)		
	copper	**brass**	**glass**
0	20	20	20
1	23·2	21·5	20·4
2	26·4	22·8	20·9
3	30	24	21·2
4	33·2	25·2	21·3
5	36·5	26·4	21·7
6	39·8	28	22
7	43·2	29·1	22·3
8	46·4	30·5	22·6
9	50	32	22·9
10	53·2	33·2	23·2
11	56·4	34·6	23·6
12	60	36	24

D. Baker's results shown as a table

A sticky problem

Mr Baker next tackles the problem of finding the strongest glue to stick on the feet of the mat. His apparatus and results are shown opposite.

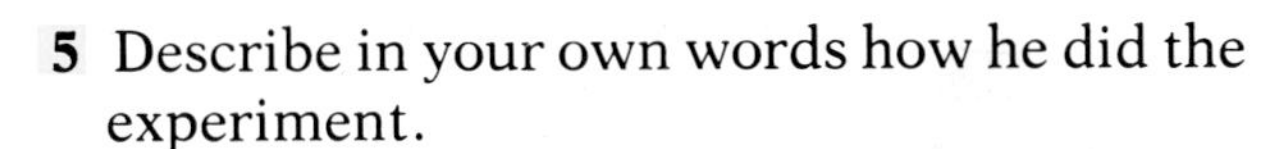

5 Describe in your own words how he did the experiment.

6 What is the strongest glue?

7 Although they seem to be the same describe how you could test to see if Nevastick was stronger than Upstick?

8 What other properties should Baker test the glues for?

9 Imagine you are Baker. Write a report to Wood describing your results. You may use diagrams and graphs in the report. Finish the report by telling Wood how the teapot mat should be made.

clamped to table

glued joint

kilogram weights

	aha	neva stick	pratt	up stick
kg weights to break joint	1	3	4	3

Glue testing and results

The right one for the job

Metals

Metals are good conductors of electricity and have many uses in industry for carrying both small and large electric currents. You can see in the photograph how aluminium is used to connect the different parts of a circuit on a silicon chip. The photograph shows transmission cables carrying electricity across the country.

Metals can also be very strong. The steel wires used to build suspension bridges such as the one shown can be pulled by great forces without breaking. This type of steel is called **high-tensile** steel.

Plastic

Although not as strong as steel, plastic is a very useful material. It is light, hard wearing, does not rot, is a good insulator of heat as well as electricity, and it can be attractively coloured. Many different types of plastic such as PVC, clear polystyrene, expanded polystyrene, phenolic resin, and nylon can be found around the home.

1 Give an example of a metal being used because it is a good conductor of electricity.

2 Give an example of a metal being used because it is very strong.

3 List as many different plastic objects as you can in the room shown below.

4 List the property of the plastic which makes it suitable for each use.

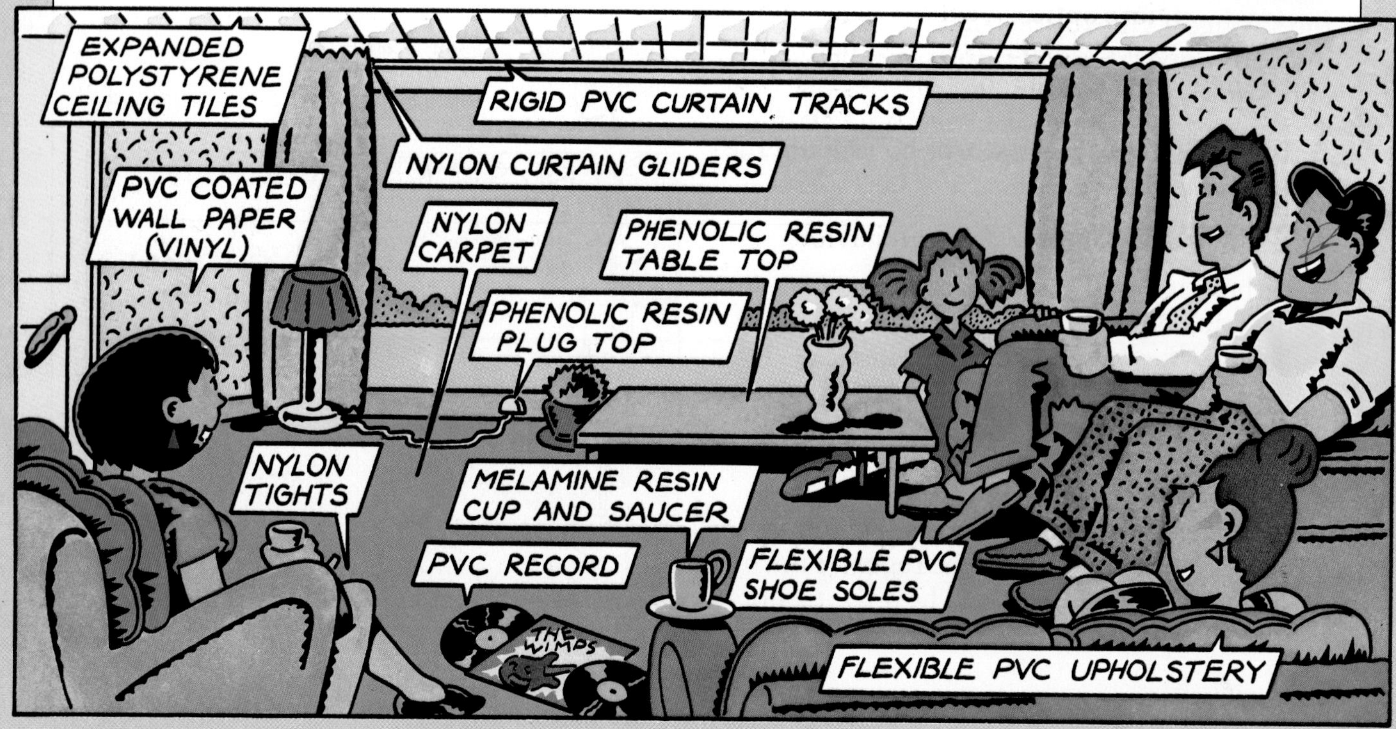

Fibres

Fibres and fabrics

Although a single fibre is not very strong a bundle of fibres can be twisted together to make a rope. Ropes made from nylon fibres are both strong and lightweight and are very useful to mountaineers.

Fibres can also be made into a **fabric** or cloth. Clothes are made from fabric because it is attractive, flexible, and warm. Fabrics keep us warm because they trap air between the fibres. Air is a good insulator of heat. Notice that the insulating property of fabrics does not depend on the fibre but how the fabric is made. The thicker the fabric the more air is trapped and the warmer it keeps us. A knitted fibre has gaps in it which allow air through to carry away body heat. A woven fibre does not do this so easily and so it is warmer than a knitted fibre.

Glass fibres

Glass is amazing stuff! Used as a window it is solid to keep out the wind and rain yet it lets through the sunshine to warm and cheer our homes.

By drawing out the molten glass during its making, glass can even be made into long flexible fibres. A beam of light will bounce along inside one of these fibres even although the fibre bends. This has led to the exciting invention of **fibre optics**. A cable made from bundles of these glass fibres can be made to carry thousands of telephone messages at the same time. This is done by using very strong light from a laser and chopping up the light beam to send the messages in code.

1 Explain why mountaineers find nylon ropes useful.

2 Which is best used for an overcoat, a knitted or a woven fabric? Explain your answer.

3 Explain why some fabrics are warmer than others?

4 Find out one other use than for telephone cables of optical fibres and write a short note about it.

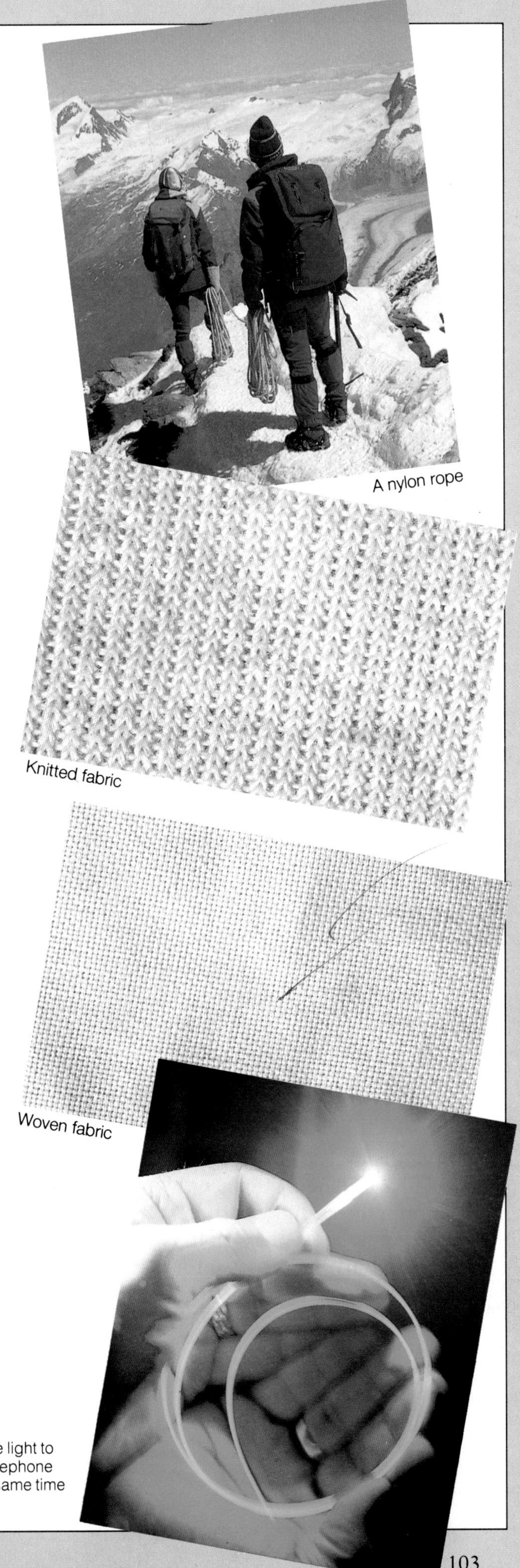

A nylon rope

Knitted fabric

Woven fabric

Fibre optic cables use light to carry thousands of telephone conversations at the same time

Choosing materials

Choosing materials

Why choose that?

The properties of a material are not the only things to be considered when deciding whether to use it for a job.

Cost

Aluminium does not rust like steel. So why aren't all cars made of aluminium? A glance at the graph gives us the answer. It would cost too much!

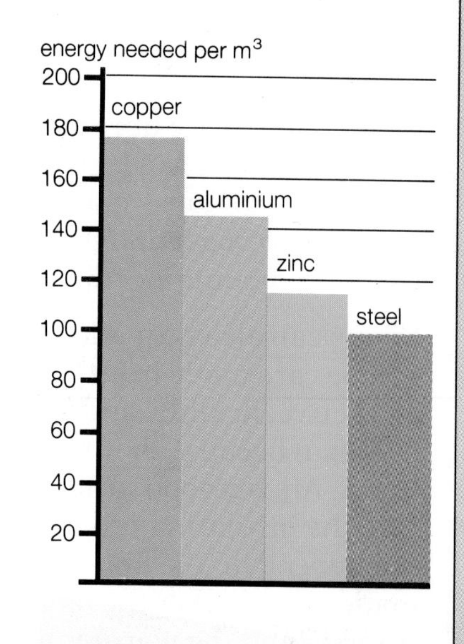

Availability

The builder of the log cabin shown would have been very foolish to use brick and mortar when there was so much wood readily available.

Log cabins are built in areas where there is plenty of wood

Appearance

Velvet is sometimes chosen for curtains because of its rich warm appearance. However it is expensive!

Velvet curtains look attractive but are expensive

Health

The use of certain materials is sometimes unhealthy. Although asbestos is an excellent fire-proof material it has recently been found that the fibres from some sorts of asbestos can cause cancer.

Safety

Expanded polystyrene tiles look nice and help stop heat escaping through the ceiling. However, in a fire they melt and drip burning pieces into the room which spreads the fire. For safety reasons it is best not to use them.

1 List 6 things which affect choice of materials.

ASBESTOS COMMITTEE POINTS TO WORKMEN'S CANCER TOLL

By Tom Forest

SIXTY-ONE workmen who were employed in building Glasgow's asbestos-ridden Red Road flats have since died – 52 of cancer.

The pressure group Clydeside Action on Asbestos has traced 180 workers who were involved in building the multi-storey flats in the 1960s. The group was not surprised to find that 60 of those identified have died over the past 20 years but it was alarmed to learn that 52 had died from cancer, which is three times the average figure.

Keeping dry

Singing in the rain

Charles Macintosh

My name is Charles Macintosh and until recently I ran a cloth-dyeing business in Glasgow. One of the jobs that we cloth-dyers hate doing is cleaning the dye off the machines. So, imagine my delight when, six years ago in 1819, I heard that naphtha cleans off the dye beautifully. Naphtha, or coal oil, is one of the things left over when coal is heated to make coal-gas. The new coal-gas companies springing up all over didn't know what to do with the stuff and were throwing it away. Smelling a bargain, I bought a quantity very cheaply from the Glasgow Gas Works to try out. And then came my stroke of luck! While cleaning some machines in the workshop, I made the remarkable discovery that naphtha dissolves rubber. When I spread the sticky solution on the table the naphtha soon dried out leaving a thin coat of rubber. Then I had the brilliant idea of spreading some of this 'liquid rubber' onto a sheet of cotton and when it had dried I found that water could hardly pass through the cotton. I then tried pressing two sheets together as I have shown in the drawing. Success! I had invented a new flexible, water-proof material.

It wasn't long before I was selling 'the new Macintosh' waterproof cape. Although it is selling really well now, at first it was criticised very heavily by doctors. They said that although it stopped rain getting in it also stopped sweat getting out and so it was very unhealthy. I think they were angry that fewer people were catching colds.

This is how Macintosh made his waterproof material

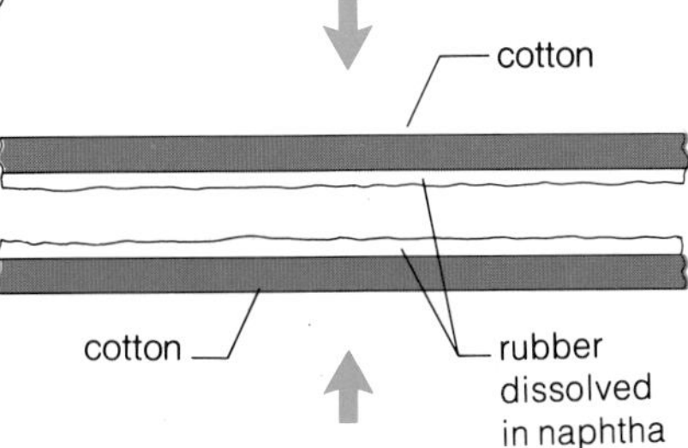

1 What is the above mainly about?
  a The discovery of naphtha.
  b Cloth dying.
  c The discovery of rubber.
  d The discovery of a waterproof material.

2 Where does the chemical naphtha come from?

3 In what year was this written?

4 What important discovery did Macintosh make which enabled him to invent the new water-proof material?

5 What piece of clothing is still named after Macintosh?

6 Explain in your own words how far Macintosh's choice of materials for his new discovery was affected by properties, costs, availability, appearance, health, and safety. Write a sentence about each.

The first waterproof garment the macintosh

Iron and steel

Iron

Iron is an **element** or pure substance which is usually found in the ground mixed with earth, rocks, and other impurities. This mixture of substances is called **iron ore**. To separate the iron from the other substances, the ore must be heated in a **smelting furnace**. In this type of furnace the iron ore is mixed with a fuel which draws off the impurities from the iron as it burns.

Wrought iron

Some furnaces remove almost all the impurities and leave behind a very pure iron called **wrought iron**. This is soft and easily hammered into different shapes. Two red-hot pieces hammered together become tightly joined so this iron is often used to make ornamental gates. However, it is too soft and easily worn away to be used for supporting heavy loads.

By melting iron ore in a different type of furnace and allowing it to mix with some **carbon** a much stronger type of iron called **cast iron** can be made. This iron can be poured while still hot into moulds and so formed into different shapes. Although it is hard, cast iron is also very brittle and it does not stand up to sudden shocks. It is useful for making, among other things, man-hole covers and garden rollers, and it was once used for making drain pipes.

Cast iron

Steel

Wrought iron contains almost no carbon and cast iron contains up to 4.5% carbon.

Steel is the name given to any alloy of iron and carbon which contains between 0.25% and 4.5% carbon. The bar chart shows the percentage of carbon contained in the main types of iron and steel.

1 What is very pure iron called?

2 Which contains most carbon: a cast-iron lamp-post or a train rail made from medium carbon steel?

3 The steel in an axe-head contains 1% carbon. What kind of steel is it?

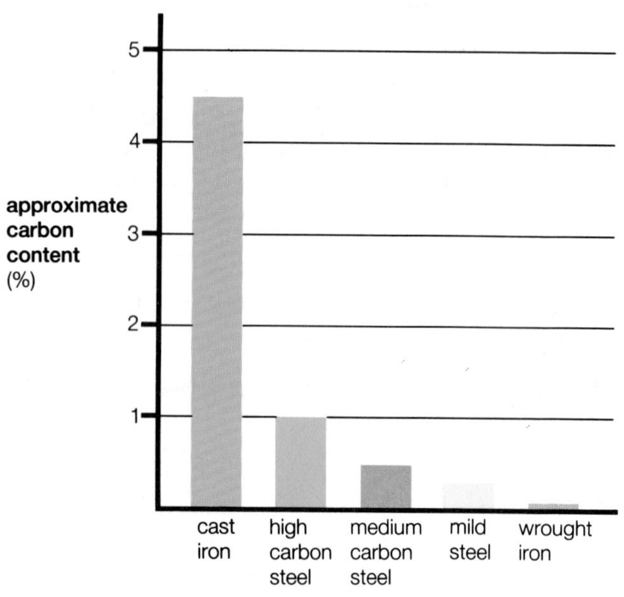

Carbon content of various iron alloys

Strong steel

Strong steel

The tensile strength of steel

The strength of a material can be measured by trying to pull it apart using a special machine. The force needed to break a piece of the material 1 square metre in area is called the **tensile strength** or simply **strength** of the material.

The graph shows how the strength of steel depends on the small amount of carbon contained in the iron. Use this and the bar chart on the previous page to answer the questions.

1 Arrange high carbon steel, mild steel, and medium steel in order of strength.

2 Which type of **steel** would you choose to make the support cables of a suspension bridge?

3 What is the tensile strength of wrought iron?

4 Use the information on page **106** to copy and extend the tensile strength graph to find out if cast iron is stronger than wrought iron.

Tensile strength is the force needed to break a piece of material whose cross-section is 1 m^3

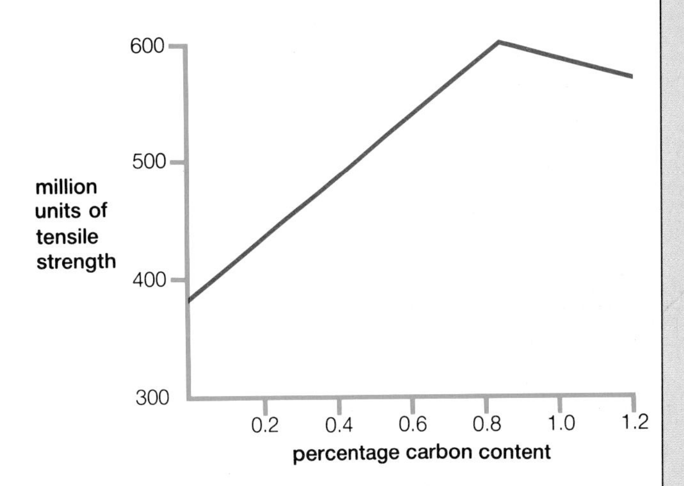

How the strength of steel is affected by the amount of carbon in the steel

Steel plus

The properties of steel can also be changed by adding small quantities of other metals while it is being made. 35% nickel added to a low-carbon steel produces an alloy called **invar**. This alloy is unusual because, unlike most metals, invar does not expand when it gets hot. Invar is used to make things which need to stay the same length even if they heat up. An example of this is a surveyor's long measuring tape.

Steel made with 1% carbon and 1.4% chromium is very hard and is used for making ball bearings.

Perhaps the best-known steel is **stainless steel** which is made from iron, 18% chromium and 8% nickel. This steel is sometimes called 18-8 stainless steel and is used to make things which must not rust.

5 Name three household objects which are made from stainless steel.

Stainless steel

Plastic

Plastic

Plastic is a name given to a whole family of man-made materials. Most plastics are made from chemicals found in oil although a few are made from other materials. Cellulose acetate for example is made from wood. Opposite is a list of some plastics. When most raw plastics are heated they become soft or 'plastic' and can be shaped into useful objects. This property gives the whole family of materials the name 'plastic' although each type of plastic has its own special name too.

All plastics are **polymers**. This means they have been made by forcing chemicals to join together to form long chains of molecules. Ethene molecules can be made to link together in long chains to form polythene. Styrene molecules linked together form polystyrene and so on. The word 'poly' means many. Plastics are made from long chains containing **many** molecules.

1 List as many plastics as you can with names beginning with poly.

polythene	melamine resin
polystyrene	polyester resin
phenolic resin	polypropylene
polytetra-fluoroethene	nylon
polyvinyl-chloride	urea resin
	acrylic
	cellulose acetate

These are all types of plastic

The effects of heat on plastics

Plastics which can be softened by heat are called **thermoplastics**. Plastics which cannot be softened by heat are called **thermosets**.

Use the key to help you answer the questions.

2 Which statement is true?
- **a** Most plastics come from oil.
- **b** Most plastics come from materials other than oil.

3 State whether the following are made from a thermoset or a thermoplastic: a formica work top, a melamine cup, a polystyrene tile, a nylon curtain rail.

4 Why does very hot water make a polythene bag sag but has no effect on a polythene basin?

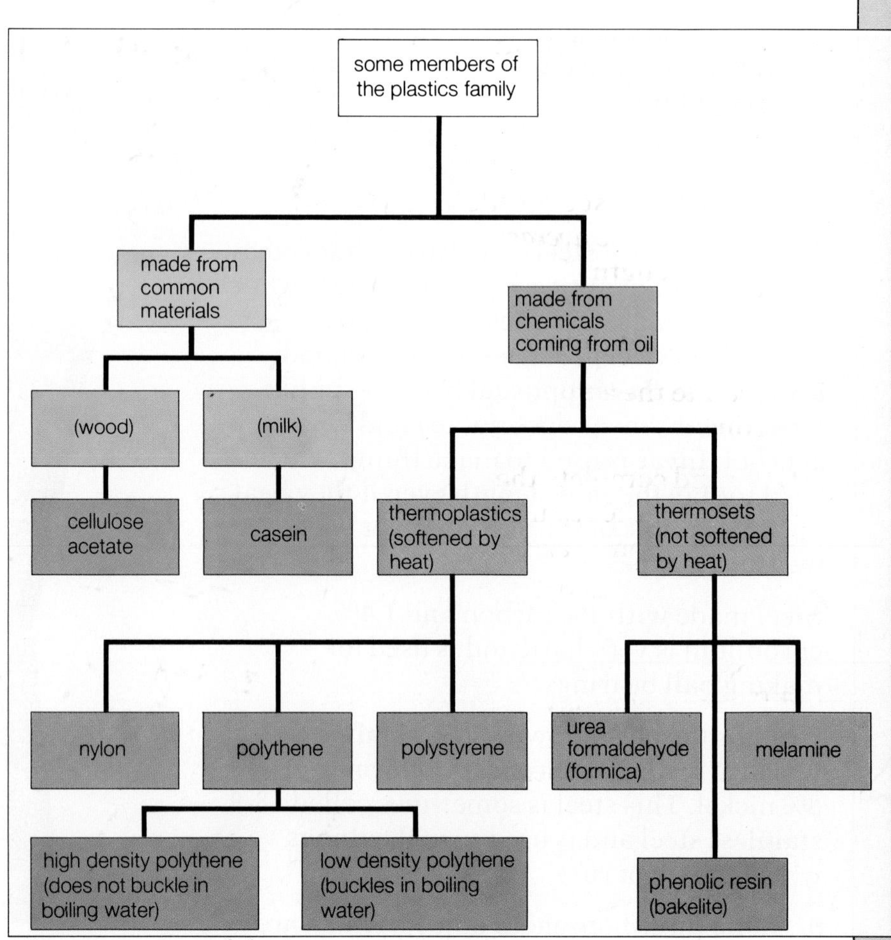

A key to some sorts of plastics

Rubber

What is rubber?

Like plastic, rubber is a polymer. However, it is neither a thermoset nor a thermoplastic. It is an **elastomer**. Rubber returns to its original shape when it is stretched and released. It behaves in an **elastic** way.

Raw rubber comes from **latex** which oozes out of the rubber tree once a groove has been cut in the bark. In its natural state rubber is not much good as it softens in heat and goes stiff in the cold. (Rather like a thermoplastic.) When rubber-coated shoes were first made in America, in the 1820s, people were disappointed to find that the shoes became soft in Summer and stiff in Winter. However, it was soon discovered that the natural properties of rubber could be changed by **vulcanization** that is, heating it with chemicals. This makes the rubber less likely to change with temperature.

Latex being collected from the rubber tree

Testing rubber

The information given is from the notebook of a scientist who works in the Bounco Rubber Company. She has been carrying out tests on different rubber samples and now must report back to her boss.

1 Use the scientist's results to calculate the *average* tensile strength of vulcanized and unvulcanized rubber.

2 Calculate the average hardness.

3 Copy and complete the table using the results from questions 1 and 2.

4 Imagine you are the scientist. Write a short report about the differences you have found between vulcanized and unvulcanized rubber.

A page from the scientist's notebook

4/11/86

Testing Rubber Samples

Sample	V or U	Property Measured	Result
1	V	T	32
2	V	H	43
3	U	T	3
4	V	T	34
5	U	T	4
6	U	H	22
7	V	H	38
8	V	T	30
9	U	H	29
10	V	H	45
11	U	T	2
12	U	H	24

Notes

1. U = Unvulcanized V = Vulcanized
2. T = Tensile strength. This is measured in MN/m^2
3. H = Hardness. This is a number measured on the hardness machine. A hard material has a high number.

Report to the boss

property	unit	unvulcanized	vulcanized
average value of tensile strength	MN/m^2		
average value of hardness	hardness number		

Strength and shape

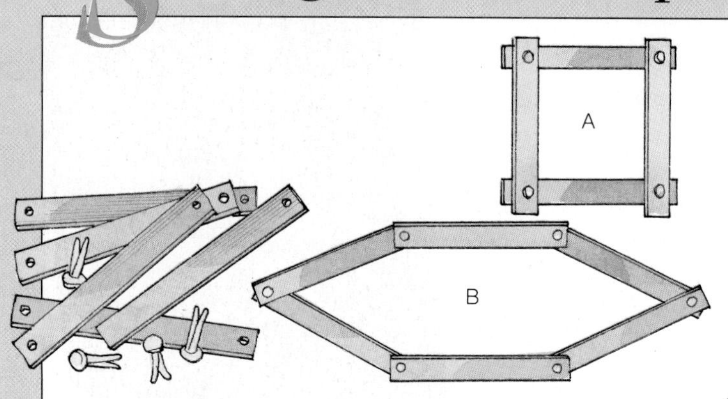

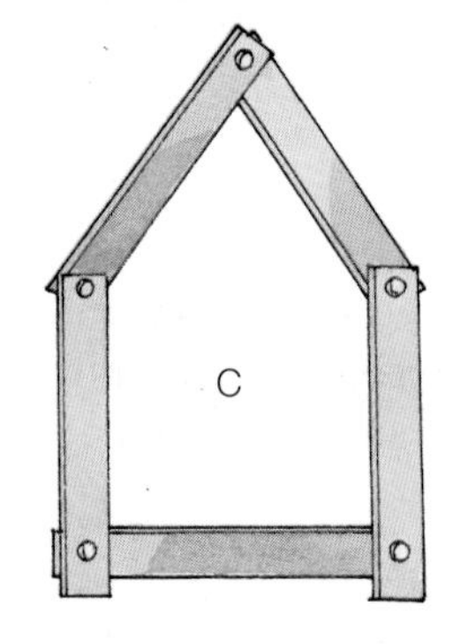

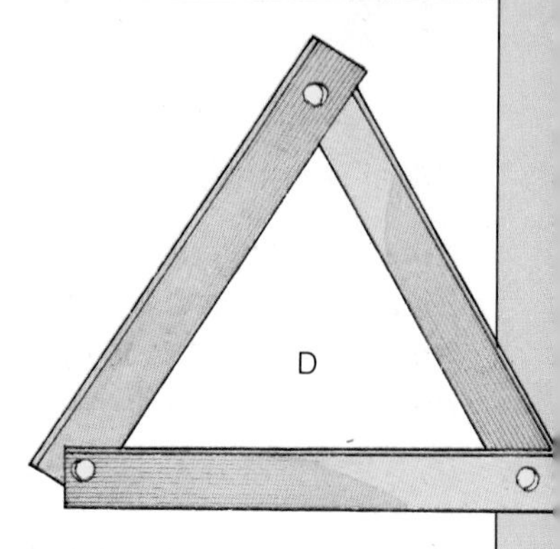

Finding a strong shape for a framework

BMX bike

Frameworks using triangles for strength

Shaping up

Cranes, bridges, electricity pylons, and house roofs are all examples of **frameworks**. A framework is a shape made from bars joined together. To be useful, a framework should be able to support both itself and some other load without falling down.

You can do some simple experiments on frameworks by loosely joining strips of cardboard with pins as shown. You will find that the only structure that will hold itself up and support any weight is a triangle. A triangular framework is a very strong shape. Other frameworks can be made strong by dividing them into triangles. Two different examples of frameworks which use triangles for strength are also shown.

1 Copy the photograph of a roof truss and colour in all the triangles you can find in it.

2 Redraw **A**, **B** and **C** from the top of the page adding extra strips inside the frameworks to make them strong.

3 What makes the BMX bike so strong?

4 From books and pamphlets supplied by your teacher find as many examples as you can of triangles being used to strengthen structures.

A roof made from corrugated plastic sheeting

Corrugations

Sheets of material can be given extra strength by folding the material into **corrugations**. The photograph shows corrugated plastic sheeting being used as the roof of a summer house.

5 Give 1 other example of corrugation being used to give strength to a sheet of material.

6 Explain in your own words why corrugation works. (Hint: triangles.)

Even stronger!

Tubes

Frameworks are often built from **tubes** rather than solid bars. A tube is stronger than a solid bar of the same weight. A tube is another example of a strong shape. Look at part of the Forth Railway Bridge. Many of the triangular shaped frameworks have been made from tubes. This makes the bridge strong without making it too heavy. Tubes are also found in nature where strength and light weight are important. An example is a plant with a hollow stem.

1 Trace the photograph of the Forth Bridge and colour in the parts made from tubes.

2 Give 2 other examples of strong tubes found in nature.

Strong building blocks

If you take a wooden stick and bend it in the middle until it breaks you will see quite clearly from the splinters that the wood at the bottom has been torn apart. Although it is not so easy to see, the wood at the top has been squashed.

When concrete, wood, or steel beams are used for building they all bend slightly even if they are only supporting their own weight! They must be designed to stand up to this strain at the top and bottom.

The strength of a building beam also depends on which way up it is used.

Steel beams used for building are often made in the shape of a letter 'I'. This shape is deep for strength yet strengthened at the top and bottom where the strains are. An I-beam is strong and light. Concrete is a very useful material often used for building. However, it has a weakness. While it can take a lot of squeezing, it does not like being stretched. To make concrete beams stronger they are often **re-inforced** (made stronger) by thin steel rods which are added to the parts likely to get stretched.

3 Explain in your words why an I-beam is strong.

Wood bent until broken *An I-beam*

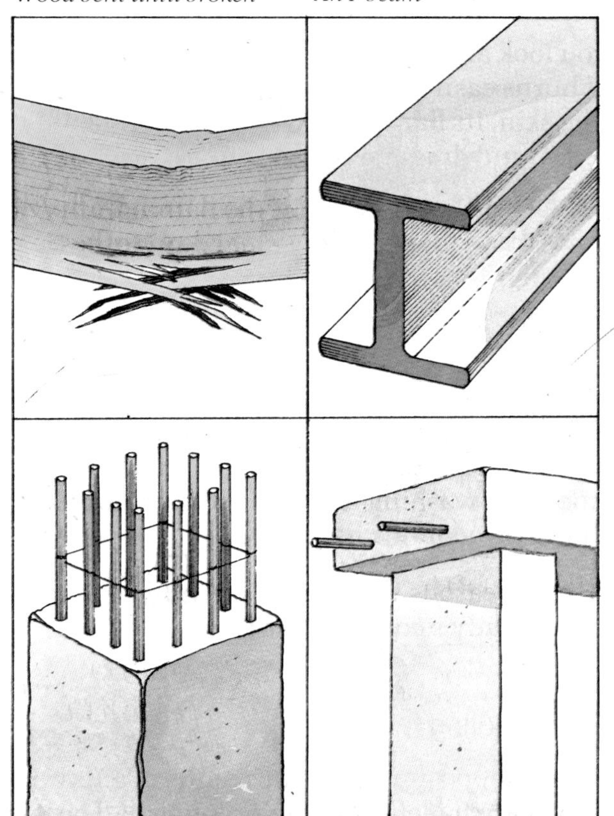

Concrete is re-inforced by steel rods

4 Why are the wooden planks used to hold up the floor in a house always used edge-on?

5 Look at the re-inforced concrete shapes. Why is the horizontal beam re-inforced only at the bottom while the vertical post is re-inforced all round the outside? (Hint: think where the stretching happens.)

Dangerous stuff

Play it safe — read the label

Safe as houses?

We all like to think of our home as a safe place to live. It comes as a shock to find that using household materials wrongly could lead to death or injury by burning, explosion, poisoning, or skin damage.

Fumes

Substances used for painting, decorating, cleaning, and repairing often contain petrol-like chemicals which give off **dangerous fumes**. These fumes may be **highly flammable** or **poisonous**, or both. Often the label carries a warning 'Not to be used in a confined space'. This means it should only be used where there is plenty of moving air to stop the fumes building up.

Glue sniffers get high by deliberately breathing the poisonous fumes which come from certain glues. This damages their bodies so much that some of them die.

GUN SIEGE BOYS HAD BEEN SNIFFING GLUE

Three boys who had been sniffing glue fired air rifles, shot guns and .22 rifles wildly causing damage estimated at tens of thousands of pounds during a siege lasting more than six hours at a gun shop.

The Lord Justice Clerk said The fact that you were sniffing glue is no excuse in the eyes of the law.

Two of the boys were given a sentence of three years and the other will be sentenced next week.

Poisons

Young children will pop almost anything into their mouths. Medicines which are quite safe for adults can poison children and should be kept in special **child-proof containers**.

Corrosive substances

A corrosive substance is one that will chemically burn anything it touches including skin. An **irritant** such as fibre-glass wool irritates the skin and can cause skin complaints if it is not handled with protective gloves. Some irritants can also damage the lungs if breathed in.

Radioactivity

Radioactive substances give off invisible but harmful rays. Such substances should always be carefully stored in lead-lined containers, marked with a special sign. Although radio-active substances are not commonly found in the home, certain types of smoke detectors use radioactive substances to detect particles of smoke.

Aerosols

Aerosol cans contain substances mixed with gas under pressure. If they are punctured or heated they can explode **even if the substance inside is non-flammable**.

1 List 5 dangerous materials which can sometimes be found in the home and write a short sentence about each.

Shaving foam. Safe or dangerous?

Avoiding danger

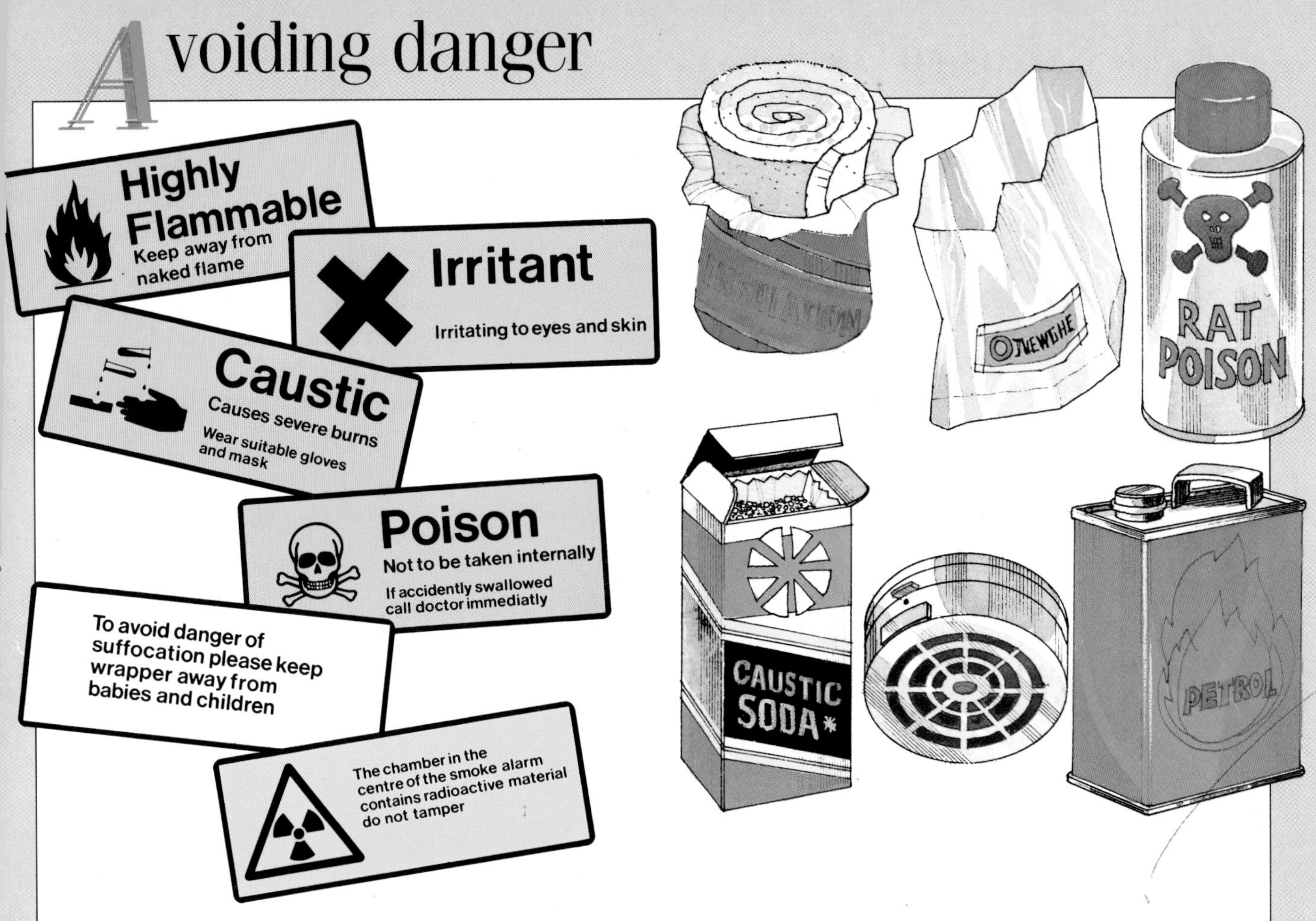

Warning labels

Dangerous substances

1 Match the labels on the left with the objects on the right.

2 Draw the symbols which are used to show danger due to:
- **a** flammability
- **b** radio-activity
- **c** corrosive substance
- **d** irritant
- **e** poison.

3 The warning shown opposite appeared on the aerosol tin of a substance used for sealing holes. Describe in your own words the dangers of using the substance.

CAUTION
Pressurised container.
Protect from sunlight and do not expose to temperatures greater than 50°C.
Do not pierce or burn even after use.
Do not spray on a naked flame.
Use in a well-ventilated place.
Avoid breathing the vapour.
Keep out of the reach of children.
Not for use with polystyrene or fibreglass.

A warning on an aerosol tin

4 Look at the part of the index for a book about housekeeping.
- **a** Which pages would you look up to find a safe way of storing flammable substances?
- **b** A person in your family has accidently swallowed some bleach. Which *two* parts of the book would you look up while waiting for the doctor to arrive?
- **c** Your friend says it is perfectly safe to throw a used aerosol tin of spray paint into a fire. You are not so sure. Where might you find advice in this book?

Acetate	140 141	Heating	72
Aerosols	99 101	Irons	225
Asbestos	131	Kitchens	205
Bedmaking	31	Jute	26
Boilers	103 104	Paint	232
Carpets	23, 57	Poisions	56
Chairs	89 90	Polish	64 67
Decorating	77	Refrigerators	94 98
First aid	3, 4	Sheets	60
Glass	58, 59	Storage	207

Part of the index from a housekeeping book

Fire hazard

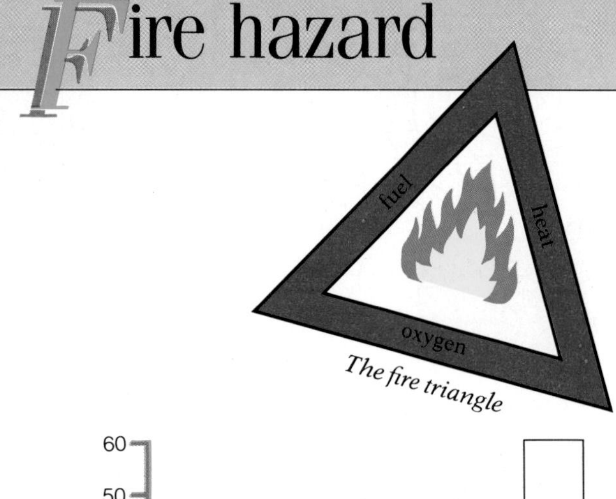

The fire triangle

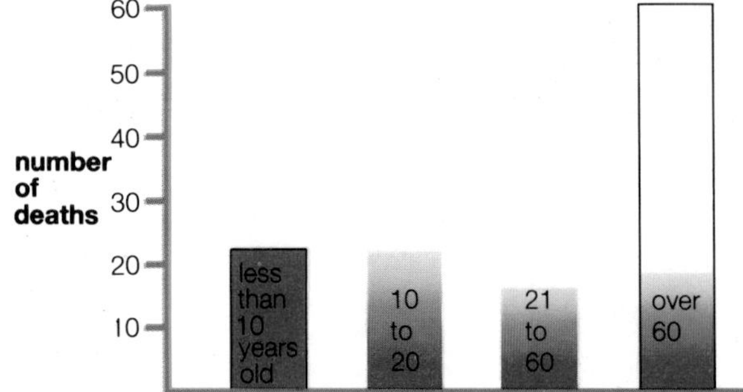

Fire deaths in Scotland in one year

Fire deaths

Fire killed 155 people in Scotland during 1983. Children under the age of 10 and people over 60 accounted for more than half the total but 58 people in the 21–60 age group also died. 22 children under the age of 10 died.

1 Copy the bar chart and add the information about the 21–60 age range.

2 *Estimate* the deaths in the 10–20 age range and in the over 60 age range and complete the chart.

A fire-resistant suit protects from heat and flames

A fireman uses a breathing set to enter a smoke-filled building

Smoke, the killer

A fire starts as a result of three things coming together, **heat**, **fuel**, and **oxygen**. These three are sometimes shown as the **fire triangle**. Each or all of these three things can play their part in causing a fire death.

The tremendous amount of heat created in a fire can burn a victim to death. Special clothing is often worn by fire-fighters to protect them from the heat and flames. Usually in a fire the victim does not die from the heat but from breathing the smoke. Many household materials which are normally quite safe give off dangerous fumes in the heat of a fire. Examples are polyurethane foam found in easy chairs, PVC, a common plastic, and rubber also common in the house. In a fire the fumes from all these can cause death.

As the fire burns, oxygen is used up and carbon dioxide is produced. The carbon dioxide causes the fire-victim to breathe quickly and so take in more of the deadly smoke. The lack of oxygen can also cause death. A handkerchief placed across the mouth and nose like you see in the films does not protect you from the poisonous gases nor does it do anything about the lack of oxygen. A fireman entering a burning building where there is a lot of smoke carries his own fresh air with him.

3 Name 3 ways death can be caused in a fire.

4 Name another way in which smoke could cause death in a fire.

Poisonous gases

Death by poison gas

The intense heat of a house fire can make household materials give off poisonous gases.

Burning wool and silk can release the poisonous gas hydrogen cyanide. This is the same gas used in some American states to execute criminals in the gas chamber. Polyurethane foam, a foam plastic widely used in plastic cushions and household furniture, releases hydrogen cyanide when burning and can cause death in seconds. A careless cigarette left smouldering on a sofa or mattress filled with this foam can cause death by poison gas even without a fire.

Another plastic, PVC (polyvinyl chloride), breaks down at high temperatures to produce deadly hydrogen chloride. Burning rubber produces a poisonous mixture of sulphur dioxide and hydrogen sulphide. This mixture is particularly deadly because sulphur dioxide is heavier than air and sinks to the floor.

When materials which contain carbon burn, the carbon joins with the oxygen in the air to form carbon dioxide. Large amounts can kill. Small amounts make you breathe faster.

When most of the oxygen has been used up in the fire then carbon monoxide is produced instead of carbon dioxide.

Experts on fires have discovered that most people killed by house fires could not find their way out because of the smoke and were then either suffocated by lack of oxygen or poisoned by carbon monoxide.

Carbon monoxide poisoning

You may remember from earlier in the book that the red blood cells carry oxygen around your body. When you breathe in carbon monoxide, during a fire for example, the carbon monoxide stops the red cells from doing their proper job of carrying oxygen. When about 2/3 of the red cells are busy carrying carbon monoxide instead of oxygen you die from lack of oxygen in the body.

Burning or smouldering furniture can give off poisonous fumes

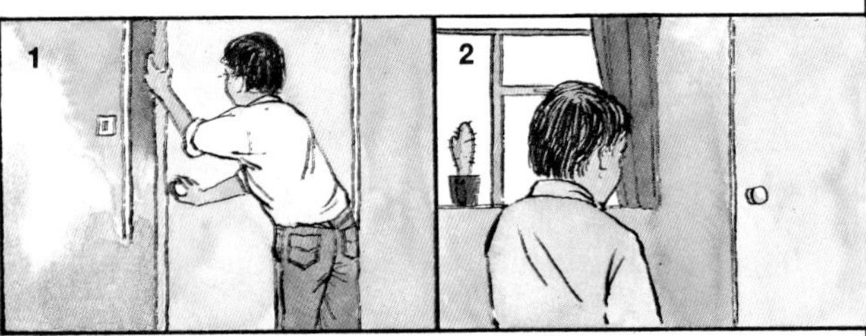

1. If there is time close doors and windows behind you
2. Each person should know at least two ways out from any room in the house

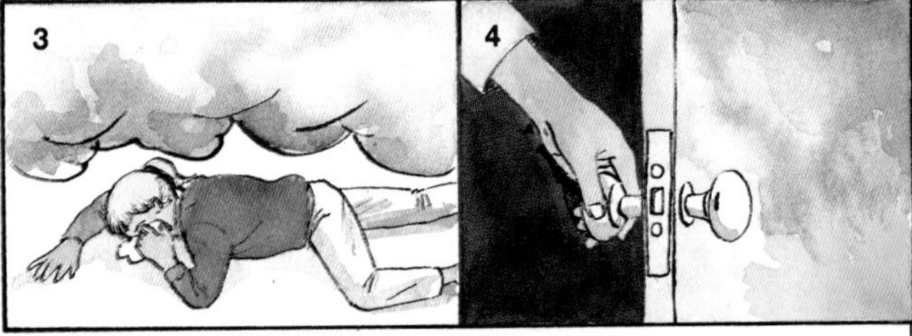

3. If the smoke is heavy crawl along the floor and try not to breath deeply
4. Never open a door which feels hot or is leaking smoke

5. Get out quickly
6. Phone for the Fire Brigade from a safe distance

What to do in a fire

1 Look at each of the above pictures in turn and explain why the captions make good sense.

2 Why would the suggestion in picture 3 not work very well if there was a lot of burning rubber in the house?

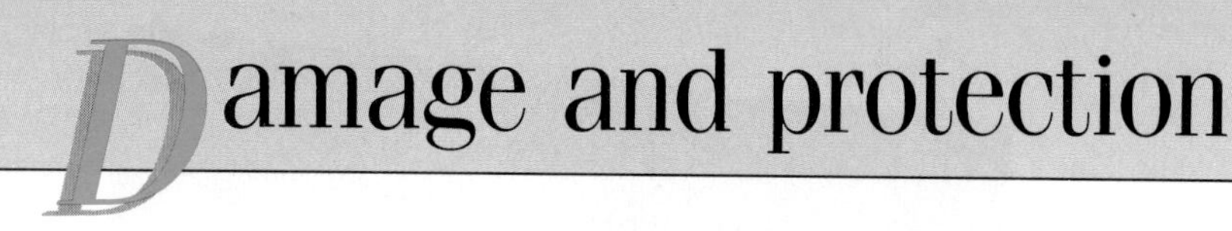

Damage and protection

Cushioning the blow

Every day the Post Office in Britain handles about 600 000 parcels. You may have seen inside a sorting office and noticed that parcels are often quite roughly treated. They are bumped along conveyor belts and thrown onto piles of other parcels. This may damage the contents of the parcels unless they are properly protected against the bumps. Some ways of doing this are shown opposite.

Expanded polystyrene foam can be shaped to fit the object exactly and so cushion it from bumps. Sometimes polystyrene chips are used to surround the object. Straw is less common nowadays and is only occasionally found in parcels. It has been replaced by shredded paper.

A very useful type of packing is a thin plastic sheet containing hundreds of air bubbles. Because air is soft and springy the sheet cushions the object it is wrapped around. This type of plastic sheet is used inside padded envelopes.

Good packing protects against damage

Protecting fabrics

Fabrics used for clothes, curtains, and furniture can be damaged in many different ways. Apart from being rubbed or torn they may also be damaged by fire or water, eaten by moths, or ruined by incorrect washing and ironing. Sometimes a fabric is 'proofed', that is, treated with special protective chemicals. **Fire-proofing** makes it less easy to burn. **Water-proofing** stops water from getting into the fabric while **moth-proofing** makes the fabric indigestible so that the moth grub dies from lack of food.

Fabrics which have been proofed usually carry a special label telling you how to treat them so that you do not destroy the proofing.

Special-care labels on clothes also tell you the correct way to wash and iron them so that you do not damage the material through too much heat while washing or ironing. One system of labelling is shown.

treatment	minimum precaution necessary	some caution necessary	special care necessary	treatment prohibited
washing	95	60	30	(crossed washtub)
bleaching (with chlorine)	Cl			(crossed triangle)
ironing	•••	••	•	(crossed iron)

washing
The figure shown in the washtub symbol is the temperature of the water in degrees Celcius

ironing
The dots show the temperature of the iron
1 Dot • cool iron
2 Dots •• warm iron
3 Dots ••• hot iron

Care-labelling

1 Cotton needs a hot iron. Silk needs a warm iron. Polyester needs a cool iron. What kind of scarf would have a label with (iron, 1 dot)?

2 What does the symbol (crossed washtub) mean on a garment?

3 What label would you expect to find on a very delicate fabric which needed a cool wash and could not be ironed?

Dry rot

A lot of rot

Dry wood lasts a long time but wet wood can be damaged by **rotting**. Rotting is caused by a fungus, that is, a plant related to a mushroom. A fungus produces millions of **spores** which float through the air to land on wood. If the wood is wet enough the spores produce fungus which feeds on the wood and breaks it down.

These wood-destroying spores are around us all the time but they only take a hold if wood becomes very damp. One common type of rot is called **dry rot** because once the wood has rotted it looks like a dry powder.

1 What two things must be present for dry rot to start?

2 Explain in your own words how dry rot spreads.

Dry rot

Wood can be protected by painting it

Stopping the rot

To prevent wood rotting it is important to stop water getting into the wood. One common way of doing this is to make the wood waterproof by covering it with several coats of paint. For wood which is outdoors this has to be repeated every few years as the paint gets chipped and cracked due to the effects of the sun, rain, and frost.

A **damp-proof course** is a waterproof barrier at the foot of a brick wall. It stops water seeping up the bricks in the wall and rotting the wooden timbers inside a house. The damp-proof course is built into the wall by the brick-layers when the house is being built.

Special air-holes are built into houses to allow air to circulate under the floors and so keep the timbers dry. In kitchens and bathrooms, where lots of water splashes about, special sealing substances are used to stop water dropping through cracks onto the floor boards.

3 List four ways of preventing dry rot in houses and write a sentence about each one.

A damp-proof course stops rising damp

Preventing water damage

Air holes allows air to circulate

Metal corrosion

Rust
Verdigris
Zinc Joints

Corrosion

Some metals **corrode** when they are left without a protective covering. A metal corrodes by slowly changing into a new substance while the original metal gets eaten away.

When iron corrodes the iron slowly joins with the oxygen in the air and changes to **iron oxide** or **rust**. Although paint can keep out the oxygen and water needed to let the metal rust, once the paint is scratched rust can form very quickly as every car-owner knows!

Copper also corrodes when left exposed to the weather. Rain and chemicals dissolved in the rain-water change the surface of the copper to **copper carbonate** or **verdigris**. You may have seen the bright green colour of verdigris on a copper roof.

Two other metals, aluminium and zinc, join very quickly with the oxygen in the air. They become covered all over with oxide. However, in their case the oxide protects them from further corrosion. For this reason aluminium and zinc are often used for jobs where corrosion would be a nuisance. For example zinc is sometimes used to form water-tight joints on roofs.

An experiment with rust

When curious Kate asked her science teacher why her Dad's car was always rusting she was given an experiment to do. She cleaned 4 iron nails and put them into 4 different test tubes filled with 4 different things. She left them for a week and then came back to look at them.

Look at the page from her laboratory notebook then answer the following questions.

1 Which nails did not rust at all?

2 Why did Kate put oil on the top of the 'oxygen free' water?

3 Which nail rusts the most?

4 Which 2 substances are needed for iron to rust?

5 In winter salt is used to melt the snow on the roads. What effect does this have on motor cars using the road?

6 How did Kate explain to her Dad why his car was always rusting?

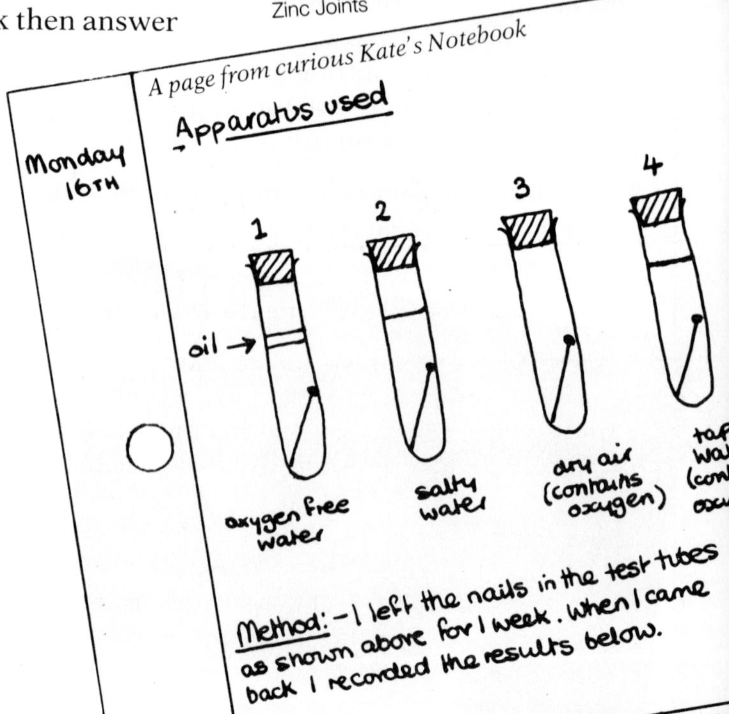
A page from curious Kate's Notebook

Monday 16TH

Apparatus used

1 2 3 4

oil →

oxygen free water

salty water

dry air (contains oxygen)

tap

Method: – I left the nails in the test tubes as shown above for 1 week. When I came back I recorded the results below.

Results

Test tube	No rust	Rusty	Very rust
1	✓		
2			✓
3	✓		
4		✓	

Protection against corrosion

Anodising

Aluminium can be forced to grow a thicker oxide layer by a special process called anodising. The protective layer of oxide can be dyed various colours to give the metal a very attractive appearance. The photograph shows part of anodised bicycle.

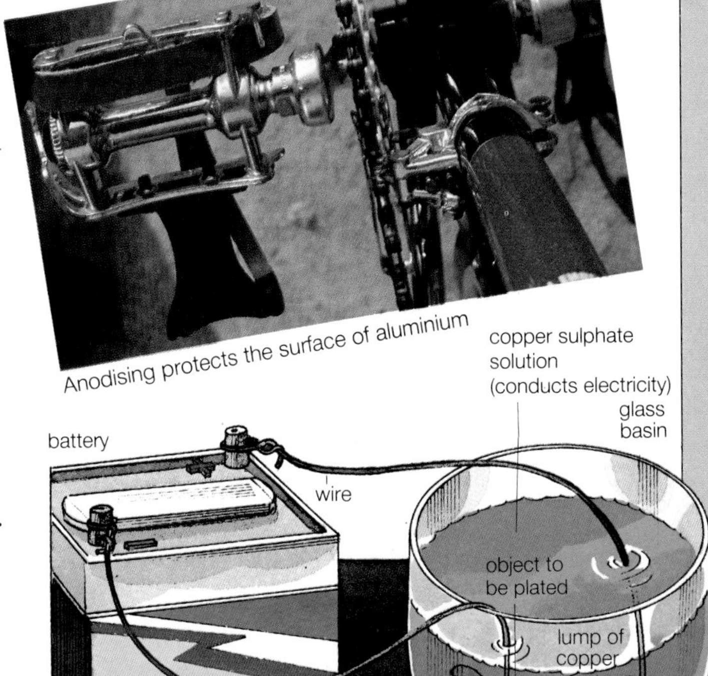

Anodising protects the surface of aluminium

Electroplating puts a thin protective layer of metal on the surface

Electro-plating

Electro-plating is a way of giving a metal object a protective covering of another metal. It is done in a special bath using electricity. Look at an object being copper plated. When the electric current flows small particles of copper move towards the object and stick to it. At the same time the lump of copper loses some copper.

Galvanising

Galvanising is a way of protecting the surface of steel from corrosion. By dipping the steel into hot molten zinc the steel is given a protective coat of zinc. Some galvanised objects are shown in the photograph.

These steel objects have all been galvanised

Physical and chemical protection of metals

Metal will not corrode if air and water are kept away from the surface of the metal. So one way of stopping corrosion is to paint the metal surface or cover it with a thin layer of protecting metal as in electro-plating. Painting and electro-plating are examples of **physical protection**. If the surface layer is scratched the metal underneath will corrode.

Chemical protection is another way to stop metals corroding. Sometimes when two different metals touch each other an unusual chemical reaction happens which allows one metal to corrode but not the other. Galvanising is a good example of chemical protection. The steel does not rust even when the zinc is scratched. Unfortunately zinc is poisonous so galvanised steel containers can't be used for food.

1 List four different ways of protecting metal against corrosion.

2 State whether the following are examples of physical or chemical protection: painting, anodising, electro-plating, galvanising.

3 'Tin cans' are made from steel covered with a layer of tin. They rust easily when scratched. Is the steel chemically or physically protected?

4 Oil rigs often have big lumps of magnesium attached to the submerged legs. Suggest why.

Index

Acknowledgements

The publishers would like to thank the following for permission to reproduce transparencies:

Heather Angel: p. 66, p. 68 (middle), p. 78 (top), p. 86, p. 87 (top), p. 90 (top); Ashmolean Museum, Oxford: p. 96; Aspect Picture Library: p. 34 (bottom), p. 88 (top); Austin Rover: p. 95 (top); Barnaby's Picture Library: p. 27 (top), p. 82 (bottom left and right), p. 102 (bottom), p. 111; Anne Bolt: p. 83 (bottom right); British Petroleum: p. 53, p. 54; British Railways Board: p. 95 (top); British Steel Corporation: p. 83 (bottom left); Cement and Concrete Association: p. 97; Central Electricity Generating Board: p. 57, p. 102 (middle); Civil Aviation Authority: p. 116 (top); John Cleare: p. 95 (2nd from bottom), p. 103 (top); Bruce Coleman/Leonard Lee Rue III: p. 90 (middle); Richard Costain Limited: p. 95 (top); Daily Telegraph Colour Library/Space Frontiers: p. 58 (bottom middle); John Dawkins: p. 67 (top), p. 68 (top), p. 70 (bottom right), p. 87 (bottom left and middle), p. 90 (bottom), p. 95 (top), p. 106, p. 109; Electricity Council: p. 39, p. 44, p. 45; Mary Evans Picture Library: p. 25; Farmer's weekly p. 89 (top); Peter Fletcher: P. 87 (middle), p. 91 (top right), p. 99 (2nd from bottom), p. 119 (bottom left); Derek Fordham: p. 34 (top), p. 88 (bottom); Forestry commission: p. 104 (right); Format/Raissa Page: p. 30 (bottom); Fothergill and Harvey plc: p. 95 (2nd from top); Alex Fraser: p. 39, p. 44, p. 70 (top left), p. 95; Terry Jennings: p. 58 (bottom left), p. 62 (bottom), p. 63 (top and bottom), p. 65, p. 76, p. 78 (bottom), p. 83 (top left), p. 89 (bottom left), p. 91 (middle), p. 112 (bottom); Frank Lane Agency: p. 53 (top), p. 70 (bottom); Sue Lloyd: p. 6; Mansell Collection: p. 105, p. 113 (top and bottom); Bob Matthews: p. 37; Metropolitan Police: p. 2 (bottom), p. 13; Ken Moreman: p. 20 (middle), p. 21 (top and bottom); NASA: p. 84; National Trust: p. 91 (bottom); North of Scotland Hydro-Electric Board: p. 58 (bottom right); Oxford Scientific Films: p. 68 (bottom), OSF/Cooke: p. 67 (bottom), OSF/Houghton: p. 69 (top), OSF/Bernard: p. 69 (middle), OSF/Thompson: p. 72 (middle), OSF/Gardener: p. 79; OSF/MacLean: p. 87 (bottom right); Press Association: p. 112 (top); Rentokill Limited: p. 119 (top); Rex Features: p. 3, p. 4 (top); St. Bartholomew's Hospital, London: p. 14, p. 29 (bottom); Science Photo Library: p. 4 (bottom), p. 28, p. 29 (top), p. 102 (top), p. 103 (bottom), Seaphot/Planet Earth: p. 41 (top and bottom); Shirley Institute: p. 100; Adrian Smith; p. 121 (top); Spectrum Colour Library: p. 62 (top), p. 89 (middle); Topham Picture Library: p. 85 (middle), p. 120 (middle); Weight Watchers (UK) Ltd.: p. 10; Wellcome Institute Library, London: p. 23; West Air Photography: p. 91 (top left); Wiggins Teape: p. 83 (top right); World Wildlife Fund/David Black: p. 72 (top), WWF/P. Grijpma: p. 73 (top), WWF/Chris Harvey: p. 73 (bottom).

Cover pictures by: Daily Telegraph Colour Library/Space Frontiers, John Dawkins, Chris Honeywell.

Illustrated by: Bob Chapman Sheila Hadley Gary Hincks Vanessa Luff Ben Manchipp Colin Meier Oxford Illustrators Peter Russell Martin Salisbury Paul Thomas

Photography by: Chris Honeywell

Photographic props loaned by:

Boswells, Oxford; J.W. Carpenter Ltd.; Glutton's Delicatessen, Oxford; C.J. Heating Ltd., Oxford; and The Prince of Wales, Oxford.

Our special thanks to:

The Civil Aviation Fire Training School, Darlington and Fire Service College, Moreton-in-Marsh for setting fire to things.